BACKPACKING
IN SOUTHWESTERN
BRITISH COLUMBIA

T0150775

BACKPACKING
IN SOUTHWESTERN
BRITISH COLUMBIA

The Essential Guide
to Overnight Hiking Trips

TARYN EYTON

GREYSTONE BOOKS

Vancouver/Berkeley

Greystone Books Ltd.
greystonebooks.com

Cataloguing data available from Library and Archives Canada
ISBN 978-1-77164-668-0 (pbk.)
ISBN 978-1-77164-669-7 (epub)

Editing by Lucy Kenward
Copy editing by Erin Parker
Proofreading by Alison Strobel
Cover design by Fiona Siu
Cover photograph by Taylor McColl
Text design by Nayeli Jimenez
Photographs by Taryn Eyton, except where credited otherwise

Printed and bound in Singapore on ancient-forest-friendly paper by
COS Printers Pte Ltd.

Greystone Books gratefully acknowledges the Musqueam, Squamish,
and Tsleil-Waututh peoples on whose land our office is located.

Greystone Books thanks the Canada Council for the Arts, the British
Columbia Arts Council, the Province of British Columbia through the
Book Publishing Tax Credit, and the Government of Canada for
supporting our publishing activities.

Canadä

PREVIOUS SPREAD: *Watersprite Tower overlooking
Watersprite Lake (Trip 13).*

CONTENTS

SAFETY NOTICE

Hiking, scrambling, backpacking, camping, and all forms of outdoor recreation involve inherent risks and an element of unpredictability. Many of the trips in this guidebook are not for novices and may not be safe for your party. There are dangers on every road, trail, and route, and conditions can change at any time. While every effort has been made to ensure accuracy, this book may contain errors. You assume full responsibility for your safety and health in the backcountry. The author, publisher, and distributors accept no liability for any loss, damage, injury, or death arising from the use of this book. Check current conditions, carry the Ten Essentials, exercise caution, and stay within your limits.

INTRODUCTION

BACKPACKING STRIPS US DOWN to our core as humans: all that matters is walking, eating, and sleeping. From my first backpacking trips on the West Coast Trail and in Garibaldi Provincial Park, I was hooked. Instead of worrying about my commute or the status of my email inbox, I spent days engrossed in the meditative rhythms of nature. I slept and woke with the rise and fall of the sun. I wandered through dense forests, scrambled up to vertiginous viewpoints, and paused often, transfixed by squirrels chasing each other up tree trunks or marmots basking on rocks. I had enjoyed the wilderness on day hikes, but the immersion of backpacking deepened the experience. Thankfully, from my home in Vancouver, I don't have to travel very far to camp in the backcountry.

Backpacking in Southwestern British Columbia is for people who want to go beyond day hiking to camp under the stars, enjoy the solitude of sunrise, and explore less-travelled areas. When I started backpacking in this region over 15 years ago, I found few details about where to camp or how to explore farther than I could walk in a day. Today, it can still be hard to find content specifically for backcountry camping. This book is the guide I've been looking for all these years. It covers some of my favourite overnight and long weekend hiking destinations from the Sunshine Coast in the west, north along the Sea to Sky Highway to the Duffey Lake area, and east along the Fraser, Coquihalla, Skagit, and Similkameen Rivers. The 40 trips in this book are in the traditional territories of the Coast Salish, Nlaka'pamux, St'at'imc, and Syilx peoples. They cover over 800 kilometres of trails, with the option to add another 600 kilometres by extending the individual trips or day hiking from their base camps.

The trips here range from easy to very challenging, to suit backpackers of various experience levels. While most people hike and backpack in the summer months in southwestern British Columbia, I've included low-elevation trails that you can hike in the spring and fall. There are must-see locations that most hikers have heard of and a handful of hidden gems for those seeking solitude or adventure. Each of the trips I've chosen highlights a different backcountry destination and gives you all the information you need: how to get there, what facilities you can expect at camp, and where you can hike farther into the backcountry from your campsite. While researching this book, I backpacked all of these trails as well as a few that didn't make the cut.

When choosing the backpacking trips for this book, I kept a few guiding principles in mind. Each trip is:

- easy to complete in two to three days.
- accessible by two-wheel-drive (2WD) vehicle (sometimes with a little bit of added road walking).
- located within a few hours of Metro Vancouver, including the Sunshine Coast.
- worth dedicating your time off to.
- easy to extend, with optional day hikes from a backcountry base camp or multiple possible campgrounds (where feasible).
- located in an area with a land manager, like a park, hiking club, or government agency.

The last point is very important to me. I am a certified Leave No Trace Master Educator and have been volunteering to teach wilderness ethics education for over a decade. When a location is featured in a guidebook, increased traffic usually results. Unfortunately, southwestern BC has a few popular locations that are getting loved to death and overrun with campfire scars, poop landmines, and braided trails. I am unwilling to contribute to adding more.

So I have deliberately chosen not to include locations on Crown land that have no formal management plan, no land manager, and no formal facilities. By including only areas with a land manager, I know that a regulatory framework is already in place to maintain trails and install infrastructure like outhouses and food caches. I have also included a section about Leave No Trace best practices. Please familiarize yourself with Leave No Trace before your next hike. Our actions as individuals matter. They can keep the wilderness wild and avoid hurting the places we love.

The first principle of Leave No Trace is "Plan Ahead and Prepare," so this book includes a section on trip planning as well as another on safety. Prepared hikers are likely to have less impact on the land and to be able to self-rescue in an emergency. They also have more fun. And having fun is the main reason we go backpacking.

BACKPACKING BASICS

TRIP PLANNING

1. WEATHER AND SEASONS

Compared to weather in the city, backcountry weather is usually colder, wetter, and windier. It's also very unpredictable. Be prepared for cold and wet weather in any season. City weather forecasts are useless in the mountains. If possible, use park or ski resort forecasts to get a better idea of what to expect. Use caution in periods of high rainfall and during the spring melt. All that extra water can cause flooding and landslides. It can also wash out bridges and trails.

In southwestern BC, July and August are the driest and warmest months and therefore the best time to plan a backpacking trip. May, June, and September can also be nice, but the weather is a bit colder and more variable. If you get a window of good weather, backpacking in April and October is a possibility if you're prepared for cooler temperatures.

Unless you have snowshoes, winter clothing, and avalanche training, backpacking during the winter months in southwestern BC is unpleasant and even dangerous. In this guide, you'll find a recommendation for which months are the best to hike each trail. In general, all the trips are snow-free from mid-July to mid-September. But lots of trips at lower elevations are accessible in spring and fall as well. The snow melts at different rates each year, so check trail conditions before you go.

2. FITNESS

Hikers of any age can enjoy backpacking as long as they are in good health. However, backpacking is more challenging than hiking, due to the extra weight of your camping gear, so it's best to ease into it. When choosing a trip, consider the fitness of each hiker in your group. Southwestern BC has some steep and rugged trails. New backpackers should start with the trips rated "easy" before tackling more challenging trails. Beginners could also consider a trip to one of the many huts described in this book to gently introduce themselves to backpacking without the added weight of a tent.

Each person hikes at their own pace. However, a good way to estimate hiking times for backpackers is 3 to 4 kilometres (1.9 to 2.5 mi) per hour, plus 15 minutes for every 100 metres (328 ft) of elevation gain. This formula is just a starting point and assumes average fitness and short breaks.

3. TRAIL CONDITIONS

Mother Nature changes our trails every year. Fallen trees, lingering snow, missing markers, overgrown sections, mud, and washed-out bridges are common, especially in the spring. In southwestern BC, we rely on volunteers and dwindling numbers of park rangers to maintain our trails. Some trails can go years without maintenance. Check the links in the Further Resources section for each trip to get an idea of trail conditions in the area before you go.

4. NAVIGATION

Most trails in this guide are easy to follow, but a few are less travelled and require more navigation skills. The maps in this guide are for reference only. For navigation, invest in a topographic map, compass, and/or GPS device or app. In the Further Resources section for each hike, you'll find listings for recommended trail maps and National Topographic System (NTS) map sheets.

Hiking in southwestern BC can test your navigation skills. Fog, unexpected snowstorms, thick forest, overgrown trails, and confusing networks of logging roads can easily disorient you. Watch for trail markers as you hike. If you think you're off track, don't keep going. Turn around and head back to the last trail marker, then try again.

5. BACKROAD DRIVING

Many of the trips in this guide involve driving on gravel forest service roads. While most of them are 2WD accessible, you may encounter potholes, steep hills, bumpy sections, unbridged creeks, and deep cross-ditches. In southwestern BC, road conditions change each year as rain, snow, and logging operations reshape the landscape. All road descriptions were current at the time of writing, but changes in the coming years are inevitable.

Drive slowly, and get out of the car to evaluate hazards before continuing. Bring a spare tire, a shovel, and a saw to assist with self-rescue. There is no cell service on most of these roads and navigation can be challenging. Use a GPS device or app with a backroad map layer, or bring a backroad map book to stay on track. You will share the roads with logging trucks, industrial traffic, and ATVs. Always drive with your headlights on and go slowly around curves. Pull over to let faster traffic pass.

View from Earl's Cabin Camp, Lower Stein Valley (Trip 29).

6. FEES AND RESERVATIONS FOR CAMPING AND HUTS

As hiking and backpacking have become more popular in southwestern BC, parks and land managers have introduced backcountry camping fees. Backpackers impact the wilderness more than day hikers with their tenting, cooking, and pooping. Camping fees are used to create and maintain infrastructure to minimize these impacts with tent pads, food lockers, and outhouses, as well as to maintain the trails. In most cases, you must pay fees online before you arrive. You can find information on whether fees are required and how to pay them in the details for each trip in this guide.

While most destinations in this guide are first-come, first-served, a few popular campgrounds in BC Parks require advance reservations. This ensures that each group has enough space to set up and limits negative impacts on the environment that come with overcrowding. Your reservation guarantees you a spot in the campground but does not reserve a particular campsite. You choose your campsite from the ones available when you arrive. Make reservations as far in advance as possible as campsites get booked up. At the time of writing, backcountry campsites in BC Parks were reservable up to four months before your trip.

A few of the trips in this guide have backcountry huts you can stay in. Some of these huts require reservations, while others are first-come, first-served. Some of them are free whereas others charge a fee. Since the huts are managed by various outdoor clubs, as well as BC Parks, policies vary from hut to hut. You can find more information about the policies for reservations and fees for each hut within the trip descriptions.

7. REGULATIONS

In many areas, regulations regarding fires, smoking, cannabis, dogs, bikes, swimming, and drones are common to minimize environmental impact and create a welcoming space for everyone. If you choose to fish, obtain the appropriate licence. Some areas have bait restrictions or seasonal closures, or require catch-and-release practices. Be a responsible backcountry citizen and check the regulations before you go. Your actions could reduce other hikers' enjoyment of these pristine locations. You can also be fined for violations.

8. BACKPACKING GEAR

Having the right gear can be the difference between a trip that is safe and fun and one that isn't. When selecting backpacking gear, choose lightweight items appropriate for the conditions. Bring only the essentials and try to carry less than 25 percent of your body weight. For clothing, go with wool or synthetics, not cotton, which holds moisture and makes you cold. For more advice on choosing backpacking gear, see my website, HappiestOutdoors.ca, or get advice from staff at an outdoor store that specializes in backcountry camping and hiking. Avoid general sporting goods stores and big-box stores, as they don't have the gear selection or staff knowledge to cater to backpackers.

You should carry the Ten Essentials on every trip to ensure you have what you need in case of accident or emergency:

1. Illumination (headlamp or flashlight with extra batteries)
2. Nutrition and hydration (extra food and water)
3. Insulation (extra clothing)
4. Navigation (map, compass, and GPS)
5. Fire starter (lighter or matches)
6. First-aid kit
7. Emergency shelter (tent, tarp, or space blanket)
8. Sun protection (hat, sunscreen, sunglasses, and long sleeves)
9. Knife
10. Communication (whistle, mirror, phone, personal locator beacon, or satellite messenger, plus extra batteries or a battery charger)

But you'll need a lot more than that to be comfortable on a backpacking trip. Here is my backpacking gear checklist for summer trips in southwestern BC. Make sure everything fits well and you know how to use it before your trip. You don't want to be hours into the backcountry and discover your boots are uncomfortable or you don't know how to use your stove.

Camping Gear

- Backpack with a rain cover or pack liner. Make sure it fits you well.
- Three-season backpacking tent with guylines and pegs
- Three-season sleeping bag rated for 0°C (32°F) or colder, and compression sack
- Sleeping pad designed for three-season use, ideally with an R-value of at least 2.5

Cooking Gear

- Single-burner backpacking stove and fuel
- Lighter, matches, or ferro rod in a waterproof container
- Pot
- Bowl, mug, and spork (combined spoon and fork)
- Knife
- Water bottles or hydration reservoir
- Water treatment (filter, purification drops, etc.)
- Food
- Lightweight dry bag for food storage
- Biodegradable soap and small microfibre cloth

Wildflower meadows on the slopes above Tenquille Lake (Trip 3).

Safety Gear
- The Ten Essentials
- Bear spray
- Repair kit, including a multi-tool, repair tape or duct tape, safety pins, needle and thread, and tent pole splint
- 12 to 15 metres (40 to 50 ft) of lightweight rope for food hangs, tarp shelters, or emergencies

Toiletries
- Sunscreen
- Toothbrush and toothpaste
- Mini trowel, hand sanitizer, toilet paper, and bag for packing out used toilet paper

Clothing
- Waterproof-breathable rain jacket and pants
- Lightweight synthetic or down-insulated jacket and/or fleece jacket
- Quick-drying t-shirt(s)
- Quick-drying hiking pants and/or shorts
- Midweight long underwear top and bottoms
- Quick-drying underwear and sports bra
- Toque and a brimmed hat
- Lightweight fleece gloves

- Sunglasses
- Wool or synthetic hiking socks
- Hiking boots

Optional Gear
- Collapsible day pack for side trips from base camp
- Backpacking pillow
- Lightweight tarp and rope to make a kitchen shelter
- Ultralight chair or foam butt cushion
- Bear canister or bear-resistant bag (to use instead of hanging food where no food storage facilities are provided)
- E-reader/paperback book or deck of cards
- Camera gear
- Insect repellent and/or head net
- Earplugs
- Swimsuit and small microfibre towel
- Trekking poles
- Sandals or camp shoes
- Gaiters

9. FOOD PLANNING

It can take a bit of practice to figure out a backpacking meal plan that works for you. In general, bring food that is lightweight, compact, easy to cook, and calorie-dense. Repackage food at home to minimize bulk and garbage. Keep in mind that you'll likely burn more calories than usual, so you may want to bring more food than you'd eat at home.

Avoid canned food. Dehydrated and freeze-dried meals made with rice, pasta, and oatmeal are ideal. You can dehydrate your own, buy dried ingredients at the grocery store, or purchase pre-packaged backpacking meals at an outdoor store. For protein, cured meats, nuts, and hard cheeses are good options. Don't forget ready-to-eat snacks like energy bars, candy, dried fruit, and trail mix. Hot liquids like tea, coffee, hot chocolate, and soup are also nice to have in cold weather. For more backpacking food tips, see my website, HappiestOutdoors.ca.

SAFETY

1. FIRST AID

Backpacking trips take you far from hospitals and medical help. Always carry a well-stocked first-aid kit and know how to use everything in it. Check your kit before every trip to restock frequently used items like Band-Aids, blister dressings, and painkillers. Consider taking a wilderness first-aid course to learn how to treat common injuries in the field.

2. LEAVE A TRIP PLAN

If you don't come home on time because you are lost or hurt, will anyone know where to look for you? Leave a detailed trip plan with a friend or family member. It could be the difference between a successful rescue and a tragedy. Use the trip planning form on the AdventureSmart app or website, or create your own. It should include the names and contact information for all group members, details about your planned route, details about the gear and supplies you have with you, and the date and time you expect to be back. Give your trip plan to a trusted friend or relative, with instructions on when to call search and rescue if you aren't back on schedule. (When you get home, don't forget to follow up with a call to those who have your trip plan.)

3. HAZARDS

Hypothermia

While bears and avalanches get a lot of press, wet and cold weather is actually the most dangerous thing backpackers can encounter, and it's common in southwestern BC. Hypothermia occurs when a person's core body temperature drops below 35°C (95°F). Mild symptoms include uncontrolled shivering, slurred speech, and loss of balance. Without treatment, people with hypothermia stop shivering, have shallow breathing and a weak pulse, and may lose consciousness.

Prevent hypothermia by packing warm, dry clothing to change into. If the weather gets bad and you have not reached your destination, pitch your tent instead of pressing on into the storm. Change into dry clothing and get into a dry sleeping bag. Eat and drink warm foods and fluids.

Getting Lost

It can be surprisingly easy to get lost while hiking. You can miss a junction, accidentally turn onto an unmarked side trail, or get off-track in overgrown areas. To avoid getting lost, carry a copy of the trail description, a trail map, and a compass or GPS, and check them frequently to make sure you're on the right track.

If you aren't sure you are on the correct trail, don't just keep hiking onwards. Ask other hikers for help. Backtrack to the last junction or trail marker and try again. If you do become truly lost, stay put. If possible, call for help and then wait. (See the How to Get Help section below for more information.) If you keep moving, it will be difficult for search and rescue to find you. Do not hike downhill, hoping it will lead you back to the road. This strategy will bring you into dangerous terrain with cliffs and waterfalls that can make rescue more difficult and has led to fatal falls.

Looking down to Rainbow Lake from Rainbow Pass (Trip 8).

Drinking Water and Hygiene

While it might be nice to think that water in the backcountry is clean and pure, you never really know if humans and animals have pooped (or died) upstream. Lakes and streams can contain bacteria, viruses, and protozoa that can make you sick. Use a backcountry water filter or use chlorine or iodine drops or tablets to treat your water.

When backpackers get sick on a trip, they often blame contaminated water. However, poor hygiene is often the actual culprit. Take care to wash your hands or use hand sanitizer after going to the bathroom and before eating.

Snow and Ice

In early season or high in the mountains, it is common to encounter snow on the trails. A simple slip and fall on a steep snow slope can result in injury or death. Melting snow can conceal hidden holes or creeks. Drowning, ankle injuries, and hypothermia are common when hikers fall through broken snow.

Check trail conditions before you go to know how much snow to expect. Leave high-elevation hikes until late in the summer when they are more likely to be snow-free. When encountering snow, use extra caution. Bring microspikes or crampons and an ice axe for better traction. Be prepared to turn back if snow conditions are more than your group can handle.

None of the trails in this book involve travel on glaciers, but some of them will take you right up to the edge of one. Unless you have mountaineering equipment and training, never walk on a glacier or go into an ice cave. They can collapse at any time or you can fall into a crevasse.

If you choose to backpack in winter or spring in southwestern BC, know that many of the trips in this book are in serious avalanche terrain. Take an avalanche course to learn how to recognize and avoid avalanche-prone terrain and to conduct a rescue if an avalanche strikes.

Trailhead Security

Unfortunately, car break-ins and vandalism are common at some of the trailheads in this guide, especially between Squamish and Pemberton and along the Chilliwack Lake Road. The only foolproof way to avoid this problem is to get dropped off and picked up at the trailhead. However, that isn't feasible for most hikers. If you do leave your car parked at a trailhead overnight, do not leave anything in your vehicle. Consider leaving the glove box and console open to show thieves you aren't hiding anything from view.

4. WILDLIFE

Insects

While more a nuisance than a danger, mosquitos and blackflies can be bad in southwestern BC, especially in June and July in wet alpine areas and near lakes. Insect repellent, a head net, and clothing that covers your arms and legs can be helpful. If you are sensitive to bites, bring a topical anti-itch cream and antihistamine tablets.

Wasps can be an issue along trails, particularly during warm and dry summers. They swarm out of their underground nests to sting unsuspecting hikers as they walk by. If you are stung, wash the area with soap and water to remove as much venom as possible. Ibuprofen and antihistamines can help with the pain and swelling. Hikers with wasp allergies should always carry their EpiPen.

Ticks are more of a hazard since they can carry Lyme disease, which is becoming more prevalent locally. They are not common on most of the trails in this guide, but use caution in the Lower Stein Valley, on the Tikwalus Heritage Trail, and on any lower-elevation trails in dry climates.

Ticks seek exposed skin where they can bite and then burrow into your flesh. Wear long pants and long sleeves. Check yourself frequently for ticks. At camp, remove your clothing and do a thorough check, paying particular attention to the areas at the edge of your clothing and your hairline. If you discover a tick, remove it carefully with tweezers. When you get home, talk to your doctor about Lyme disease testing and treatment.

Bears

Your chances of seeing a bear while hiking are small, though they are more likely in areas that have higher concentrations of bears. Black bears live throughout southwestern BC. Grizzly bears are only found in a few areas covered by this guide, namely on the west side of Highway 99, and in the Stein Valley, Manning Park, and Coquihalla regions. Bears are usually not aggressive and will run away when they see people. Bears are more likely to bluff charge or attack if they are surprised, have cubs with them, or are defending food.

To avoid surprising a bear, talk or sing as you hike, especially in dense vegetation like berry bushes. Travel in a group and keep your dog on a leash. If you come across a dead animal, leave the area immediately. To avoid attracting a bear to your campsite, follow the tips in the Food Storage section below.

If you see a bear, give it lots of space. Stay still and talk calmly to the bear. Don't run. If you are attacked or bluff charged, use bear spray at close range if you have it. If that doesn't work, lie down and play dead. A territorial bear will leave you alone. However, if the bear keeps attacking after you play dead, fight back as the bear is predatory. If you have a negative encounter and the bear poses an immediate threat or danger to public safety, report it to the BC Conservation Officer Service by calling 1-877-952-7277 (RAPP).

Cougars

While cougar sightings are infrequent, the local cougar population is large. It is very rare for cougars to attack adults, but they will sometimes attack children and dogs. If you see a cougar, don't run. Back away slowly. Gather together in a group and pick up small children. Try to look big by waving your arms over your head. If the cougar doesn't retreat, shout at it and throw things. If it attacks, fight back.

Mountain Goats

Even though they are herbivores, mountain goats can be dangerous. They have sharp horns and may use them to defend their personal space. Mountain goat sightings are rare in most parts of southwestern BC, but there is a resident herd in Cathedral Provincial Park (Trip 40). Unfortunately, this herd has become habituated to humans and actively seeks out food from campers. The goats also crave salts and have discovered they can lick salt from sweat on hikers' clothing or from urine.

For your safety, and to keep the goats wild, stay at least 50 m (164 ft) away from them. If a mountain goat approaches, slowly move away. If necessary, chase goats away by yelling, waving your arms, or throwing rocks. To avoid attracting goats, never feed them and do not leave clothing or gear unattended. And always pee in outhouses. If you aren't near an outhouse, pee on rocks, bare soil, or snow at least 50 m (164 ft) from a trail.

Food Storage and Backcountry Cooking: Protecting Your Food From Animals

In many backcountry campgrounds, animals have realized that humans are a source of food. In southwestern BC, these critters include mice, squirrels, and birds, as well as larger, more dangerous animals like bears.

Widgeon Falls on the way to Widgeon Lake (Trip 22).

To avoid attracting animals to your campsite, always cook 100 m (328 ft) away from your tent. Clean up all food scraps after eating. Never burn food scraps in a fire, as this can attract animals. Store all food, cooking equipment, and scented items, such as toiletries and sunscreen, in a food locker, food hang, or bear canister. Any clothing that is smelly from food or toiletries should be cached as well. Never leave these items in your tent or backpack.

Many of the backcountry campgrounds in this guide have food storage lockers or huts to store food inside. Others have food-hanging poles or wires, which suspend your food out of reach of bears but leave it exposed to the elements and to clever birds or rodents. Bring a weather- and chew-resistant bag like a lightweight dry bag to prevent small animals from getting at your food. You can also purchase bear- and critter-resistant bags called Ursacks. While these bags are made of super-strong Spectra fabric that can resist being chewed or clawed, they aren't odour-proof, waterproof, or crush-proof. The manufacturer recommends lining them with a specially designed odour-proof bag and aluminum liner.

In campgrounds without provided food storage, you will need to construct your own food hang with a rope and carabiner to keep your food away from bears. Suspend your food from a tree branch at least 1.5 m (5 ft) from the hanging branch and the tree trunk and 4 m (13 ft) off the ground. This technique sounds straightforward but takes a lot of practice to get right. It can also be very difficult to find trees with suitable branches, especially at high elevations. Consider investing in a bear canister. These sturdy hard plastic containers require tools and thumbs to open. Thankfully bears have neither. Bear canisters hold less food and are heavier and more expensive than food-hang gear. However, they are much easier to use.

5. HOW TO GET HELP

No one plans to get injured or lost on a hike, but it happens to even the most prepared people. If you need to call for help, remember that search and rescue is completely free in BC. There is no charge for rescue. If you have cell service, call 911. The dispatcher will help coordinate search and rescue. However, many of the trails in this guide do not have cell service.

Consider carrying a personal locator beacon (PLB) or a satellite messaging device like a Garmin inReach to call for emergency help. Carry a whistle to alert other hikers in the area or help rescuers locate you. Shouting will make your voice hoarse, but you can keep blowing a whistle for hours. As well, the sound of a whistle carries farther than the human voice. A mirror, flares, and matches to make a signal fire can also help rescuers see you from the air. If you are unable to call for help at all, your trip plan is your lifeline. Your emergency contact will call 911 to trigger a rescue if you do not return on time.

Looking down to Garibaldi Lake (Trip 9) from Panorama Ridge.

WILDERNESS ETHICS AND LEAVE NO TRACE

As more and more people go into the wilderness, we must all do our part to keep our wild places wild. Recreationists are increasingly using helicopters and other motorized means to access the alpine and other more remote areas, yet this practice increases our impact on fragile ecosystems and wildlife populations. In the 1970s, the US Forest Service developed the concept of Leave No Trace. Its seven principles guide wilderness users to leave as little impact on the land as possible. Today, non-profit Leave No Trace education organizations exist in countries all over the world. I am a certified Leave No Trace Master Educator and have been volunteering with Leave No Trace Canada since 2006. If you want to learn more about Leave No Trace, or if you want to take a Leave No Trace Awareness Workshop, visit LeaveNoTrace.ca.

Whether you are new to backpacking or are an experienced hiker, familiarize yourself with the Leave No Trace principles below.

1. PLAN AHEAD AND PREPARE

Check the weather forecast, trail conditions, and park regulations before your hike. This helps ensure that you will have a safe and fun hike, while also minimizing your impact on nature. Leave a trip plan and pack a first-aid kit and the Ten Essentials in case something goes wrong. Portion and package food at home to reduce the chance of leaving garbage on the trail.

2. TRAVEL AND CAMP ON DURABLE SURFACES

Hike and camp on durable surfaces like rocks, gravel, bare soil, and snow. Avoid alpine meadows, marshes, and other sensitive surfaces where the vegetation can take years to grow. Stay on the trail. Cutting switchbacks or walking off-trail to avoid mud causes erosion and tramples vegetation. If there is no trail, have your group spread out to avoid creating one.

If possible, camp in a designated or previously used campsite, preferably on a wooden tent platform or earthen tent pad. If there are no designated or previously used campsites, pitch your tent on gravel, bare dirt, snow, or dry grass to minimize your impact. Try to camp 70 m (230 ft) away from water sources since the vegetation in these areas is fragile and animals need uninterrupted access routes to water. Most of the trips in this guide have established campsites. Where there are none, I have recommended the most low-impact place to camp.

3. DISPOSE OF WASTE PROPERLY

Be responsible when disposing of trash, human waste, and soap in the wilderness. All of these can pollute water, making it unsafe to drink or killing plants and fish. Animals that learn to eat human food or waste may stop eating their natural food. It can also make them sick. Plus garbage and poop on the trails look disgusting!

Bring a plastic bag to pack out your trash, including food waste like fruit peels and eggshells. These can take months to biodegrade, and in the meantime they attract animals. A good rule is: "If it didn't grow here, it doesn't go here." Never burn your trash. It doesn't burn well, so it leaves a mess and can attract animals.

When washing dishes or yourself, try using just a warm, wet cloth. If you do use soap, choose the biodegradable kind. Don't wash directly in a river or lake: use a pot as a dish basin instead. Strain out any large particles, then dump the dirty water 70 m (230 ft) away from water sources. Biodegradable soap needs to filter through soil to break down. Don't dump it directly in a water source where it can kill fish and plants.

A dip in a wilderness lake is a fun way to cool off on a hot day. But if we aren't careful, we can also harm fragile ecosystems. Before you jump in, head 70 m (230 ft) away from the shore and use water and a cloth to wash bug spray and sunscreen off your skin. Their chemicals can kill plants and fish. If the lake is tiny and the only water source for a nearby campground, consider skipping the swim. Most campers don't want to drink someone else's swimming water, even after it is filtered or purified.

Use a toilet for human waste whenever possible. If there is no outhouse, pick a spot 70 m (230 ft) from trails, campsites, and water sources. Pee on bare ground, soil, or rocks to avoid damaging vegetation. If you have to poop, use a small trowel, stick, or tent peg to dig a hole 15 cm (6 in) deep. Poop into the hole and then bury it. The best practice is to bring a resealable plastic bag to pack out your toilet paper, but you can also bury it with your poop. Don't burn it since you can accidentally start a forest fire.

Don't bury used menstrual supplies or dump them in outhouses. They don't biodegrade so you need to pack them out. Store used toilet paper and menstrual supplies in a sealed plastic bag securely with your food and other toiletries at night to avoid attracting animals. If you use a menstrual cup, bury the fluid in a cat hole or pour it into an outhouse.

If you are backpacking with a dog, pack out their poop or bury it like you would human poop. Dog poop contains bacteria and parasites that aren't normally found in the backcountry. Leaving it in the wilderness can make wildlife sick.

4. LEAVE WHAT YOU FIND

Leave the wilderness as you found it to keep ecosystems intact and let other hikers enjoy them too. If we all picked flowers or brought home rocks or historical items, there wouldn't be any left. Take a photo instead.

Good campsites are found, not made. Don't build structures, cut down trees, or dig trenches. When you leave your camp, it should look like you were never there. Please don't leave graffiti or build piles of rocks. Other hikers may mistake your "art" for trail markers or cairns and be led astray. As well, many animals and insects live under rocks. When you move them, you destroy their homes.

5. MINIMIZE CAMPFIRE IMPACTS

In the last decade, forest fires have become more common and more destructive in BC. Careless campfires accidentally start many forest fires. Campfires can also have other negative impacts, such as scorching soil or leading to dead branches being overharvested from the forest. It can take damaged ecosystems decades to recover. Plan to cook on a stove, not over a fire. It's quicker, more fuel efficient, and has less impact on the wilderness. Consider foregoing a fire and gathering around a small lantern instead.

If you do have a fire, learn to minimize your impact. Check regulations before you go to find out if fires are permitted in the park or the region. Many parks have year-round fire bans to protect sensitive ecosystems with fragile soils, short growing seasons, and a lack of firewood.

Use an existing fire ring and avoid building new ones. Ensure the soil under the fire is protected with gravel, rocks, or ash to avoid scorching soil or burning tree roots. When gathering firewood, stick to the "4 Ds": dead, down, dinky, and distant. Dead and downed wood burns best: never cut live

Lightning Lakes and Hozomeen Mountain from Despair Pass, Skyline Trail (Trip 38).

trees. Dinky branches help keep your fire small and mean you don't need to carry an axe. Gather your firewood from a place distant from your camp to avoid overharvesting.

Most importantly, make sure your fire is completely out when you leave it. Bring a collapsible bucket or water container and make campfire soup: douse the fire, stir up the ashes, test to see if it feels warm, then repeat until it's cool to the touch.

6. RESPECT WILDLIFE

The wilderness is home to many animals. You are just a visitor, so treat wildlife with respect. Never feed animals, either intentionally or by leaving your food unattended. Human food can make them sick. If they develop a taste for it, they may lose their ability to find food on their own. They may also attack people in the hope of getting food. Some animals like squirrels and whisky-jacks may look super cute and beg for handouts, but don't give in!

Wild animals need space to maintain their natural behaviour. Observe them from a respectful distance using binoculars or use the zoom lens on your camera to get a better look. If an animal changes their behaviour, you are too close. Keep your dog on a leash and under control so they don't harass wildlife. Off-leash dogs can also be dangerous if they chase a predator, and then the predator follows the dog back to you. Many negative bear encounters begin with an off-leash dog. While dogs are permitted on many trips in this book, they are not recommended in areas with high bear activity.

7. BE CONSIDERATE OF OTHERS

We all share the trails, huts, and campsites. Respect the way other people wish to experience nature, and do not let your behaviour negatively impact someone else's experience. Learn and follow basic backcountry etiquette. Yield to others on the trail. Step off the trail to take breaks so you aren't in someone's way. Give other groups space at viewpoints, popular photo spots, or in camp. Keep your voice low and avoid yelling. Leave the music at home: most campers want to enjoy the sounds of nature. Backpack in small groups of fewer than 10 people to minimize your impact on the environment and others. But above all else, be kind. Being nice goes a long way when you're sharing space.

HOW TO USE THIS BOOK

THE TRIPS IN this book are divided into geographic regions. Each regional section begins with an overview of its climate, geography, and culture, as well as practical information like where in the area to buy supplies and camp. Each hike includes a map, photo, statistics, ratings, driving directions, a trail description, camping details, information on how to extend your trip, and a list of further resources. (Please note: The trail and road conditions are written for summer conditions.)

Below are definitions for the ratings and statistics used in this book:

Outstanding Trip ★: While all of the trips in this book are worthwhile, a select few are truly spectacular.

DIFFICULTY
A guide to how challenging each trip will be.

● **Easy:** Trips that are short and flat.

■ **Moderate:** Trips that are longer with more than 400 m (1312 ft) of elevation gain on non-technical terrain.

◆ **Challenging:** Trips that have more than 700 m (2297 ft) of elevation gain, and may be longer and have some technical terrain or route-finding challenges.

◆◆ **Very challenging:** Trips with more than 1100 m (3609 ft) of elevation gain, very technical terrain, and/or some route-finding.

STATISTICS
Duration: The recommended number of days you should allow to complete the trip. This includes your hike to the campground and back, as well as

recommended day hikes from a backcountry base camp. I have assumed six to eight hours of hiking at most each day, though many trips are much shorter.

Distance: The round-trip distance you'll cover on the hike from the trailhead to the campground and back to the trailhead. Trips with multiple options are expressed as a range, with the precise distance to each location noted in the trail description. This statistic does not include day hikes from a backcountry base camp.

Elevation Gain: Elevation gain is the difference between the highest and lowest points on the trip. Trips with multiple route options show elevation gain as a range, with each option noted in the trail description. Where your route climbs straight up a mountain, this statistic is straightforward. However, on cross-country routes, this number does not encompass all of the small (or large) ups and downs you will encounter.

High Point: The highest elevation you'll reach on the trip. For trips with multiple routes, this is the highest point on any of them. Remember that snow can stay late into the season in the mountains, so use this statistic along with the best months recommendation to pick the ideal time to hike each trail.

Best Months: The best months to hike each trail without encountering significant snow or freezing temperatures overnight.

Fees and Reservations: Any user fees and/or reservations required for the trip.

Regulations: Any restrictions on fires, smoking, cannabis, dogs, bikes, swimming, and drones.

Caution: Unique hazards, such as challenging navigation, exposed terrain, wildlife, shared trails with mountain bikes, or extreme weather, that you might encounter.

KEY TO MAP SYMBOLS

P Parking

T Toilet

△ Designated Camping

▲ Informal Camping
   (no facilities)

   Food Storage

   Waterfall

   Viewpoint

   Ferry Dock

   Backcountry Hut

   Backcountry Shelter

   Hotel/Lodge

4WD 4-Wheel-Drive Road

⚠ Warning

99 Primary Highway

▲ Mountain Peak

→ Direction of Travel/
   Off-Map Destination

Road

Track

Trail

Described Route

Described Route (off trail)

Alternative Route

Alternative Route (off trail)

Ski Lift

Railroad

800 Major Contour Line (100 m/328 ft)

Minor Contour Line (20 m/65 ft)

Stream/Creek

Forest

Ocean, Lake, Major River/Creek

Alpine (1000 m/3280 ft and higher)

Wetland

Glacier/Permanent Snow

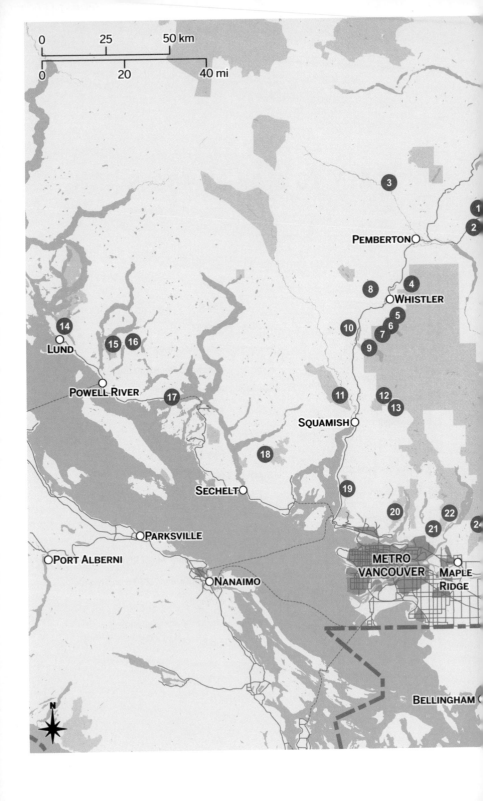

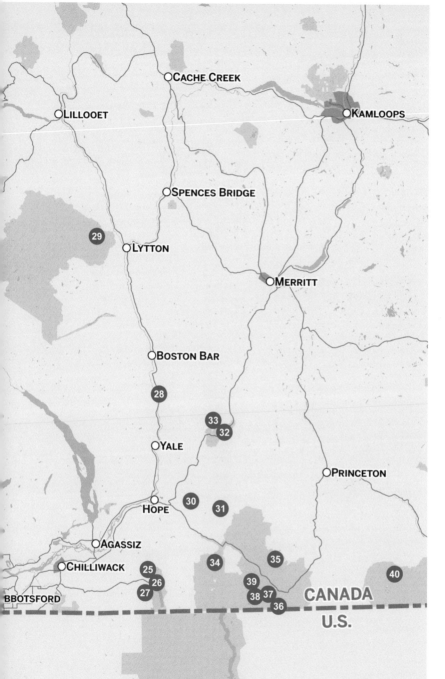

Trip	Difficulty	Duration	Distance	Elevation Gain	High Point
1 Marriott Meadows	■	2 days	10 km (6.2 mi)	420 m (1378 ft)	1820 m (5971 ft)
2 Joffre Lakes	■	2 days	10 km (6.2 mi)	320 m (1050 ft)	1570 m (5151 ft)
3 Tenquille Lake	■/◆◆	2–3 days	12–19 km (7.5–11.8 mi)	460–1460 m (1509–4790 ft)	1710 m (5610 ft)
4 Wedgemount Lake	◆◆	2 days	13 km (8.1 mi)	1160 m (3806 ft)	1970 m (6463 ft)
5 Russet Lake	◆	2 days	25–29 km (15.5–18 mi)	305–1280 m (1001–4199 ft)	2181 m (7156 ft)
6 Cheakamus Lake	●	2 days	7–14 km (4.3–8.7 mi)	50 m (164 ft)	900 m (2953 ft)
7 Helm Creek	■	2–3 days	17 km (10.6 mi)	700 m (2297 ft)	1550 m (5085 ft)
8 Rainbow Pass	■	2–3 days	13–20.6 km (8.1–12.8 mi)	445–890 m (1460–2920 ft)	1430 m (4692 ft)
9 Garibaldi Lake and Taylor Meadows	■	2–4 days	15–18 km (9.3–11.2 mi)	900 m (2953 ft)	1500 m (4921 ft)
10 Brew Hut	◆	2 days	12 km (7.5 mi)	566 m (1857 ft)	1686 m (5531 ft)
11 Lake Lovely Water	◆◆	2–3 days	11 km (6.8 mi)	1135 m (3724 ft)	1150 m (3773 ft)
12 Elfin Lakes and Rampart Ponds	■	2–4 days	22–42 km (13.7–26.1 mi)	610 m (2001 ft)	1590 m (5217 ft)
13 Watersprite Lake	■	2 days	17 km (10.6 mi)	660 m (2165 ft)	1470 m (4823 ft)
14 Manzanita Bluff	●/■	2 days	7–16 km (4.3–9.9 mi)	295 m (968 ft)	365 m (1198 ft)
15 Confederation Lake and Fiddlehead Landing	■/◆	2–3 days	15–30 km (9.3–18.6 mi)	600 m (1969 ft)	690 m (2264 ft)
16 Tin Hat Hut	◆	2 days	12 km (7.5 mi)	700 m (2297 ft)	1170 m (3839 ft)
17 Saltery Bay Loop	■	2–3 days	18 km (11.2 mi)	570 m (1870 ft)	570 m (1870 ft)
18 Tetrahedron Plateau	■	2–3 days	12–17 km (7.5–10.6 mi)	280–680 m (919–2231 ft)	1500 m (4921 ft)
19 Howe Sound Crest Trail	◆◆	2–4 days	31.7 km (19.7 mi) one way	660 m (2165 ft)	1548 m (5079 ft)
20 Elsay Lake	◆◆	2 days	20 km (12.4 mi)	575 m (1886 ft)	1250 m (4101 ft)

Best Months	Driving Distance	Fees	Reservations	Hut	Dogs Allowed	Food Storage
July to September	190 km (118 mi)	Y	Y for hut only	Y	Y but not in the hut	Y
Late June to early October	185 km (115 mi)	Y	Y	N	N	Y
July to September	182 km (113 mi)	N	N	Y	Y but not recommended	Y
July to September	138 km (86 mi)	Y	Y	Y	N	Y
Mid-July to September	125 km (78 mi)	Y	Y	Y	N	Y
May to November	124 km (77 mi)	Y	Y	N	N	Y
July to September	124 km (77 mi)	Y	Y	N	N	Y
June to October	124 km (77 mi)	N	N	N	Y but not on the Rainbow Lake Trail	Y
July to September	102 km (63 mi)	Y	Y	N	N	Y
July to September	106 km (66 mi)	Y for hut only	N	Y	Y	Y
Late June to early October	72 km (45 mi)	Y for hut only	Y for hut only	Y	Y but not in the hut	Y but not at Sandspit
July to September	84 km (52 mi)	Y	Y	Y	N	Y
Mid-June to October	84 km (52 mi)	Y for hut only	Y for hut only	Y	Y but not in the hut	Y
March to November	200 km (124 mi)	N	N	Y	Y	N
April to November	191 km (119 mi)	N	N	Y	Y on leash at Confederation Lake	Y
June to October	183 km (114 mi)	N	N	Y	Y	Y
April to November	142 km (88 mi)	N	N	Y	Y	Y but not at Rainy Day Lake
Mid-June to October	89 km (55 mi)	Y	N	Y	N	Y
Mid-July to September	30–45 km (19–28 mi)	N	N	N	Y but not recommended	N
June to October	31 km (19 mi)	N	N	Y	Y on leash	Y

Trip	Difficulty	Duration	Distance	Elevation Gain	High Point
21 Dennett Lake	■/◆	2–3 days	11–18 km (7.1–11.2 mi)	725–860 m (2379–2822 ft)	1075 m (3527 ft)
22 Widgeon Lake	◆	2–3 days	19 km (11.8 mi)	800 m (2625 ft)	800 m (2625 ft)
23 Gold Creek Canyon	●	2 days	9.6–19.4 km (6–12 mi)	170–275 m (558–902 ft)	375 m (1230 ft)
24 Golden Ears	◆◆	2–3 days	21 km (13 mi)	1180 m (3871 ft)	1370 m (4495 ft)
25 Lindeman and Greendrop Lakes	●/■	2 days	3.4–11 km (2.1–6.8 mi)	200–350 m (656–1148 ft)	990 m (3248 ft)
26 Flora Lake	◆	2 days	14 km (8.7 mi)	1060 m (3478 ft)	1740 m (5709 ft)
27 Radium Lake	◆	2–3 days	19 km (11.8 mi)	900 m (2953 ft)	1515 m (4970 ft)
28 Tikwalus Heritage Trail	◆	2 days	13 km (8.1 mi)	790 m (2592 ft)	910 m (2986 ft)
29 Lower Stein Valley	●	2 days	4–26 km (2.5–16.2 mi)	30–350 m (98–1148 ft)	600 m (1969 ft)
30 Manson Ridge	● to ◆	2–3 days	12–15.5 km (7.5–9.6 mi)	200–600 m (656–1969 ft)	950 m (3117 ft)
31 Palmers Pond	●	2 days	6–12 km (3.7–7.5 mi)	190–385 m (623–1263 ft)	1855 m (6086 ft)
32 Falls Lake	●	2 days	2 km (1.2 mi)	50 m (164 ft)	1300 m (4265 ft)
33 Little Douglas Lake	●	2 days	3.5 km (2.2 mi)	100 m (328 ft)	1330 m (4364 ft)
34 Skagit River Trail	●	2 days	8 km (5 mi)	75 m (246 ft)	670 m (2198 ft)
35 Heather Trail	■	2–5 days	10–45 km (6.2–28 mi)	320 m (1050 ft)	2120 m (6955 ft)
36 Frosty Mountain	■	2–3 days	14 km (8.7 mi)	670 m (2198 ft)	1910 m (6266 ft)
37 Lightning Lakes	●	2 days	13 km (8.1 mi)	none	1250 m (4101 ft)
38 Skyline Trail	■	2 days	25 km (15.5 mi)	520 m (1706 ft)	1890 m (6201 ft)
39 Poland Lake	■	2 days	16 km (9.9 mi)	465 m (1526 ft)	1835 m (6020 ft)
40 Cathedral Lakes	◆	3–4 days	29–31 km (18–19.3 mi)	1360 m (4462 ft)	2190 m (7185 ft)

Best Months	Driving Distance	Fees	Reservations	Hut	Dogs Allowed	Food Storage
July to October	37 km (23 mi)	N	N	N	Y on leash but not recommended	N
Mid-June to October	52 km (32 mi)	N	N	N	Y on leash but not recommended	N
April to November	62 km (39 mi)	Y	N	N	Y on leash	N
July to September	62 km (39 mi)	Y	N	N	Y on leash	Y but not at Alder Flats
May to October	136 km (84 mi)	Y	N	N	Y on leash	Y
Mid-July to September	136 km (84 mi)	Y	N	N	Y on leash	Y
July to September	137 km (85 mi)	Y	N	N	Y on leash	Y
May to October	196 km (122 mi)	N	N	N	Y	Y
April to October	266 km (165 mi)	N	N	N	Y on leash but not recommended	Y
June to October	163 km (101 mi)	N	N	N	Y	Y
July to September	252 km 157 mi)	N	N	N	Y	Y
July to September	200 km (124 mi)	N	N	N	Y on leash	Y
Late June to October	215 km (134 mi)	N	N	N	Y	Y
April to November	185 km (115 mi)	N	N	N	Y on leash	Y
July to mid-September	232 km (144 mi)	Y	N	N	Y on leash	Y
July to early October	219 km (136 mi)	Y	N	N	Y on leash	Y
June to October	221 km (137 mi)	Y	N	N	Y on leash	Y
July to September	221 km (137 mi)	Y	N	N	Y on leash	Y
July to September	221 km (137 mi)	Y	N	N	Y on leash	Y
July to September	367 km (228 mi)	Y	N	N	N	Y

Middle Joffre Lake, Joffre Lakes (Trip 2).

PEMBERTON AND WHISTLER

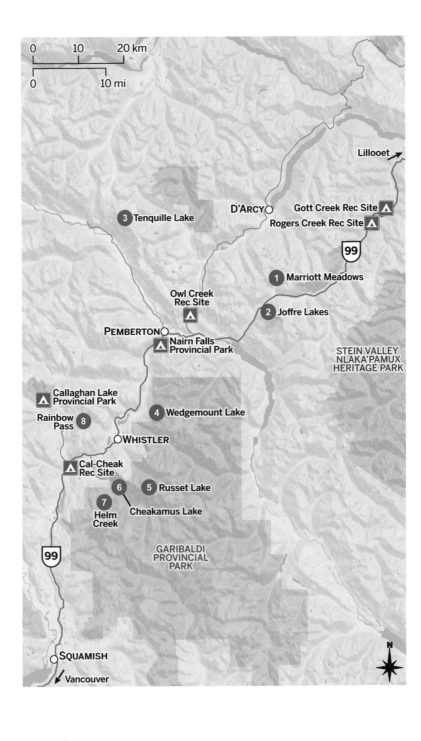

WHEN I FIRST saw the glaciated summits near Whistler and Pemberton from the valley floor, they seemed impossibly distant. But with trails snaking their way up the precipitous slopes, walking amongst these lofty peaks is achievable. You'll discover a completely new landscape up above the treeline: aquamarine lakes shine like jewels. Brilliantly coloured wildflowers cling tenaciously to the smallest patches of soil amongst jagged scree. Pikas and marmots chirp and whistle as they scamper across meadows. And crevassed glaciers rumble downhill from rocky spires. Spend the night at a backcountry campground or hut to allow yourself more time in these special places.

Most of the hikes in the Whistler and Pemberton region are accessed off Highway 99, also known as the Sea to Sky Highway. The ski resort village of Whistler is the region's hub, but the town of Pemberton to the north also supports a small community.

The region sits high in the Coast Mountains, so the trails here do not melt out until early summer. The climate is characterized by cold and wet winters with dry, warm summers. North of Pemberton, the landscape is more influenced by the Interior climate, making it a bit hotter and drier in the summer.

This region is the traditional territory of the Skwx̱wú7mesh Úxwumixw (Squamish) and Lı́lwat7úl (Lı́l'wat) Nations. Squamish territory extends north from the town of Squamish to the Whistler Valley. The heart of Lı́l'wat territory is the village of Mount Currie, where most of the Nation live today. Their traditional territory extends from the Whistler Valley in the south, north to the Duffey Lake Road and the Pemberton Valley. To learn more about their culture, history, and art, visit the Squamish Lı́l'wat Cultural Centre in Whistler.

Supplies: Whistler has several large grocery stores, gas stations, and well-stocked outdoor stores. Pemberton has a grocery store, several gas stations, and a small outdoor store.

Accommodation: Whistler and Pemberton offer lots of choice for hotels. Camping is a bit harder to arrange. Nairn Falls Provincial Park just south of Pemberton accepts camping reservations. There are several first-come, first-served campgrounds in the area: Cal-Cheak Rec Site off Highway 99 south of Whistler, Callaghan Lake Provincial Park in the Callaghan Valley, Owl Creek Rec Site north of Mount Currie, and Rogers Creek and Gott Creek Rec Sites on the Duffey Lake Road.

1
MARRIOTT MEADOWS

Difficulty: ■
Duration: 2 days
Distance: 10 km (6.2 mi)

Elevation Gain: 420 m (1378 ft)
High Point: 1820 m (5971 ft)
Best Months: July to September

Fees and Reservations: Hut and camping fees are $25/person/night, payable online. The hut requires reservations. Camping is first-come, first-served.

Regulations: No dogs inside the hut.

Caution: The mosquitos and blackflies can be bad in July.

EXPERIENCE THE TRANSITIONS from wet coastal forest to alpine tundra as you hike up to Marriott Meadows. From the end of the well-built trail at the 16-bunk Wendy Thompson Hut, choose your own adventure. Enjoy the wildflowers and babbling brook next to the hut. Hike a few minutes uphill to enjoy views across the valley to the Matier Glacier and Joffre Lakes (Trip 2). Or for those comfortable with off-trail exploration, take a day trip to one of the many brilliant blue alpine lakes in the rocky bowl below Mount Marriott. Relax after your adventures in the well-appointed hut or in the nearby informal campground.

GETTING THERE
Head north on Highway 99 past Pemberton and Mount Currie. About 26 km (16.2 mi) past Mount Currie (and 3 km/1.9 mi past the Joffre Lakes parking

Hiking above the lake.

lot), shortly after a bridge, look for an unsigned gravel road branching off the highway to the left. If you pass a large maintenance shed on the right side, you've gone too far. Low-clearance **2WD vehicles** should park on the highway shoulder. It's a 2.5-km (1.6-mi) hike with 100 m (328 ft) of elevation gain to the trailhead.

Turn left onto the gravel road and go left at a fork. After 0.8 km (0.5 mi), arrive at a small **parking lot**. If you have a **4WD vehicle**, continue along the bumpy and narrow road, ignoring a right-hand fork, to the road's end, about 2.5 km (1.6 mi) from where you left the highway. There is space for two or three cars here. You can also park in one of several pullouts along the way, and walk the rest of the way to the trailhead.

TRAIL

TRIP PLANNER

0 km (0 mi)	Trailhead
1 km (0.6 mi)	Rohr junction
3 km (1.9 mi)	Lake
5 km (3.1 mi)	Wendy Thompson Hut

The trail starts at the end of the gravel road. The first 0.5 km (0.3 mi) travels through a lush Douglas-fir and western hemlock forest in a valley bottom with several creek crossings on small bridges. It can be very muddy, so step carefully. But the wet section is over quickly as you climb steeply up the slope.

About 1 km (0.6 mi) from the trailhead, arrive at a **junction**. Your route to Marriott Meadows heads straight. The trail to the right goes to Rohr Lake. Just after the junction, cross a small creek on a log bridge. Continue hiking up the steep trail, then cross the larger Cayoosh Creek on another log bridge around 2 km (1.2 mi) from the start. This one has a handline to help you keep your balance.

As you continue uphill, the forest transitions from coastal forest to the smaller trees of the subalpine zone, where Engelmann spruce and subalpine fir dominate. The forest starts to thin out around 3 km (1.9 mi) from the trailhead, with thickets of black huckleberry and carpets of heather replacing the trees. The grade eases here too, which is a welcome change. A few minutes later, an unnamed **lake** comes into view. Scramble through talus fields, watching for cairns and orange flagging high above the shore of the lake for about 0.5 km (0.3 mi).

The trail descends to the lakeshore at the west end of the lake. Cross a stream entering the lake, then head along the shoreline for a few metres. Look for a trail with orange flagging heading up the slope into the trees. Follow the trail through open forest for another 0.5 km (0.3 mi) to reach the **hut and camping area**. It's set in a beautiful rocky bowl interspersed with patches of grassy meadow. A babbling stream runs through the centre with wildflowers clustered on its banks.

CAMPING AND HUT

The Whistler section of the Alpine Club of Canada (ACC) built this gothic-arched backcountry hut in 2000. The hut is named in honour of Wendy Thompson, a local paramedic who was killed in a helicopter crash in 1995. It was built to support backcountry skiing, but the trail travels through serious avalanche terrain and, in winter, is recommended for experienced parties only. To minimize impact on the sensitive terrain, the ACC prefers that visitors sleep in the hut rather than pitch tents. However, you can camp in the meadows and use the hut facilities if you pay camping fees.

Campsites: Several near the hut. Take care to avoid crushing fragile vegetation. The lowest-impact sites are amongst the boulders on the other side of the stream.

NATURE NOTE

The hillside on the opposite side of the lake is almost bare with a few patches of trees growing in straight lines. If you look carefully, you'll see that the trees occupy slightly higher ground. Each winter, avalanches thunder down these chutes, uprooting trees and bushes. Only the hardy trees on the higher ground survive.

Camping amongst the boulders near the Wendy Thompson Hut.

Hut Sleeps: 16 on bunks in the loft
Toilet: Outhouse near the hut
Water: Collect from the stream beside the hut.
Food Storage: On hooks inside the hut
Other Amenities: The hut has foam mattresses, a wood stove, tables, benches, a kitchen counter with grey-water sinks, cooking utensils, plates, cups, pots, and solar lighting.

EXTENDING YOUR TRIP

Upper Marriott Basin: Hikers with good map-and-compass skills can spend a couple hours exploring in the trails of upper Marriott Basin above the treeline. There are numerous small lakes and tarns within a few kilometres of the hut, but careful navigation is required through the boulder fields. A faint cairned route leads towards the summit of 2725-m-high (8940 ft) Mount Marriott about 6 km (3.7 mi) away, best for experienced scramblers only. The mountain is named as a memorial to RCAF Flying Officer Terence James Marriott, killed in action in World War II.

Rohr Lake: The short hike to Rohr Lake is a worthy side trip. The beautiful blue lake is set in a subalpine bowl. From the junction, gain 220 m (722 ft) over 1 km (0.6 mi) on a steep and muddy trail past blueberry bushes, boulders, and a waterfall.

FURTHER RESOURCES

ACC Whistler: info, hut fees, and reservations https://accwhistler.ca/Wendy Thompson.html
NTS Map: 092J08

2
JOFFRE LAKES

Difficulty: ■

Duration: 2 days

Distance: 10 km (6.2 mi)

Elevation Gain: 320 m (1050 ft)

High Point: 1570 m (5151 ft)

Best Months: Late June to early October

Fees and Reservations: Reservations are required to camp and cost $6/night for each tent pad. Camping fees are $5/person/night. Both reservation and camping fees are payable online.

Regulations: No fires. No dogs. No drones. No smoking, vaping, or cannabis.

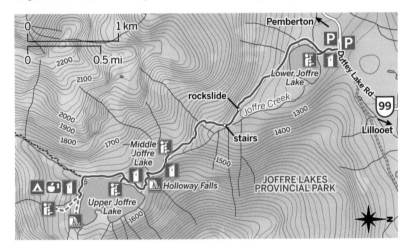

JOFFRE LAKES PROVINCIAL PARK is one of the most popular parks in BC, and for good reason. It's a relatively easy hike past a chain of three brilliant turquoise lakes with glaciers hanging high above. On weekends, the lakes teem with hordes of day trippers posing for selfies to add to the thousands already on social media. But if you score a coveted campground reservation, you'll be able to enjoy dusk and dawn in this beautiful place—without the crowds. The fragile subalpine environment is already overstressed from current levels of use, so please tread lightly and hike responsibly. And consider visiting midweek to lessen your impact.

GETTING THERE

Drive north on Highway 99 past Pemberton and Mount Currie. About 23 km (14.3 mi) after Mount Currie, look for the Joffre Lakes parking lot on your right. This small parking lot fills very early in the day. If it's full, park in the

The view of Upper Joffre Lake from above the waterfall.

overflow lot on the other side of the highway. Parking on the highway shoulder is not permitted and your car will get towed. There are outhouses at the main parking lot. See the Further Resources section for shuttle bus services that will take you from Vancouver or Whistler to Joffre Lakes.

TRAIL

TRIP PLANNER

0 km (0 mi)	Trailhead
0.3 km (0.2 mi)	Lower Joffre Lake viewpoint junction
1.8 km (1.1 mi)	Rockslide
3 km (1.9 mi)	Middle Joffre Lake
3.6 km (2.2 mi)	Holloway Falls
4 km (2.5 mi)	Upper Joffre Lake viewpoint junction
4.8 km (3 mi)	Junction with Tszil mountaineering route
5 km (3.1 mi)	Campground and junction with waterfall trail (0.3 km/0.2 mi away) and moraine viewpoint trail (1 km/0.6 mi to viewpoint)

A wide and fairly flat path heads through the forest from the trailhead. Within 0.3 km (0.2 mi), reach a junction. The main trail to Upper Joffre Lake continues to the right. But for now, go straight for a few metres to reach a **viewpoint on Lower Joffre Lake** where you can see the glaciers on Joffre Peak far above.

Holloway Falls.

Retrace your steps to the junction and turn left onto the main trail. Within a few minutes you'll cross a large wooden bridge over Joffre Creek as it drains from the lake. Catch a last glimpse of Lower Joffre Lake through the trees to your left as the trail begins to climb.

About 1.8 km (1.1 mi) from the start, reach an open area of **rockslide**. Extensive trail work in this section over the last decade has rendered the formerly challenging scramble across car-sized boulders into a literal walk in the park. Hike through the rockslide and head back into the forest. This section has the steepest grades and even some stairs to help you up the slope. Look for a stump carved into an owl about 2.6 km (1.6 mi) from the trailhead. When you see it, you'll know you're almost at the top of the climb.

Reach the shores of **Middle Joffre Lake**. There are a few places to get down to the lakeshore for a photo op. Cross a bridge over the lake outlet creek and pass a spur trail to an outhouse. Continue along the lakeshore for a few minutes to find the famous Joffre Lake floating log. A line of hikers is often waiting their turn to walk out onto the log to pose for pictures.

Continue along the lakeshore, past a stump carved into the shape of a raven, and begin the short climb to Upper Joffre Lake on switchbacks and stairs. This section of trail was rerouted in 2014 and reaches **Holloway Falls**, a beautiful stair-stepped waterfall.

A few minutes past the waterfall, cross a bridge over the outlet from Upper Joffre Lake. You'll get your first view of Upper Joffre Lake through the trees a few minutes later. Continue on the rocky path set back from the lakeshore. About 4 km (2.5 mi) into the hike, a spur trail leads to an outhouse on your right. Another trail on your left goes to a **lakeside viewpoint** in a boulder field. Many day hikers stop here, content with the spectacular view of huge glaciers tumbling down a rocky slope towards the turquoise waters of Upper Joffre Lake.

Your trail to the campground heads along the western shore of Upper Joffre Lake for another kilometre, crossing rocks and roots as it undulates along the lakeshore. At 4.8 km (3 mi) from the trailhead, cross a bridge over a creek. A sign marks a **junction with the route to Tszil Mountain**, a

NATURE NOTE

The impressive Stonecrop and Matier Glaciers tower above Upper Joffre Lake. Watch and listen carefully and you'll likely hear and see chunks of ice calving off the glaciers, especially on warm days. Look around you to see how these glaciers shaped the landscape when they extended into the valley you hiked up. The bedrock outcrops have been worn down by centuries of grinding ice. And the crumbling ridges of rocks nearby, called moraines, mark the former edges of the glaciers.

mountaineering route. Continue on the main trail, passing a helipad, and arrive at an outhouse a minute later. The main **campground** is just ahead of you, across a creek with stepping stones to aid in crossing.

CAMPING

The campground at Upper Joffre Lake is spread along the shoreline at the southwestern corner of the lake. A handful of campsites are located on a gravel beach, but most sites are flat spots carved out of the rocks of a moraine.

Campsites: 26 flat gravel sites
Toilet: Outhouse located 100 m (328 ft) before the campsite
Water: Collect from the stream between the outhouse and campground.
Food Storage: Large metal bearproof locker with numbered buckets to keep each campsite's food organized

EXTENDING YOUR TRIP

No marked trails lead beyond Upper Joffre Lake. However, there are several informal trails. Use caution in this area, as rocks and ice can fall from the glacier above at any time. In May 2019, two massive landslides rumbled down the eastern slopes of Joffre Peak just over the ridge from the lakes, spreading debris across a 5-km-long (3.1 mi) path that stretched nearly to Highway 99.

Waterfall: Follow a faint trail through the campground, parallel to the lakeshore, to reach a waterfall cascading over rocks into Joffre Lake. It's a 0.6-km (0.4 mi) round trip.
Moraine Viewpoint: Hike up the crest of a moraine behind the campground on a steep and well-worn trail through the rocks. It leads to a climbers' route on the glacier, which is for experienced mountaineers only. But hikers can follow the first section to get amazing views of the lake from above. The round trip is about 1 km (0.6 mi) with 150 m (492 ft) of elevation gain.

FURTHER RESOURCES

Joffre Lakes Provincial Park: info, fees, reservations http://bcparks.ca/parks/joffre-lakes/
Visit Joffre Lakes: shuttles and parking info https://www.visitjoffre.ca/home
Joffre Lakes Bus: shuttles https://www.joffrelakes.ca/
Trail Map: Stein to Joffre Trail Map by Trail Ventures BC
NTS Map: 092J08

3
TENQUILLE LAKE

Difficulty: ■/◆◆
Duration: 2 to 3 days
Distance: 12 to 19 km (7.5 to 11.8 mi)

Elevation Gain: 460 to 1460 m
(1509 to 4790 ft)
High Point: 1710 m (5610 ft)
Best Months: July to September

Fees and Reservations: No fees. The hut and camping are both first-come, first-served.

Regulations: Dogs permitted but not recommended.

Caution: Watch for mountain bikes. Grizzly bears are common in this area. The mosquitos can be bad here.

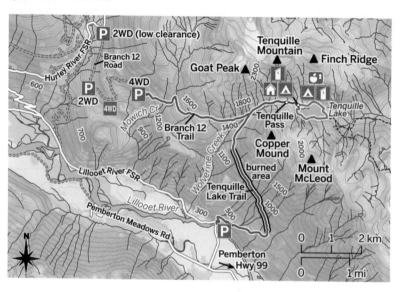

CRYSTAL-CLEAR TENQUILLE LAKE sits cradled amongst numerous craggy peaks. This subalpine lake features some gorgeous camping spots as well as a large hut to sleep in. However, the real draw here is the wildflowers in mid-summer. The open slopes around the lake light up with blooms of almost every imaginable colour, including red paintbrush, blue lupine, and white western anemone. From your base camp at the lakeside cabin and campground, fish for rainbow trout, explore the flat trail around the lake, or head up the trail-less slopes to summit nearby peaks. With two trails to choose from, you can access Tenquille Lake with either a 2WD or 4WD vehicle.

Looking down on Tenquille Lake from the slopes of Finch Ridge.

GETTING THERE

Turn off Highway 99 onto Pemberton Portage Road into the town of Pemberton and reset your odometer. Continue through town, then head north on Pemberton Meadows Road. Follow it through farmland for 26 km (16.2 mi). Turn right onto the Lillooet River Forest Service Road and continue for 1.5 km (0.9 mi) to a bridge. Immediately after the bridge, the road turns to gravel. Park here for the **Tenquille Creek trailhead**.

For the Branch 12 Trail, continue on Lillooet River FSR for another 7.5 km (4.7 mi). Turn right onto the Hurley River Forest Service Road. This road is graded each year and while it is steep and bumpy, it is usually fine for 2WD vehicles. Check road conditions online before attempting it.

Reset your odometer and drive up this road for approximately 10.5 km (6.5 mi). At a sharp hairpin bend, turn right on a road signed "Hurley River/ Tenquille Branch." This road is also known as Branch 12. **2WD vehicles** without good clearance should park here. Branch 12 is a decommissioned logging road with lots of bumps, steep sections, and water bars. With a high-clearance 2WD vehicle, you can drive the first 1.9 km (1.2 mi) to a parking lot. The remaining 3.1 km (1.9 mi) to the **Branch 12 trailhead** is **4WD only** due to deep water bars and creek crossings.

TRAIL

Three trails lead to Tenquille Lake. The Tenquille Lake Trail is the traditional route that climbs steeply from the Lillooet River. In recent years, the more moderate Branch 12 Trail has become the most popular since it is shorter and has much less elevation gain. Both trails are described below. A third trail via Tenquille Creek in the east requires a lot of 4WD driving and is not officially sanctioned, so it is not included here.

TRIP PLANNER

0 km (0 mi)	Tenquille Lake trailhead
7.5 km (4.7 mi)	Junction with Branch 12 Trail
9.5 km (5.9 mi)	Tenquille Lake Cabin and campground

The original route to Tenquille Lake, which began as a miners' access trail nearly 100 years ago, is challenging. It gains 1470 m (4823 ft) on a 9.5-km-long (5.9 mi) punishing ascent from the Lillooet River, but it is a good option for those with low-clearance 2WD cars who don't want to drive on gravel roads. Much of this trail was burned in a 2009 forest fire, and while it has been reopened, it is less travelled and is becoming overgrown. Use caution on windy days, as the burned trees can easily blow over. Keep an eye out for mountain bikers who descend this trail from the lake.

From the parking area near the Lillooet River bridge, walk east along the road for 50 m (164 ft) to the trailhead. The trail heads east in a rising traverse for the first 2.5 km (1.6 mi). As it starts to swing around to the north, enter the burned section of forest. Continue climbing steeply through the regenerating burn for the next few kilometres, crossing several streams that run dry later in the summer. This section of trail can be quite brushy with young aspen and alder trees that thrive in the full sun of the recovering burn. Watch for the pink blooms of fireweed in mid-summer.

About 6.5 km (4 mi) from the car, exit the burn zone and re-enter the forest as the trail moves closer in to the valley of Wolverine Creek. Continue climbing up the creek valley, crossing a large avalanche slope. About 1 km (0.6 mi) after you entered the forest, cross Wolverine Creek.

Immediately afterwards, reach a **junction with the Branch 12 Trail**. Turn right to head towards Tenquille Lake. While you still have some uphill left, the worst is over. Continue up the trail beside Wolverine Creek, passing

NATURE NOTE

In mid-summer, the pass and the slopes above the lake are covered in wild-flowers, especially western anemone. In bloom, their round white flowers are beautiful but unremarkable. But as they go to seed, they turn into shaggy mop-tops, reminiscent of characters straight out of a Dr. Seuss book. Watch for hoary marmots munching on blooms on the slopes behind the cabin.

underneath several avalanche chutes to Tenquille Pass. From the pass, it's an easy descent to the western end of Tenquille Lake, where you'll find the **cabin and campsites.**

BRANCH 12 TRAIL

TRIP PLANNER

0 km (0 mi)	Branch 12 trailhead
1.5 km (0.9 mi)	Mowich Creek
4.5 km (2.8 mi)	Junction with Tenquille Lake Trail
6 km (3.7 mi)	Tenquille Lake Cabin and campground

It's only 6 km (3.7 mi) to Tenquille Lake on the moderate Branch 12 Trail, which gains 460 m (1509 ft) of elevation from the 4WD-only trailhead. (Add another 3 to 5 km/1.9 to 3.1 mi and 260 to 350 m/853 to 1148 ft of elevation gain from the 2WD parking spots.) It can be very buggy at the trailhead and on the first few kilometres of trail, especially in the early summer.

The trail begins with a couple of tight switchbacks before beginning a more gradual rising traverse to the east. About 1.5 km (0.9 mi) from the car, the trail detours north into the valley of **Mowich Creek**, crossing the stream on a bridge. After the creek, the trail heads through the forest and gradually uphill. Over the next 3 km (1.9 mi), you'll cross countless small streams. Many of the footbridges have collapsed over the years, but they are still easy to cross without getting wet. This section provides spectacular views down to the Pemberton Valley.

About 4.5 km (2.8 mi) from the end of the road, reach a **junction** near Wolverine Creek. The path to the right is the steep Tenquille Lake Trail from the Lillooet River valley far below. Head left to continue east, ascending into the meadowy slopes of Tenquille Pass. The **cabin and campsites** near the shore of Tenquille Lake are just below you.

CAMPING AND HUT

The main camping area and cabin are located in a stand of trees at the east end of Tenquille Lake. More campsites are available near the lakeshore about 0.3 km (0.2 mi) to the east of the cabin. Follow the trail across an avalanche chute and a stream to find them. In 2011, the Pemberton Wildlife Association replaced a dilapidated log cabin used by local horseback riders and hunters since the 1940s.

Campsites: Lots of flat spots for tents near the cabin. And two camping areas 0.3 km (0.2 mi) to the east of the hut, with room for a few tents at each.
Hut Sleeps: About 16 on the loft floor

Swimming in Tenquille Lake near the hut.

Toilets: Outhouse near the cabin and another near the camping area to the east
Water: Collect from the streams flowing into the lake.
Food Storage: On hooks in the cabin or in the food lockers at each camping area
Other Amenities: The cabin has a wood stove, propane Coleman stove (bring your own 1L green propane cylinders), picnic tables, cooking counters, and LED lighting (bring your own AA or D batteries). The camping areas have metal firepits.

EXTENDING YOUR TRIP

Tenquille Lake Loop: Take an easy hike around Tenquille Lake on a 3-km (1.9-mi) loop trail. The flat path follows the lakeshore and is popular with anglers in the early morning and late evening. Bikes and horses are permitted on the south side of the lake only.

Explore Nearby Peaks: Experienced hikers with off-trail navigation skills will find lots of worthy objectives in the area. The meadowy slopes surrounding Tenquille Lake lead easily up to the top of several nearby peaks, though you will need to be comfortable scrambling over boulders and scree. The most straightforward peaks are Finch Ridge above the northwest corner of the lake and Mount McLeod above the southeast side of the lake.

FURTHER RESOURCES

Recreation Sites and Trails BC: info, maps http://www.sitesandtrailsbc.ca/
I Survived the Hurley: road conditions for the Hurley FSR https://isurvived thehurley.com/
Pemberton Wildlife Association: Tenquille Lake Hut info http://www. pembertonwildlifeassociation.com/news/2011/8/31/tenquille-lake-cabin-rules/
Driving Map: Vancouver, Coast & Mountains BC Backroad Mapbook
NTS Map: 092J10

4
WEDGEMOUNT LAKE

Difficulty: ♦♦
Duration: 2 days
Distance: 13 km (8.1 mi)

Elevation Gain: 1160 m (3806 ft)
High Point: 1970 m (6463 ft)
Best Months: July to September

Fees and Reservations: Reservations are required to camp and cost $6/night for each tent pad. Camping fees are $10/person/night. Both reservation and camping fees are payable online.

Regulations: No dogs. No fires. No drones. No smoking, vaping, or cannabis.

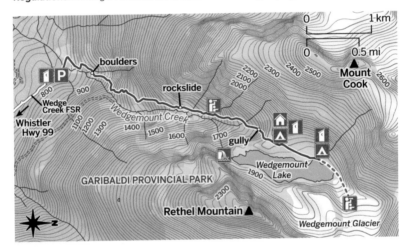

A TURQUOISE LAKE, snow-capped peaks, wildflowers clinging to rocks, campsites with incredible views, and an easily accessible glacier all await at Wedgemount Lake. The punishingly steep climb is well worth the effort. The trail ascends through the forest to a rocky headwall. At the top, the Wedgemount Glacier tumbles down between Wedge Mountain and Mount Weart, nearly reaching the lake. Enjoy the pink and purple alpenglow on the surrounding peaks at sunset from campsites on the lake or on a rocky knoll above it.

GETTING THERE

Head north from Whistler on Highway 99. A few minutes past the end of Green Lake, turn right onto a gravel road signed for Wedgemount Lake. Immediately cross the railway tracks and then a single-lane bridge. On the other side of the bridge, turn left onto Wedge Creek Forest Service Road,

The view of Wedgemount Lake and Wedgemount Glacier from a tent platform at the upper camping area.

which is a bit bumpy and steep but 2WD accessible. Reach another fork a few hundred metres later and go uphill to the right to stay on Wedge Creek FSR. About 150 m (492 ft) later, ignore a steep road heading uphill and stay left. Reach a large gravel parking lot 2 km (1.2 mi) from the highway. There's an outhouse here. If you are staying in Whistler, you can also take a taxi to the trailhead.

TRAIL

TRIP PLANNER

0 km (0 mi)	Trailhead
4.75 km (3 mi)	Rocky bowl
5.5 km (3.4 mi)	Bluff high point
6 km (3.7 mi)	Wedgemount Lake Hut and campground
6.5 km (4 mi)	Lakeshore campground
7.5 km (4.7 mi)	Wedgemount Glacier toe

From the north end of the parking lot, follow the gravel road across a new bridge over Wedgemount Creek. After the bridge, watch for the trail leaving the road to the right. This new section of trail dates to 2014 when the original trail was rerouted to accommodate a hydroelectric power project. It gains elevation gradually in long switchbacks and passes beneath a boulder field.

About 1 km (0.6 mi) from the car, the route merges with the old trail and the climbing begins in earnest. The trail ascends the slope on a rough trail with lots of big steps and tight zigzags. About 3.5 km (2.2 mi) along, the grade eases slightly as you cross a rockslide. Continue climbing steeply through the forest. You'll get a few glimpses of the valley ahead, including 300-m-high (984 ft) Wedgemount Falls. About 4.75 km (3 mi) from the trailhead, the forest opens up into a **rocky bowl** with the best view of the falls. You can also see a steep rocky gully directly above you. This is your ascent route to the lake.

Head across the open bowl and begin scrambling up the gully. It has some very steep spots that can be loose in dry weather, so use caution. Listen for the peep of pikas as you climb. These squirrel-sized rodents make their homes in the gaps between rocks at high elevation. In the summer, they collect grass in miniature hay piles to dry it out so they can eat it during the long winter.

Top out on a **rocky bluff**. The brilliant turquoise waters of Wedgemount Lake are below you. Turn around for a great view of your ascent route and Cougar Mountain across Highway 99.

The landscape changes drastically here as the forest vegetation gives way to rocks and sensitive alpine plants, clinging to the smallest bits of soil for survival. Watch your step as you walk, to prevent squishing them. In early August, the wildflowers are in full display. Look for bright pink and purple river beauty in wet areas near the lake and streams. The **hut and first camping area** are nearby, 6 km (3.7 mi) from the start. To reach the **lakeside camping area**, follow the trail downhill through the rocks for another 0.5 km (0.3 mi).

CAMPING

UPPER CAMPGROUND AND HUT

The upper camping area sits on a rocky knoll above the lake that can be windy. A small and basic hut, built by the British Columbia Mountaineering Club (BCMC) in 1970 and subsequently donated to Garibaldi Provincial Park, stands nearby. To sleep in the hut, make a backcountry camping reservation for Wedgemount Lake (there are no separate bookings for the hut). Bunks in the hut are first-come, first-served.

NATURE NOTE

In the 1990s, the Wedgemount Glacier spilled into the east end of Wedgemount Lake, calving chunks of ice into the water. Since then climate change has caused the glacier to melt and shrink. The ice has retreated about 400 m (1312 ft) from the edge of the lake and 100 m (328 ft) uphill in less than 30 years, exposing the bedrock beneath.

Campsites: 10 wooden tent pads near the hut and on a spur trail to the north

Hut Sleeps: 6 in the loft

Toilet: Large wooden outhouse next to the hut

Water: Collect from a stream flowing into the lake near the lakeside campground.

Food Storage: On food-hanging poles near the hut.

LAKESIDE CAMPGROUND

The lakeside campground is on the gravel flats near the east end of the lake, about 0.5 km (0.3 mi) from the hut and upper campground. These campsites are directly next to the lakeshore.

Campsites: 10 flat gravel campsites

Toilet: BC Parks erects a temporary toilet in the summer with a tent privacy structure. If the toilet is not installed, walk to the outhouse near the hut 0.5 km (0.3 mi) away.

The retreating toe of the Wedgemount Glacier and its meltwater pond.

Water: Collect from the stream flowing into the lake near the campground.

Food Storage: On food-hanging poles near the temporary outhouse.

EXTENDING YOUR TRIP

Wedgemount Glacier: From the lakeshore campground, follow a faint trail east along the water's edge. At the end of the lake, go uphill through rocky rubble to a pond formed from the melting toe of the glacier. It's a 2-km (1.2-mi) round trip with 100 m (328 ft) of elevation gain.

FURTHER RESOURCES

Garibaldi Provincial Park: info, fees, reservations http://bcparks.ca/explore/parkpgs/garibaldi/

NTS Map: 092J02

5
RUSSET LAKE

Difficulty: ◆
Duration: 2 days
Distance: 25 to 29 km (15.5 to 18 mi)

Elevation Gain: 305 to 1280 m (1001 to 4199 ft)
High Point: 2181 m (7156 ft)
Best Months: Mid-July to September

Fees and Reservations: Reservations are required to camp and cost $6/night per tent pad. Camping fees are $10/person/night. Both reservation and camping fees are payable online. The Kees and Claire Hut requires online reservations and costs $45/person/night.

Regulations: No dogs. No fires. No drones. No smoking, vaping, or cannabis.

Caution: The lower portion of the Singing Pass Trail passes through busy mountain bike trails.

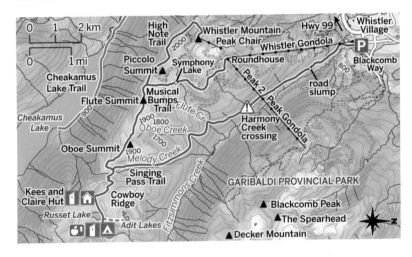

THE ALPINE MEADOWS at Russet Lake in Garibaldi Provincial Park are some of the best in the region. And since they're deeper into the backcountry than most day trippers venture, you won't have to contend with crowds. Head here in late July or early August to enjoy pink heather, red paintbrush, and indigo lupines. You're almost guaranteed to see chubby marmots too. The alpine flowers are one of their favourite foods. The lake is nestled in a subalpine bowl with great views of Decker Mountain to the north and the Overlord Glacier. The dramatic reddish rocks of Fissile Peak rise above the east shore of the lake. To get to Russet Lake, choose between two lift-accessed high-alpine

Looking down at Cheakamus Lake from Flute Summit on the Musical Bumps Trail.

routes or a forested climb. Camp beside the calm waters of Russet Lake or book a bunk in the eco-conscious Kees and Claire Hut nearby.

GETTING THERE
In Whistler, head to Whistler Village parking lot 4, off Lorimer Road. On the west side of the lot near Blackcomb Way, park in one of six parking spots reserved for BC Parks visitors marked "Singing Pass Overnight Parking." Follow the instructions on the sign to pay for overnight parking by phone. You must also leave a copy of your backcountry reservation on your dash. If the designated spots are occupied, park as close to them as possible. You can also get to Whistler via ride-sharing services or private shuttle buses from Vancouver.

TRAIL
Several different routes lead to Russet Lake. For incredible mountain views and wildflower meadows en route, pay to ride the gondola up to the Musical Bumps or High Note Trails. Be sure to check gondola opening dates and times before you go. For a low-impact, human-powered approach, follow the rushing waters of Fitzsimmons Creek uphill through the forest and into the subalpine along the Singing Pass Trail.

TRIP PLANNER

0 km (0 mi)	Whistler Mountain Roundhouse
1 km (0.6 mi)	Harmony Lake
3.5 km (2.2 mi)	Symphony Lake
4.75 km (3 mi)	Junction with High Note Trail
5.5 km (3.4 mi)	Flute Summit
7.5 km (4.7 mi)	Oboe Summit
9.4 km (5.8 mi)	Junction with Singing Pass Trail
11.5 km (7.1 mi)	Kees and Claire Hut
12.5 km (7.8 mi)	Russet Lake campground

This route has only 305 m (1001 ft) of net elevation gain, but you will gain and lose much more than that along the rolling 12.5-km (7.8-mi) trail. This route is called the "Musical Bumps" because it passes over three summits named for instruments. In the 1960s, local mountaineer Karl Ricker of the Alpine Club of Canada christened the peaks Oboe, Flute, and Piccolo in order of pitch from lowest to highest.

Buy a ticket and take the gondola up Whistler Mountain to the Round-house, gaining 1175 m (3855 ft) in 25 minutes. From the Roundhouse, head left across the plaza and follow signs to **Harmony Lake**. Admire the great views of Blackcomb Peak across the valley. Leaving the lake, follow the High Note Trail up through meadows and across gravelly slopes. Pass under a ski lift and gain 160 m (525 ft) of elevation climbing over the rocky shoulder of Harmony Ridge.

Next, lose 100 m (328 ft) of elevation descending through forest and scree slopes to reach the meadows again. About 3.5 km (2.2 mi) from the start, arrive at **Symphony Lake**. This beautiful alpine bowl erupts in wildflowers in late July and early August. Look for bright yellow daisy-shaped arnica near the stream and the tiny white and pink blooms of heather spreading across

NATURE NOTE

Watch for hoary marmots munching grasses or sunning themselves on rocks. These large ground squirrels live in burrows in alpine meadows and rock slides. They are sometimes known as "whistle pigs" for the high-pitched call they use as a danger signal. Whistler Mountain's original name was London Mountain since, like London, the peak is often shrouded in fog. The mountain was renamed for the marmot's shrill call, to attract more tourists and avoid implications of bad weather.

the slopes. This is the last reliable water source on this route before Russet Lake, so fill up here on hot days.

Climbing up through the open meadows from Symphony Lake, pass under another ski lift, then reach the junction with Burnt Stew Trail. Continue straight on the High Note Trail on flatter terrain through the saddle between Piccolo and Flute Summits. At 4.75 km (3 mi) from the Roundhouse, reach a three-way **junction** and meet up with the western portion of High Note Trail coming from Whistler Mountain.

From the junction, head left (east) onto the Musical Bumps Trail. At this point, leave the Whistler Resort alpine trails and head into the less-travelled backcountry of

The view of Russet Lake from the lower slopes of Fissile Peak.

Garibaldi Provincial Park. Ascend 120 m (394 ft) to the top of 2015-m-high (6611 ft) **Flute Summit,** the highest point on the trail. Stop to savour the views from the top. The turquoise waters of Cheakamus Lake (Trip 6) are below you. Across the lake, you can see the route up Helm Creek (Trip 7) towards Black Tusk and Garibaldi Lake.

Descend from Flute Summit, losing 150 m (492 ft), to a flat saddle, then immediately gain 80 m (262 ft) climbing to the top of **Oboe Summit**. At this point, you are 7.5 km (4.7 mi) from the start. Head downhill from Oboe towards Singing Pass. As you drop steeply down into the valley, the vegetation changes from alpine rocks to subalpine meadows and finally to open forest. You will have dropped 225 m (738 ft) in elevation once you arrive at the pass, where you reach the **junction** with the Singing Pass Trail ascending from Whistler Village.

Turn right (east) to begin the climb of Cowboy Ridge, the last obstacle between you and Russet Lake. Over the next 2 km (1.2 mi), gain 250 m (820 ft) as you work your way up the ridge on a switchbacking trail. As you emerge above the treeline, the views really open up. Look south across Cheakamus Lake to the massive Cheakamus Glacier between Castle Towers Mountain and Mount Davidson.

About 11.5 km (7.1 mi) from the beginning of the trail, top out on the shoulder of Cowboy Ridge. As the trail curls around to the northeast, you'll get your first glimpse of Russet Lake 80 m (262 ft) below you. The **Kees and Claire Hut** is just a few metres away. Continue downhill alongside marmot burrows through spectacular wildflower meadows to find the **campground** on the north shore of the lake.

HIGH NOTE TRAIL

TRIP PLANNER

0 km (0 mi)	Whistler Mountain summit
3 km (1.9 mi)	Junction with Half Note Trail
4.75 km (3 mi)	Junction with Musical Bumps Trail
5.5 km (3.4 mi)	Flute Summit
7.5 km (4.7 mi)	Oboe Summit
9.4 km (5.8 mi)	Junction with Singing Pass Trail
11.5 km (7.1 mi)	Kees and Claire Hut
12.5 km (7.8 mi)	Russet Lake campground

Another spectacularly scenic lift-accessed option is to take the newer High Note Trail from the top of Whistler Mountain, then meet up with the Musical Bumps route 4.75 km (3 mi) into the hike. Even though the High Note Trail starts higher than the Musical Bumps route, it still has lots of ups and downs. You'll gain a total of 550 m (1804 ft) and descend 805 m (2641 ft) on this route.

To start, ride the gondola up to the Roundhouse, then use the Peak chair to ascend another 230 m (755 ft) to the summit of Whistler Mountain. Check out the views of Whistler Valley from the suspension bridge and viewing platform, then follow the signs for the High Note Trail at the southeast end of the summit area.

The hike begins by dropping steeply off the summit. You'll descend 250 m (820 ft) in the first 2 km (1.2 mi) as you head downhill and trend east through alpine rocks, then subalpine meadows. The side of the trail drops away steeply at some points, so use caution. The views down to the turquoise waters of Cheakamus Lake and across to Black Tusk's distinct stratovolcanic pinnacle are sublime.

Gradually, regain about 100 m (328 ft) of elevation as you climb to the Cheakamus Lake viewpoint near the **junction with the Half Note Trail**, 3 km (1.9 m) from the start. Stop to admire the view of the Cheakamus and Castle Towers Glaciers high above the lake, then head straight at the fork to stay on the High Note Trail.

Over the next 1 km (0.6 mi), gently descend 100 m (328 ft) through open meadows as you contour the side of Piccolo Summit. Approximately 4.75 km (3 mi) from the trailhead, reach the **junction with the Musical Bumps Trail**. Turn right to follow that trail towards Russet Lake, using the description above.

SINGING PASS TRAIL

TRIP PLANNER

0 km (0 mi)	Singing Pass trailhead
4.5 km (2.8 mi)	Old parking lot
5 km (3.1 mi)	Harmony Creek
7 km (4.3 mi)	Flute Creek
8 km (5 mi)	Oboe Creek
12.5 km (7.8 mi)	Junction with Musical Bumps Trail
14.6 km (9.1 mi)	Kees and Claire Hut
15.6 km (9.7 mi)	Russet Lake campground

The 15.6-km-long (9.7 mi) Singing Pass Trail is an old prospector's trail that gains a staggering 1280 m (4199 ft). As long as 10,000 years ago, Indigenous people quarried obsidian in what is now Garibaldi Provincial Park, and settlers mined gold, copper, and silver in the last century. Watch for evidence of abandoned mine shafts as you climb up the Fitzsimmons Creek valley. Most of the trail is easy walking, though it involves some challenging scrambles across an unbridged creek and a landslide. Without the limitations of the gondola schedule, however, you can go at your own pace, on your own time. This route is also a great option during late spring and early fall when the gondola isn't running.

The trailhead is located next to the Whistler Gondola bus loop on Blackcomb Way. However, the Whistler section of the Alpine Club of Canada and the Federation of Mountain Clubs of British Columbia have proposed a trail that will begin near the Whistler Sliding Centre's bobsleigh track at Blackcomb Base II (parking lot 8) and head upstream high above the east side of Fitzsimmons Creek to a new footbridge. After crossing the bridge, the new trail will head upslope to join the Singing Pass Trail, about 3.5 km (2.2 mi) from the current trailhead.

From the current trailhead, the first 1.3 km (0.8 mi) of trail is on a former mining road turned ski resort access road that passes underneath the Excalibur Gondola and crosses several mountain bike trails. At 2.6 km (1.6 mi) from the start, reach a large landslide where the old road has slumped away. The area was repaired in 2018 but is prone to washing out, so use caution.

A hoary marmot emerges from its burrow near Russet Lake.

About 4.5 km (2.8 mi) from the trailhead, pass underneath the Peak 2 Peak Gondola. Shortly afterwards, reach the end of the old road. Until the early 1990s, you could drive up this road, but it is now impassable. An **old parking lot** here marks the original trailhead.

Continue climbing on the trail and reach **Harmony Creek** at 5 km (3.1 mi). Take care here because the sides of the creek bed are steep and unstable and there is no bridge. In spring and after heavy rainfall or snowmelt, the creek can be impassable. If the water is low enough, cross the creek bed carefully. Watch your footing on boulders and downed trees, which can be slippery.

Shortly after the creek, arrive at the Garibaldi Provincial Park boundary. Cross **Flute Creek**. Then cross **Oboe Creek**. Both of these creeks have bridges, but they often wash out. Be prepared to scramble across if the bridges are damaged.

At 10 km (6.2 mi) from the start, the trail runs close to Melody Creek, which it follows all the way to Singing Pass. As you walk along the creek, the forest thins out and subalpine meadows begin to dominate. You'll reach the pass and the **junction with the Musical Bumps Trail** 12.5 km (7.8 mi) and 1040 m (3412 ft) of elevation gain from the trailhead. Turn left to begin ascending the Russet Lake trail up Cowboy Ridge using the description above.

CAMPING AND HUT

RUSSET LAKE CAMPGROUND
The campground is located on a slight rise on the north side of Russet Lake near the lake's outlet.

Campsites: 7 campsites around the north end of the lake
Toilet: Outhouse near the northwest corner of the lake
Water: Collect from Russet Creek near the lake outlet.
Food Storage: In metal food lockers located between the campground and the outhouse

KEES AND CLAIRE HUT

This hut opened in 2019 as part of a community project by the Spearhead Huts Society to build three memorial huts along the Spearhead Traverse, a ski-touring route that travels from Whistler to Blackcomb through the backcountry. The hut is named for Cornelius "Kees" Brenninkmeyer and Claire Dixon, Alpine Club of Canada volunteers who perished in a mountaineering accident. It's a beautifully modern building with a low-energy Passivhaus design.

Hut Sleeps: 38 in bunks spread over 6 separate sleeping areas
Toilets: Urine-diversion toilets in an attached building
Water: Fundraising continues to build a well for the hut. Until then, melt snow from the designated snow collection area in early season and haul buckets of water up from the lake in summer.
Food Storage: Cubbies on the wall in the kitchen area
Other Amenities: The hut has LED lighting, a heater, 4-burner stoves with propane, dishes, cutlery, and wash sinks.

EXTENDING YOUR TRIP

Adit Lakes: An informal cairned route leads north from Russet Lake to the Adit Lakes, two small alpine lakes in a rocky bowl. From the outhouse at the Russet Lake campground, pick up a faint trail across the bottom of a rocky slope. Watch for cairns as the trail contours the side of the ridge before arriving above the lakes. It's 1 km (0.6 mi) each way to the lake.

FURTHER RESOURCES

Garibaldi Provincial Park: info, fees, reservations http://bcparks.ca/explore/parkpgs/garibaldi/
Whistler Blackcomb: gondola info and fees https://www.whistlerblackcomb.com/
Spearhead Huts Society: Kees and Claire Hut info and reservations http://spearheadhuts.org/
Trail Map: Garibaldi Provincial Park Map by Clark Geomatics
NTS Map: 092J02

6
CHEAKAMUS LAKE

Difficulty: ●

Duration: 2 days

Distance: 7 to 14 km (4.3 to 8.7 mi)

Elevation Gain: 50 m (164 ft)

High Point: 900 m (2953 ft)

Best Months: May to November

Fees and Reservations: Reservations are required to camp and cost $6/night for each tent pad. Camping fees are $10/person/night. Both reservation and camping fees are payable online.

Regulations: No dogs. No fires. No drones. No smoking, vaping, or cannabis. Bikes permitted.

Caution: Black bears are very active in this area in the spring.

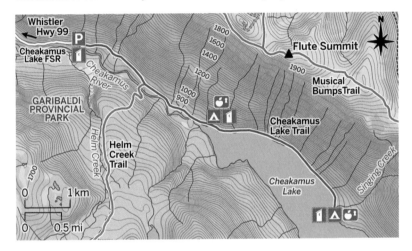

THE SHORT HIKE to Cheakamus Lake in Garibaldi Provincial Park is a great spring or fall destination thanks to its low elevation. A flat and easy trail leads through old-growth forest to two campgrounds beside the lake's turquoise waters, so this is an ideal trip for beginners or families with young children. A quick dip in the glacially fed lake is refreshing on a hot day. Paddlers willing to put in a bit of effort will appreciate the extra work of portaging a kayak, canoe, or stand-up paddleboard to the lake to explore the shoreline.

GETTING THERE

On Highway 99 south of Whistler, go east at the traffic light onto Cheakamus Lake Road towards the Cheakamus Crossing neighbourhood. Make a

Early morning reflections at Cheakamus Lake. Photo: Andy Gibb

left turn 0.5 km (0.3 mi) later onto Cheakamus Lake Forest Service Road. This gravel road is 2WD accessible despite some potholes and steep sections. Ignore all side roads and stay on the Cheakamus FSR for 7 km (4.3 mi) until it ends at a parking lot. If you are staying in Whistler, you can also take a taxi to the trailhead.

TRAIL

TRIP PLANNER

0 km (0 mi)	Trailhead
1.5 km (0.9 mi)	Junction with Helm Creek Trail (see Trip 7)
3.5 km (2.2 mi)	Cheakamus Lake campground
7 km (4.3 mi)	Singing Creek campground

The trailhead is at the east end of the parking lot near an information kiosk. There is an outhouse several steps down the trail too. The hike begins by heading through a few stands of beautiful old-growth western hemlock, amabilis fir, and western red cedar, typical of the temperate coastal rainforest.

You'll also cross a few areas with no trees and lots of brush. These are avalanche paths. Each winter, the steep slopes of Whistler Mountain above send cascades of snow all the way down to the valley bottom, sweeping huge trees along in their wake. Be bear aware and make noise as you hike through the brushy sections, especially along the banks of the Cheakamus River. Bears have excellent hearing (about twice as sensitive as humans'), but they can still get startled around loud running water.

About 1.5 km (0.9 mi) from the parking lot, arrive at a **junction**. Your path goes straight and the trail to Helm Creek (Trip 7) heads right. Continue through more old-growth forest, using small bridges to cross several creeks.

Soon you'll begin to hear the roar of the Cheakamus River getting louder. You've arrived at the **Cheakamus Lake campground** at the lake outlet. Follow the trail along the lakeshore. In the next kilometre (0.6 mi), pass more campsites and another outhouse.

If you have the time or energy to go farther, continue past the lakeside campsites on the main trail. The path undulates along the lakeshore through groves of Douglas-fir until it ends at the **Singing Creek campground**. Allow another hour for the hike.

CAMPING

CHEAKAMUS LAKE CAMPGROUND

At only 3.5 km (2.2 mi) from the trailhead, this campground is a great choice for beginners or families with young children. The tent sites are close to the trail and the lake, but since they are spread out over a kilometre (0.6 mi), some of them do feel a bit more private. Be aware that some of the lakeside sites flood in the spring or after heavy rain.

Campsites: 10 cleared campsites spread along the trail
Toilets: 2 outhouses: one near the lake outlet, another a few hundred metres down the trail
Water: Collect from the lake.
Food Storage: On food-hanging wires near both outhouses

SINGING CREEK CAMPGROUND

An easy 7-km (4.3 mi) hike from the trailhead, Singing Creek campground is located where Singing Creek empties into Cheakamus Lake, creating a small

INDIGENOUS KNOWLEDGE

The Líl'wat name for Cheakamus Lake is Nsqwitsu and, traditionally, they visited the area to pick bog cranberries. The Squamish called the lake Tseearkamisht, meaning "people who use the cedar rope fishing net," which was later anglicized to Cheakamus. The Squamish Nation has identified most of the Cheakamus watershed (which they call Kwáyatsut) as a Wild Spirit Place of cultural, spiritual, and ecological significance.

Cow parsnip along the lakeshore. Photo: Sarah Pawliuk

gravel beach. If you want to brave the chilly water to go for a swim, avoid the creek outlet: it's even colder than the lake!

Campsites: 7 cleared campsites close together on both sides of the creek, or depending on the water level, on the beach
Toilet: Outhouse north of the trail
Water: Collect from Singing Creek.
Food Storage: On food-hanging wires near the outhouse

FURTHER RESOURCES
Garibaldi Provincial Park: info, fees, reservations http://bcparks.ca/explore/parkpgs/garibaldi/
Trail Map: Garibaldi Provincial Park Map by Clark Geomatics
NTS Map: 092J02

7
HELM CREEK

Difficulty: ■

Duration: 2 to 3 days

Distance: 17 km (10.6 mi)

Elevation Gain: 700 m (2297 ft)

High Point: 1550 m (5085 ft)

Best Months: July to September

Fees and Reservations: Reservations are required to camp and cost $6/night for each tent pad. Camping fees are $10/person/night. Both reservation and camping fees are payable online.

Regulations: No dogs. No fires. No drones. No smoking, vaping, or cannabis.

Caution: The campsite is known for mosquitos. Bring insect repellent or a head net.

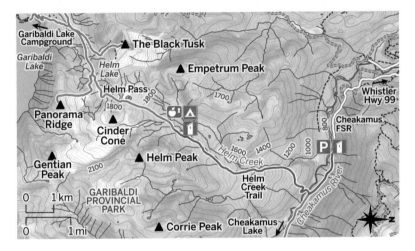

HIKE THE LESS-TRAVELLED Helm Creek Trail into the heart of Garibaldi Provincial Park. This route, nicknamed the "back door" to Garibaldi Lake, climbs steeply from the Cheakamus River up to a meadow campsite near Helm Pass with a spectacular view of the park's iconic Black Tusk. Helm Creek is a great spot to base yourself for day hikes to the fascinating volcanic Cinder Flats at Helm Pass or the incredible views of Garibaldi Lake from atop aptly named Panorama Ridge. And unlike the popular Garibaldi Lake area, it's much easier to get campsite reservations for the Helm Creek campground.

GETTING THERE
On Highway 99 south of Whistler, go east at the traffic light onto Cheakamus Lake Road towards the Cheakamus Crossing neighbourhood. Make a

Helm Lake and the Cinder Flats from Helm Pass.

left turn 0.5 km (0.3 mi) later onto Cheakamus Lake Forest Service Road. This gravel road is 2WD accessible despite some potholes and steep sections. Ignore all side roads and stay on the Cheakamus FSR for 7 km (4.3 mi) until it ends at a parking lot. If you are staying in Whistler, you can also take a taxi to the trailhead.

TRAIL

The trail starts at the east end of the parking lot near an information kiosk and outhouse. The first section of trail heads through some beautiful old-growth forest and crosses a few avalanche paths. Reach a **junction** 1.5 km (0.9 mi) from the trailhead. The trail straight ahead leads to Cheakamus

Lake (Trip 6). Turn right onto the Helm Creek Trail and begin descending slightly to the Cheakamus River.

Before the large bridge was built here in the 1990s, the only way across the river was on a cable car. On the other side, recent maintenance has improved the trail surface as you ascend several switchbacks up the steep hillside. About 3.5 km (2.2 mi) from the parking lot, the grade begins to ease as you climb more gently through the forest.

Around 7 km (4.3 mi), the forest starts to open up as the vegetation transitions from mountain hemlock forest into subalpine meadows of grass, lichen, and low shrubs like crowberry. Reach the **Helm Creek campground**.

CAMPING

The campground at Helm Creek is set in a beautiful open meadow next to its namesake creek and has views of Black Tusk.

Campsites: 30 wooden tent platforms
Toilet: Outhouse on the east side of the trail
Water: Collect from Helm Creek on the west side of the campground.
Food Storage: On food-hanging poles near the outhouse

EXTENDING YOUR TRIP

Helm Pass: Continue up Helm Creek to its source at Helm Lake and discover the unique volcanic landscape of Helm Pass, formerly called Desolation Valley. The lush alpine meadows give way to a flat and barren land of rocks and ash, a legacy of Mount Garibaldi's explosive past. The glacial outlet streams here change course every year, so use caution when crossing. They can be deep, fast, and icy cold. It's an 8-km (5-mi) round trip to Helm Pass from the campsite with 200 m (656 ft) of elevation gain.

Panorama Ridge: This viewpoint is one of the most spectacular in BC. From its lofty perch, the entirety of Garibaldi Lake is visible, along with the glaciated volcanic peaks that encircle it. Walk through the unique Cinder Flats near Helm Lake, then ascend the ridge on a challenging trail. The return trip from Helm Creek camp is 14 km (8.7 mi) with 580 m (1903 ft) of elevation gain.

NATURE NOTE

In the Squamish language, Black Tusk is known as t'ak't'ak mu'yin tl'a in7in'a'xe7en, which means "landing place of the thunderbird." Geologists explain that the tusk is the remains of an extinct stratovolcano. Viscous lava bubbled up from the earth, eventually solidifying into a dome. Over millennia, the loose cinder on the outside has eroded away, leaving the harder core behind.

Black Tusk towers over the glacial meltwater streams near Helm Pass.

Helm Creek Crossover: Combine this trip with Trip 9 (Garibaldi Lake) to make a traverse across Garibaldi Park. You'll cover 24 km (14.9 mi) and gain 1200 m (3937 ft) of elevation. Give yourself three days to make the crossover trip so you'll have time to include day hikes of Black Tusk or Panorama Ridge.

FURTHER RESOURCES

Garibaldi Provincial Park: info, fees, reservations http://bcparks.ca/explore/parkpgs/garibaldi/
Trail Map: Garibaldi Provincial Park Map by Clark Geomatics
NTS Maps: 092J02, 092J03, 092G14, 092G15

8
RAINBOW PASS

Difficulty: ■
Duration: 2 to 3 days
Distance: 13 to 20.6 km (8.1 to 12.8 mi)

Elevation Gain: 445 to 890 m
(1460 to 2920 ft)
High Point: 1430 m (4692 ft)
Best Months: June to October

Fees and Reservations: Camping is free and all campsites are first-come, first-served.

Regulations: No swimming in Rainbow Lake. No dogs on the Rainbow Lake Trail. Dogs permitted on the Rainbow-Madeley Trail but not recommended.

Caution: This is prime habitat for both black and grizzly bears. Check Municipality of Whistler bulletins online for area closures due to high grizzly bear activity. Hanging Lake can be very buggy in early summer.

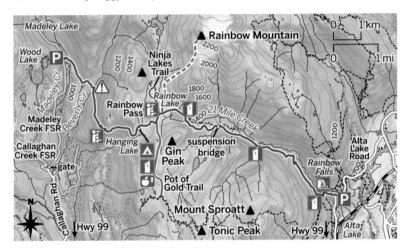

THE CAMPSITE AT subalpine Hanging Lake is set amongst wildflower meadows. In late July and August, they are ablaze with yellow large-leaved avens, white partridgefoot, broad green false hellebore, and red leather-leaved saxifrage. Hanging Lake sits on the opposite side of the valley from Whistler Mountain and Blackcomb Peak and is therefore much quieter than most campsites in the area. The swimmable lake and its well-appointed campsite lie just over Rainbow Pass, underneath imposing Rainbow Mountain and just a short walk to picturesque Rainbow Lake.

Most hikers approach via the popular Rainbow Lake trail from Whistler's Alta Lake area. But you can also hike in via the rougher Rainbow-Madeley

Walking through wildflower meadows above the west shore of Hanging Lake.

Trail from the Callaghan Valley. It's a much quieter route, and as a bonus, it's shorter and has less elevation gain than the Rainbow Lake Trail. With two cars, you could combine the two trails into a traverse. Both options are described below.

GETTING THERE

RAINBOW-MADELEY TRAILHEAD

North of Squamish, turn onto Callaghan Road from Highway 99, following signs for Whistler Olympic Park. Follow the paved road for about 10 km (6.2 mi). Just after you pass a sign for Alexander Falls, turn left onto Callaghan Creek Forest Service Road. The road turns to gravel and has a few loose sections and bumps, but it should be fine for 2WD vehicles.

Zero your odometer and cross the bridge. A network of gravel roads in this area double as cross-country ski trails in the winter, so a backroad map book or GPS can be helpful for navigation. When in doubt, follow signs for Madeley Lake. Turn right through a gate onto Madeley Creek FSR at 0.4 km (0.2 mi). If the gate is locked, you will have to park at a pullout here and walk the remaining distance to the trailhead. This will add 4.2 km (2.6 mi) and 180 m (591 ft) of elevation gain to your hike.

If the gate is unlocked, drive through it and stay on the main gravel road. Go right at 2.8 km (1.7 mi). Go left at 4.3 km (2.7 mi). Reach the trailhead on your right at 4.6 km (2.9 mi). There is a large signboard and room for a few cars in pullouts on both sides of the road.

The view of Rainbow Lake and Rainbow Mountain from Rainbow Pass.

RAINBOW LAKE TRAILHEAD

In Whistler, go west from Highway 99 onto Alta Lake Road. Follow it for about 6 km (3.7 mi) past Alta Lake. The parking lot and trailhead are next to a large "Rainbow Lake Trail" sign. Hikers without a car could arrange a taxi to the trailhead.

TRAIL

RAINBOW-MADELEY TRAIL

TRIP PLANNER

0 km (0 mi)	Rainbow-Madeley trailhead
2 km (1.2 mi)	Beverly Creek
6.5 km (4 mi)	Hanging Lake campground
7.3 km (4.5 mi)	Rainbow Pass

The Rainbow-Madeley Trail takes you to Hanging Lake in about 6.5 km (4 mi) with 445 m (1460 ft) of elevation gain. From the trailhead signboard, the trail heads slightly downhill and crosses a log bridge over Madeley Creek. At the junction immediately after the bridge, turn right onto the Hanging Lake Trail. Left goes to Madeley Lake.

The first kilometre (0.6 mi) of trail travels through a fairly flat area with lots of blueberry bushes and a few bridges over small streams. Make noise through here as bears are common. Next, start to climb gently, passing two ponds and ascending a rocky gully. Around 2 km (1.2 mi) from the trailhead, reach **Beverly Creek**. The old log bridge has washed out, so for the time being you'll have to ford the creek. It's an easy wade in mid-summer but could be challenging in high water.

A few hundred metres past the bridge, arrive at a huge old-growth hemlock tree. Continue onwards past some boulders and then through the forest on a rising traverse along the slope. About 3.8 km (2.4 mi) from the start, emerge from the forest into an open area of boulders and dead trees below a slope. Watch carefully for trail markers making a sharp left turn and ascending the slope. Don't continue straight!

Just beyond the boulder area, reach the first viewpoint. Look over the tops of the trees to the Metal Dome, Brandywine Mountain, Mount Cayley, and Powder Mountain on the other side of the Callaghan Valley. After the viewpoint, the trail continues to climb steeply for another 2 km (1.2 mi), crossing several small creeks and avalanche paths.

Eventually, the trail starts to curve north as it enters the Hanging Lake valley. The trees thin out and alpine meadow flowers dominate. The trail traverses above the west shore before descending to the north end of Hanging Lake. Your destination is the **campground** on a flat area of land just above the north shore.

RAINBOW LAKE TRAIL

TRIP PLANNER

0 km (0 mi)	Rainbow Lake trailhead
6 km (3.7 mi)	Suspension bridge
7.5 km (4.7 mi)	Rainbow Lake
9 km (5.6 mi)	Junction with Rainbow Mountain route (3 km/1.9 mi to the summit)
9.5 km (5.9 mi)	Rainbow Pass
10.3 km (6.4 mi)	Hanging Lake campground

NATURE NOTE

The Rainbow Pass trails are part of Whistler's alpine trail network, opened in 2017. However, the municipality is currently rethinking their trail strategy as endangered grizzly bears, thought to have been extirpated from the region, are recolonizing the west side of the Whistler Valley. While the return of the bears is a win for conservation, hikers in the region will need to learn how to coexist with these large mammals.

The view down to Hanging Lake and across to Metal Dome and Brandywine Mountain from Rainbow Pass.

The Rainbow Lake route is slightly longer at 10.3 km (6.4 mi) with 890 m (2920 ft) of elevation gain. From the trailhead sign, follow the path into the forest. The trail climbs next to 21 Mile Creek before briefly joining a road. Shortly after that, look for a side trail heading down to the right. It's a short and worthwhile detour of a few minutes to Rainbow Falls.

After the side trail to the falls, continue uphill to another gravel road. Stay on the road, passing by a water supply building. Ignore junctions with the Rainbow-Sproatt Flank Trail and mountain bike trails. Soon you'll pass the first of three outhouses along the route. The 21 Mile Creek watershed, which includes Rainbow Lake, supplies most of Whistler's drinking water, so it's very important to use the outhouses on this trail.

About 3 km (1.9 mi) from the trailhead, pass a wooden gate as the old road turns into a hiking trail. A regenerating second-growth forest gradually becomes a more mature western hemlock forest with lush ferns and devil's club. Several small bridges help you over wet sections of the trail.

After another kilometre (0.6 mi) of steady uphill walking, pass an outhouse and then cross a large bridge with a great view of a waterfall. The trail keeps climbing through the forest, using a newly built section to bypass an old boggy one.

Cross the **suspension bridge** over Gin and Tonic Creeks. The Municipality of Whistler removes the metal decking in the winter to protect it from snow-loading. This area gets a lot of snow!

Past the bridge, the trail enters an open meadow area, then climbs one last hill up to the shores of Rainbow Lake. Follow the trail to a bridge over 21 Mile Creek as it empties out of **Rainbow Lake**. Pause at the outhouse here if necessary, then follow the trail around the northern shore of the lake. Camping and swimming are prohibited at Rainbow Lake to protect the water supply.

Stay on the main trail through the meadows, ignoring a trail branching to the right to Rainbow Mountain. Ascend to **Rainbow Pass**, the high point of your hike. Rainbow Lake is below you to the east, with Rainbow Mountain towering above. You can also see Hanging Lake down the trail to the west and the peaks of the Callaghan Valley in the distance. Follow the trail for another 0.8 km (0.5 mi) to the **campground at Hanging Lake**, losing 70 m (230 ft) in elevation.

CAMPING

Hanging Lake is the only place to camp in this area. Look for the tent pads at the north end of the lake.

Campsites: 10 numbered campsites
Toilet: Outhouse just upslope of the tent pads
Water: Collect from creeks on the north side of the lake.
Food Storage: In metal bearproof food lockers

EXTENDING YOUR TRIP

Ninja Lakes Loop: This short trail heads north from Rainbow Pass to several small tarns along a rocky ridge. It's a 2.5-km (1.6-mi) loop with 110 m (361 ft) of elevation gain. Expect to see mountain bikes on this multi-use trail.

Pot of Gold: Follow this trail south from Rainbow Pass around the side of Gin Peak for great views of Hanging Lake, the Callaghan Valley, and the peaks of Garibaldi Provincial Park. The 3.4-km-long (2.1 mi) multi-use trail gains 130 m (427 ft) and links up with mountain bike trails in the Rainbow-Sproatt alpine network.

Rainbow Mountain: Experienced hikers with navigation skills can try the ascent of 2314-m-high (7592 ft) Rainbow Mountain. It's a challenging scramble route, so don't expect a groomed and marked trail. It's 3 km (1.9 mi) one way from the trail junction at the north end of Rainbow Lake. The route gains 850 m (2789 ft) over that distance.

FURTHER RESOURCES

Municipality of Whistler: trail info https://www.whistler.ca/culture-recreation/trails/alpine-trail-program/alpine-trail-network
Trail Map: Callaghan Valley Area Map by Clark Geomatics
Driving Map: Vancouver, Coast & Mountains BC Backroad Mapbook
NTS Map: 092J03

SQUAMISH

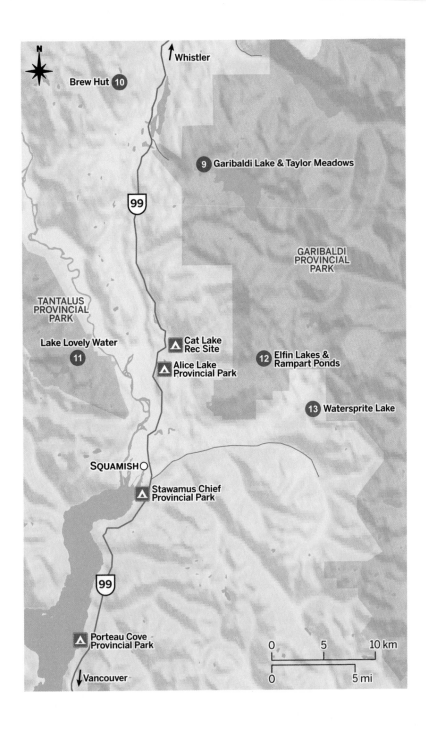

THE GEOLOGICAL HISTORY of the Squamish region is dominated by fire and ice. Centuries of explosive volcanoes, grinding glaciers, and rushing water have shaped this dramatic landscape. Glacier-capped mountains rise sharply from the deep valleys of the Squamish and Cheakamus Rivers. Hikers hardy enough to tackle the steep and sometimes rugged trails can look forward to brilliant turquoise glacial lakes, well-appointed huts, and incredible views. Many of the trails here can be busy with day trippers, but by late afternoon the solitude of the mountains is yours to enjoy.

Squamish was once a gritty industrial town. In recent years, it has been reborn as an adventure hub, with thousands flocking to the area for rock climbing, mountain biking, and hiking. Located halfway between Vancouver and Whistler on Highway 99, it's easy to get to. The town of Squamish is windy, with weather funnelling up and down the long fjord of Howe Sound. It also receives a lot of precipitation, so be prepared for rain even on the nicest of summer weekends and for snow in the winter. The local mountains can hold snow into early summer.

The Squamish and Cheakamus River Valleys, along with Howe Sound and Burrard Inlet are the traditional territory of the S̲kwx̲wú7mesh Úxwumixw (Squamish) people. They share the northern part of their territory around Black Tusk and the Whistler Valley with the Lílwat7úl (Líl'wat) Nation. Visit the Squamish Líl'wat Cultural Centre in Whistler to learn more about their history, art, and culture.

Supplies: Squamish has several grocery stores, gas stations, and outdoor stores.

Accommodation: There are lots of hotels in Squamish. You can reserve campsites at Porteau Cove Provincial Park south of Squamish, or Alice Lake Provincial Park north of town. First-come, first-served campsites are available at Stawamus Chief Provincial Park in Squamish, Cat Lake Rec Site north of town, and Cal-Cheak Rec Site south of Whistler.

9
GARIBALDI LAKE
AND TAYLOR MEADOWS

Difficulty: ■
Duration: 2 to 4 days
Distance: 15 to 18 km (9.3 to 11.2 mi)

Elevation Gain: 900 m (2953 ft)
High Point: 1500 m (4921 ft)
Best Months: July to September

Fees and Reservations: Reservations are required to camp and cost $6/night for each tent pad. Camping fees are $10/person/night. Both reservation and camping fees are payable online.

Regulations: No dogs. No fires. No drones. No smoking, vaping, or cannabis.

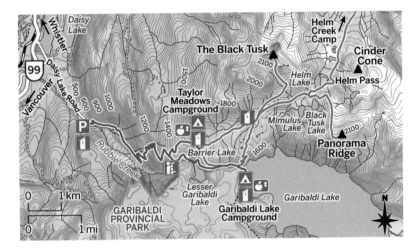

GARIBALDI LAKE IS a pretty awe-inspiring place: a gorgeous blue lake, alpine meadows, tumbling glaciers, and fascinating volcanic geology. Located just north of Squamish in the heart of Garibaldi Provincial Park, it's a popular hiking destination. But if you stay the night, the crowds go home and the backpackers have it all to themselves. It's also a great spot to base yourself to tackle some of southwestern BC's best day hikes. If possible, try to time your visit between late July and mid-August to catch the peak wildflower bloom. Choose from one of two backcountry campgrounds: quieter Taylor Meadows or iconic Garibaldi Lake, where views of the surrounding snow-capped mountains are plentiful from the beach.

Black Tusk from the summit of Panorama Ridge.

GETTING THERE

About 30 km (18.6 mi) north of Squamish on Highway 99, follow the signs for Garibaldi Lake to turn right onto Daisy Lake Road. Follow it to its end at a parking lot, 2.5 km (1.6 mi) from the highway. There is an outhouse at the trailhead. The parking lots can fill up, so you may have to park on the shoulder. Remove all valuables from your car as, unfortunately, break-ins are common here.

TRAIL

TAYLOR MEADOWS ROUTE

TRIP PLANNER

0 km (0 mi)	Trailhead
6 km (3.7 mi)	Junction with Garibaldi Lake Trail
7.5 km (4.7 mi)	Taylor Meadows campground
7.6 km (4.7 mi)	Junction with Trail to Garibaldi Lake
9.6 km (6 mi)	Junction with Trail to Garibaldi Lake
10 km (6.2 mi)	Junction with Black Tusk Trail (2.5 km/1.6 mi to viewpoint)
11.5 km (7.1 mi)	Junction with Panorama Ridge Trail (2.5 km/1.6 mi to top)
16 km (9.9 mi)	Helm Creek campground (see Trip 7)

The forested trail starts with a couple of short, steep switchbacks before the grade eases a bit. A signpost at the 2.5-km (1.6-mi) marker points the way up the hill to the left. From here, the trail switchbacks steeply for a few kilometres. Just after the 6-km (3.7-mi) marker, you'll reach a major **junction** with an information kiosk and outhouse. The trail to the left goes to Taylor Meadows and the one to the right to Garibaldi Lake.

The trail to Taylor Meadows climbs steadily but never too steeply for another 1.5 km (0.9 mi) from the junction. When the trail turns to boardwalk and you see the wooden signboard, you'll know you've arrived at the **Taylor Meadows campground**.

GARIBALDI LAKE ROUTE

TRIP PLANNER

0 km (0 mi)	Trailhead
6 km (3.7 mi)	Junction Taylor Meadows Trail
6.1 km (3.8 mi)	Junction with Barrier Viewpoint Trail
6.4 km (4 mi)	Barrier Lake
7.2 km (4.5 mi)	Lesser Garibaldi Lake
9 km (5.6 mi)	Garibaldi Lake campground
11.2 km (7 mi)	Junction with Taylor Meadows Trail
11.6 km (7.2 mi)	Junction with Black Tusk Trail (2.5 km/1.6 mi to viewpoint)
13.1 km (8.1 mi)	Junction with Panorama Ridge Trail (2.5 km/1.6 mi to top)
17.6 km (10.9 mi)	Helm Creek campground (see Trip 7)

Follow the directions for the Taylor Meadows route above, until you reach the 6-km (3.7-mi) **junction**. Go right for Garibaldi Lake. A few minutes later, take the short side trail slightly downhill for to a great **viewpoint** of the Barrier, a wall of crumbling volcanic rock.

After you've enjoyed the Barrier viewpoint, retrace your steps to the main trail. Head towards **Barrier Lake**, just a few minutes away. Skirt around the shores of the lake on a flattish trail before climbing a small hill to your

NATURE NOTE

Nine thousand years ago, nearby Clinker Peak erupted, sending lava cascading downhill. Glaciers in the Cheakamus Valley below halted the lava flows abruptly, forming a giant wall of volcanic rock. When the ice melted, it left a steep cliff below the wall and a big lake—Garibaldi Lake—behind it. Today the solidified lava of the Barrier is a dam that holds back the waters of Garibaldi Lake. However, the Barrier is not solid. If you linger at the viewpoint, you'll hear and see small sections of it crumble. A large section of the Barrier collapsed in 1855, creating the rock-strewn landscape that gave Rubble Creek its name.

first view of **Lesser Garibaldi Lake**. Cross a tall bridge over Taylor Creek, and continue through a beautiful forest of western hemlock trees draped in witch's hair lichen for another 1.5 km (0.9 mi), passing a **junction** with a trail to Taylor Meadows along the way.

Reach a signposted **junction** with the trail to Black Tusk and Panorama Ridge. Turn right here and head downhill for your first view of the lake. Cross the bridge over the lake outlet, then follow the shoreline for a few minutes to the **Garibaldi Lake campground**.

CAMPING

TAYLOR MEADOWS CAMPGROUND

Taylor Meadows campground is located in the alpine meadows above Garibaldi Lake. It is a little bit less popular than Garibaldi Lake campground, so it's easier to get reservations. And it's just a 2-km (1.2-mi) walk to Garibaldi Lake campground. Camping up in the meadows also makes day hiking to Black Tusk or Panorama Ridge a few minutes shorter.

Campsites: 40 sites, most on wooden platforms. Sites 23–40 are on a spur trail along the creek that's a bit more private.
Toilets: Several outhouses
Water: Collect from the creek.
Food Storage: On food-hanging wires with pulleys near the kitchen shelters
Other Amenities: 2 kitchen shelters. Each has a couple of picnic tables, metal counters for cooking, and washbasins for grey water.

GARIBALDI LAKE CAMPGROUND

The campground is right on the shore of Garibaldi Lake near its outlet. The campsites are set well back in the trees, but many benches and picnic tables line the lakeshore. If you're brave, go for a swim. The water is brutally cold, but the warmest patches are in the small bay between the islands and the shore. If you fish, the shoreline at the campground is a good place to cast for native cutthroat trout or rainbow trout, which were introduced to the lake in the 1920s.

Campsites: 50 sites, some on wooden platforms. Most sites are up short steep trails and some sites are very close together. Sites 23–27 are the closest to the lake.
Toilets: Several outhouses
Water: Collect from the lake.
Food Storage: On food-hanging wires with pulleys near the kitchen shelters
Other Amenities: 4 kitchen shelters. Each has a couple of picnic tables, metal counters for cooking, and washbasins for grey water. Outdoor picnic tables are located near 2 of the shelters.

Sunset alpenglow on the Sphinx Glacier and the peaks on the east side of Garibaldi Lake.

EXTENDING YOUR TRIP

It's worth planning for a few extra days in the Garibaldi Lake area to do some day hikes.

Black Tusk: Head to the viewpoint at the base of this prominent volcanic mountain. (It's strictly a rock-climbing route to the very top.) The black tooth-shaped peak is the remains of an ancient volcano. The Squamish people know Black Tusk as t'ak't'ak mu'yin tl'a in7in'a'xe7en, which means "landing place of the thunderbird." It's 10 km (6.2 mi) return from Taylor Meadows or 11 km (6.8 mi) return from Garibaldi Lake, with 700 m (2297 ft) of elevation gain.

Panorama Ridge: Walk through alpine meadows full of flowers, then ascend the ridge for the best views of Garibaldi Lake and no fewer than seven volcanoes. Cinder Cone is to the north, Black Tusk to the northwest, and Mount Price and Clinker Peak are across the lake to the southwest. To the south, look for the flat top of The Table with Glacier Pikes and the massive bulk of Mount Garibaldi (Nch'kay) behind. The hike is 13 km (8.1 mi) return from Taylor Meadows or 14 km (8.7 mi) return from Garibaldi Lake, with a 600-m (1969-ft) elevation gain.

Helm Creek Crossover: Combine this trip with Helm Creek (Trip 7) to make a traverse across Garibaldi Park. You'll cover 24 km (14.9 mi) and 1200 m (3937 ft) of elevation gain. Give yourself three days to make the crossover trip so you'll have time to include day hikes to Black Tusk or Panorama Ridge.

FURTHER RESOURCES

Garibaldi Provincial Park: info, fees, reservations http://bcparks.ca/explore/parkpgs/garibaldi/
Trail Map: Garibaldi Provincial Park Map by Clark Geomatics
NTS Map: 092G14

10
BREW HUT

Difficulty: ◆

Duration: 2 days

Distance: 12 km (7.5 mi)

Elevation Gain: 566 m (1857 ft)

High Point: 1686 m (5531 ft)

Best Months: July to September

Fees and Reservations: Hut fees are $10/person/night and can be paid online or left in the dropbox in the hut. The hut is first-come, first-served, but users are asked to register visits on the Varsity Outdoor Club (VOC) website. Camping is free and all campsites are first-come, first-served.

Regulations: No fires. Dogs permitted on the lower floor of the hut only with the consent of all guests. No dogs in the loft.

Caution: Only experienced hikers should attempt this trip. The final 2 km (1.2 mi) to the hut (50°02'24" N, 123°11'28" W) is an off-trail route requiring navigation skills and can be very challenging in bad weather. Be sure to carry a map and compass or GPS and know how to use them.

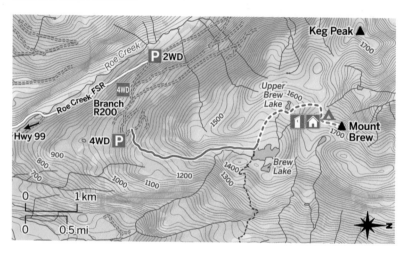

PERCHED HIGH ON a rocky ridge above beautiful heather meadows, cozy Brew Hut has a commanding view of the surrounding mountains and is perfectly positioned to catch both sunrise and sunset. Situated on the west side of the Sea to Sky Highway, this less-travelled trail rewards those who persevere. A marked trail begins high up a 4WD logging road and climbs through windswept forest and meadows to the boulder-strewn shallow waters of Brew Lake. From that point, the challenge begins. Navigate off-trail across gravel, around enormous boulders, and over meadowy slopes for 2 km (1.2 mi) to reach the hut just below the summit of Mount Brew.

Melting snow and ice in boulder-strewn Brew Lake.

GETTING THERE

About 30 km (18.6 mi) north of Squamish on Highway 99, turn left onto Chance Creek Forest Service Road, marked with a sign for cat skiing tours. The road is gravel with some bumps and steep sections. The lower portion is 2WD accessible, but you will need 4WD to get all the way to the trailhead.

Reset your odometer when you leave the highway. Cross the Cheakamus River on a single-lane bridge, then pass over two sets of railway tracks. Stay on the main road, ignoring side branches as it switchbacks uphill. Three kilometres (1.9 mi) from the highway, turn left onto the Roe Creek Forest Service Road. Continue on this road, ignoring branch roads. At 5.9 km (3.7 mi), cross a bridge over Roe Creek. This bridge may be deactivated in the near future, making this the de facto trailhead. **Low-clearance 2WD vehicles** should park here, about 4 km (2.5 mi) from the trailhead.

Vehicles with standard clearance can cross the bridge if it remains drivable. About 8.3 km (5.2 mi) from the highway, Branch R200 heads uphill to the right on a sharp hairpin bend. If you have a **2WD or AWD vehicle**, park on the shoulder here and continue on foot. With a **high-clearance 4WD**, turn right and continue up a very steep road with some deep cross-ditches. Stay right at 9 km (5.6 mi) and 9.2 km (5.7 mi). Keep left at 9.4 km (5.8 mi), then go right at 9.6 km (6 mi). At 9.8 km (6.1 mi), the road forks. Park here. Walk 0.3 km (0.2 mi) uphill along the left branch to reach the trailhead, about 10 km (6.2 mi) from Highway 99.

TRAIL

Three trails from different trailheads converge at Brew Lake before the final ascent to Brew Hut. The route described here provides the most straightforward road access and the shortest and easiest hike.

The trailhead is on the right side of the road in the middle of a clear-cut. Look for a large stump with orange diamond markers. The first few minutes of the hike climb through the cutblock, but you soon reach a stand of old-growth western hemlock and spruce trees. The trail climbs steadily through the forest, across several bluffs and talus sections. Watch for markers carefully in the rocky sections.

About 3 km (1.9 mi) from the start, the grade eases as you reach the banks of a small creek. Follow the trail through a wet section, crossing the creek several times. The vegetation transitions from tight forest to heathery meadows as you ascend beside the stream.

At 4 km (2.5 mi), reach the shores of **Brew Lake** in a bowl strewn with boulders. The lake is fairly shallow, making it much warmer than most other mountain lakes. On a hot day, it's a great place to stop for a swim. A faint trail leads downhill from the southeastern corner of the lake. It's the start of an alternate trail from the rough Brew Lake FSR to the north and another (illegal) trail originating on the railway tracks near Brandywine Falls.

The trail markers end at Brew Lake. In some places ahead, a faint footbed is visible through the meadows, and cairns sometimes mark the route through rocky sections. The open alpine terrain makes navigation fairly straightforward in clear weather. However, foggy weather or whiteout conditions can roll in at any time of year and it can be challenging to find the right route.

NATURE NOTE

From the hut and the nearby summit of Mount Brew, you can see several mountains in the Cascade Volcanic Complex, a string of volcanoes stretching along the Pacific Coast from California to BC. Look for Mount Garibaldi and Black Tusk to the east and the jagged peaks of Mount Fee and Mount Cayley to the northwest.

Follow a faint trail west-northwest up into the alpine over heather slopes and boulder fields for about 1 km (0.6 mi) to tiny **Upper Brew Lake**. Traverse around to the north side of the lake, then head due north for 1 km (0.6 mi) up a draw to a saddle. At the top of the saddle, you'll see the hut up the hill atop a boulder-covered ridge to the east. Walk a few minutes to **Brew Hut**, passing a small meltwater tarn on the way. The views from here are spectacular.

CAMPING AND HUT

UBC's Varsity Outdoor Club (VOC) built the Brew Hut in 2005, primarily for use as a winter destination for experienced backcountry skiers. Unlike most mountain huts, it's fully insulated, making it a warm place to get out of the wind. This is actually the third incarnation of the Brew Hut. The earlier huts suffered extensive damage from huge snow loads. The newest version of the hut is on a windy ridgetop to avoid snow buildup.

Hut Sleeps: 10 on the floor of the loft, plus 3 more on wide benches downstairs
Campsites: No formal campsites but flat spots for 2 or 3 tents near the hut
Toilet: Urine-diversion outhouse north of the hut
Water: Collect from a tarn 100 m (328 ft) west of the hut.
Food Storage: On hooks inside the hut
Other Amenities: The hut has a wood stove and stocked woodshed (for winter use only), table, benches, countertop, and solar lighting.

EXTENDING YOUR TRIP

Mount Brew: Hikers with the aptitude for off-trail navigation and a bit of scrambling should make the 1-km (0.6-mi) round trip to the summit of 1757-m-high (5764 ft) Mount Brew for even better views. Head north from the hut to the base of the mountain, then turn left and look for a cairn leading to a faint trail through the bushes. From there, scramble over rocks to the summit.

FURTHER RESOURCES

Varsity Outdoor Club: Hut info, fees, and visitor registration https://www.ubc-voc.com
Driving Map: Vancouver, Coast & Mountains BC Backroad Mapbook
NTS Map: 092J03

11.
LAKE LOVELY WATER

Difficulty: ◆◆
Duration: 2 to 3 days
Distance: 11 km (6.8 mi)

Elevation Gain: 1135 m (3724 ft)
High Point: 1150 m (3773 ft)
Best Months: Late June to early October

Fees and Reservations: Camping is free and all campsites are first-come, first-served. The hut is locked. Reservations are required to get the hut access code. Hut fees are $35/person/night. Make reservations and pay online.

Regulations: No fires. No drones. No smoking, vaping, or cannabis. No sound systems or loud music. No inflatable watercraft or paddleboards. Dogs permitted on leash. No dogs in the hut.

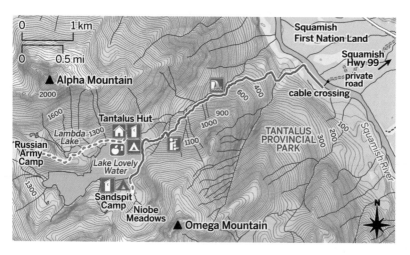

THIS BREATHTAKING BLUE subalpine lake in Tantalus Provincial Park sits beneath glaciated peaks that are a favourite destination for mountaineers. Hikers will enjoy the incredible views as well as the vibrant wildflowers as a reward for this challenging hike. Relax in the well-equipped Alpine Club of Canada hut or in one of the nearby campgrounds, and then day hike to nearby meadows and lakes.

GETTING THERE

To get to the trailhead, start by driving to Squamish via Highway 99. You can also take a ride-sharing service or the Skylynx or Squamish Connector buses.

You'll need to cross the river by boat and a few options are available. The easiest (but most expensive) option is to hire Squamish RiverJet to shuttle you from the Brackendale area of Squamish up the river to the trailhead. You can also hire Patrick Lewis of the Squamish First Nation to take you across the river. He launches from private Squamish First Nation land directly opposite the trailhead.

If you have your own canoe, you can also paddle across the river. However, the Squamish River is very deep and fast-flowing, so this option is recommended for experienced canoeists only. The closest launch points to the trailhead are on First Nations land, so you need to ask permission from the Squamish Nation. You can also launch farther upstream along Squamish Valley Road.

Some campers forego the steep hike in to the lake entirely, flying directly to Lake Lovely Water via helicopter or floatplane. Check the BC Parks website for companies with permits to land in the park. Expect to see more elaborate camp set-ups from the fly-in crowd. If that's you, by all means bring your fancy meals and camp chairs, but please leave the boom box and party plans at home to show respect for other users and the integrity of the wilderness.

TRAIL

TRIP PLANNER

0 km (0 mi)	Trailhead
5.4 km (3.4 mi)	Junction with Niobe Meadows Trail (1 km/0.6 mi to Sandspit campground, 1.5 km/0.9 mi to Niobe Meadows)
5.5 km (3.4 mi)	Tantalus Hut and Lake Lovely Water campground
7.25 km (4.5 mi)	Lambda Lake
9.75 km (6.1 mi)	Russian Army Camp

This hike is almost as steep as Vancouver's Grouse Grind. You'll gain over 1100 m (3609 ft) in just 5.5 km (3.4 mi). Give yourself plenty of time to enjoy the waterfalls and old-growth forest on the ascent, and take care coming back down. Hiking poles can be very helpful to save your knees.

The trail begins on a small beach on the west side of the Squamish River, just upstream from a pair of metal towers supporting a water survey cable over the river. Follow flagging tape and cairns as the trail climbs up and away from the river. About 0.6 km (0.4 mi) from the start, the trail crosses a rocky creek bed and then climbs steeply into an old-growth forest. The trail continues to ascend steadily into the forest as it heads into a deep creek valley. You'll follow this valley upstream all the way to Lake Lovely Water.

At roughly the trail's halfway mark, pause to admire a waterfall and rest your legs. You still have over 500 m (1640 ft) of elevation to ascend. After

Lake Lovely Water and the Tantalus Range from the boat dock at the Tantalus Hut.

the waterfall, the trail continues to climb, crossing several creeks. You'll know you're close to the top when you pass by a viewpoint of the Squamish River Valley and Black Tusk, then a waterfall, hidden in a deep canyon.

The final few metres of trail flatten out a bit as you travel next to the creek. At a **junction**, go right over a shaky suspension bridge to arrive at the **Lake Lovely Water campground** and the **Tantalus Hut**. Drop your pack and head down to the dock to admire the views of the lake and surrounding mountains of the Tantalus Range.

If you want a quieter camping experience, go left before the suspension bridge on the Niobe Meadows Trail for 1 km (0.6 mi). It's a rugged trail with lots of steep ups and downs. Eventually, you'll arrive at the **Sandspit campground** where Niobe Creek empties into Lake Lovely Water.

CAMPING AND HUT

TANTALUS HUT

The Alpine Club of Canada's Tantalus Hut is a great base for a few days at the lake. Downstairs is a common room with a wood stove and a fully equipped kitchen, and upstairs are two bunk rooms with mattresses. Best of all, the hut comes with exclusive access to the ACC's canoes and rowboats. Paddling this serene backcountry lake is sure to be the highlight of your trip. Book far in advance, as the hut is usually fully reserved.

Sleeps: 16 bunks with mattresses, in 2 rooms upstairs
Toilet: Urine-diversion outhouse near the hut's front door
Water: Collect from the lake.
Food Storage: In plastic bins in the hut to protect your food from mice
Other Amenities: Canoes and rowboats with paddles and PFDs, benches, tables, wood stove, propane cooking stoves, dishes and cutlery, wash sink, sleeping mattresses, propane lanterns

LAKE OUTLET CAMPGROUND

A backcountry campground lies just north of the hut. In 2018 BC Parks upgraded and expanded this site. Wooden tent platforms are spread amongst the trees, a few with great views of the lake. Note: Campers are not allowed to use the hut or its amenities.

Campsites: 15 wooden tent platforms
Toilet: Urine-diversion outhouse near the hut's front door
Water: Collect from the lake.
Food Storage: On food-hanging wires at the north end of the campground
Other Amenities: A food-prep counter and bench near the food-hanging wires

SANDSPIT CAMPGROUND

This small shoreline campground is 1 km (0.6 mi) south along the lake from the Tantalus Hut area, so it can be a bit more secluded. The views are amazing, but this area has fewer facilities and no privacy if you're sharing it with other hikers.

Campsites: Space for 6 tents close together on the sandspit, but it varies with fluctuating water levels
Toilet: Throne-style pit toilet on a short trail uphill from the spit
Water: Collect from the creek that flows next to the spit.
Food Storage: Bring rope to hang your food in a tree, or bring a bear canister.

HISTORY

The mountains of the Tantalus Range are named after King Tantalus of Greek mythology, who tried to serve his own son first at a feast with the gods. As punishment, Zeus made him stand in a pool of water under a fruit tree, but the water receded when he tried to drink and the fruit was always just beyond his grasp. From this story comes the word "tantalizing." World War II–era climber Basil S. Darling saw the close but inaccessible peaks in this range from the Squamish Valley and found parallels with the legend.

EXTENDING YOUR TRIP

Niobe Meadows Trail: This short hike leads to a tiny basin tucked between Mount Niobe and Omega Mountain. In mid-summer, the meadows light up with colourful flowers. From the sandspit camp on the south side of the lake, follow a faint trail upstream along the creek, hopping over lots of small boulders, to the meadows 0.5 km (0.3 mi) away.

Lambda Lake and Russian Army Camp: This trail leads around the lake to the northwest, then up through the forest to reach Lambda Lake. Follow cairns through the boulders to a challenging scramble up a steep rock face with a fixed chain for assistance. After the chain, cross a talus slope, and walk through the

A glimpse of Lake Lovely Water through the front window of the Tantalus Hut.

forest to the lakeshore. Continue past Lambda Lake and climb up to an area of open talus slopes nicknamed Russian Army Camp. Historically, mountaineers bivouacked here before scrambling up the nearby peaks. Hikers will appreciate the spectacular views of Mount Niobe and Omega Mountain across Lake Lovely Water. It's 6 km (3.7 mi) return from the hut.

FURTHER RESOURCES

Tantalus Provincial Park: info http://bcparks.ca/explore/parkpgs/tantalus/
Squamish RiverJet: http://www.squamishriverjet.ca/
Patrick Lewis Squamish River Ferry: 604-898-9107
Alpine Club of Canada Vancouver Section: Tantalus Hut info and reservations http://accvancouver.ca
NTS Map: 092G14

12
ELFIN LAKES
AND RAMPART PONDS

Difficulty: ■
Duration: 2 to 4 days
Distance: 22 to 42 km (13.7 to 26.1 mi)

Elevation Gain: 610 m (2001 ft)
High Point: 1590 m (5217 ft)
Best Months: July to September

Fees and Reservations: Reservations are required to camp or stay in the hut and cost $6/night for each tent pad or hut booking. Camping fees are $10/person/night, and hut fees are $15/person/night. Both reservation and camping fees are payable online.

Regulations: No fires. No dogs. No drones. No smoking, vaping, or cannabis. Bikes permitted as far as Elfin Lakes only.

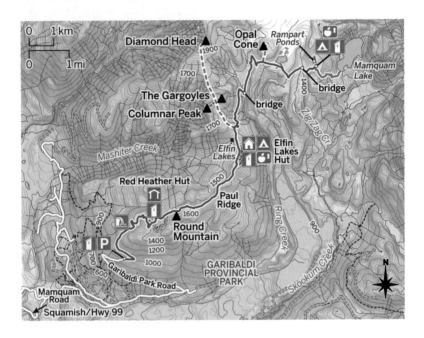

ON THIS TRIP in the southern portion of Garibaldi Provincial Park, you'll amble along a ridgeline with views of the surrounding mountains, including the imposing Mount Garibaldi (Nch'kay to the Squamish people). Camp beside two tiny alpine lakes with mountain views or book a spot in the large, busy, and comfortable hut. The hut is a great destination for beginners, shoulder season, and snowshoeing trips, but you'll need avalanche training in

Elfin Lakes with the Garibaldi Neve icefield behind. Photo: Romeo Taras

winter. Head to Elfin Lakes for an overnight backpacking trip, or stay longer and use it as a base camp for day hikes. Those seeking more adventure and solitude can continue on the trail to camp at Rampart Ponds, passing through a unique volcanic moonscape with signs of glaciation all around you.

GETTING THERE

In Squamish, go east from Highway 99 onto Mamquam Road, then turn left to go up the hill on Highland Way. At the roundabout, go right onto The Boulevard. Go straight through the next roundabout and stay on the main road as it curves through Quest University. Turn right at the next roundabout, then immediately left back onto Mamquam Road.

The pavement ends and the remaining 8.5 km (5.3 mi) to the trailhead are on gravel. Continue on the main road, ignoring side roads as it climbs through the forest. When the road reaches a few houses, go left onto the marked Garibaldi Park Road, which climbs all the way to the large parking lot at the trailhead. There's an outhouse at the trailhead.

TRAIL

TRIP PLANNER

0 km (0 mi)	Trailhead
5 km (3.1 mi)	Red Heather Hut
11 km (6. 8 mi)	Elfin Lakes Hut and campground
11.8 km (7.3 mi)	Junction with trails to The Gargoyles (2.5 km/1.6 mi away) and Diamond Head (5.5 km/3.4 mi away)

14 km (8.7 mi)	Ring Creek bridge
16 km (9.9 mi)	Junction with Opal Cone Trail (1 km/0.6 mi to top)
18.6 km (11.6 mi)	Zig Zag Creek bridge
22 km (13.7 mi)	Rampart Ponds campground
23.5 km (14.6 mi)	Mamquam Lake

The trail begins at the far end of the parking area. The first 5 km (3.1 mi) follow an old road with occasional peekaboo views over the valley and a waterfall about halfway along. The more interesting part of the trip begins when the trail emerges from the forest near the **Red Heather Hut day-use shelter** at 5 km (3.1 mi). In the winter, the shelter is usually crammed with ski tourers having lunch or warming up by the wood stove. An outhouse stands a few metres down the trail from the hut, its long staircase a clue to how much snow the region gets every winter.

In the summer, the blueberry bushes in the Red Heather area attract the largest concentration of black bears in Garibaldi Provincial Park. That's why snow camping is permitted in this area from December to April, but no camping is allowed during the rest of the year. Make lots of noise and remain bear aware as you hike through this area.

Past Red Heather Hut, go left on a more scenic hiking trail leaving the old gravel road to the left. (Mountain bikers must remain on the road.) The trail climbs up to the shoulder of Round Mountain and rejoins the old road less than a kilometre (0.6 mi) later. For the next 5 km (3.1 mi), follow the road as it undulates across the top of Paul Ridge. On clear days, there are beautiful views of snow-capped Mount Garibaldi to the north and Mamquam Mountain to the east.

The trail gradually descends slightly to reach Elfin Lakes, two small lakes tucked into a fold in the ridge. The **Elfin Lakes campground**, a ranger station, and the **Elfin Lakes Hut** lie just north of the lakes. On a warm day, you can swim in the south Elfin Lake. (There's no swimming in the north lake, as it is the drinking water source for the campground and hut.)

To continue to Rampart Ponds, stay on the trail as it heads north. You'll quickly reach a **junction**. Turn right. (Left goes to Diamond Head and The Gargoyles.) The trail crosses a few creek beds before a steep descent into the rocky **Ring Creek Valley**.

HISTORY

This road used to service the Diamond Head Chalet, a private backcountry lodge at Elfin Lakes run by the Brandvold family until 1972. The chalet attracted thousands of visitors over three decades. Today a plaque and a small section of the log structure are all that remain.

The tent platforms at Elfin Lakes have incredible views of Mamquam Mountain. Photo: Romeo Taras

The bridge over the creek sits at an elevation of 1270 m (4167 ft), 200 m (656 ft) lower than both Elfin Lakes and Rampart Ponds. That means this portion of the hike will literally be uphill both ways! After crossing the bridge, begin a long and gradual climb out of the valley. The trail travels beside the creek as the terrain switches to a moonscape of volcanic rock, scoured by glaciers and dotted with pockets of tenacious wildflowers like yellow monkey flower and pink river beauty.

About 2 km (1.2 mi) from the bridge, you'll enter a small patch of trees and pass the junction with the **Opal Cone Trail**. The next few kilometres of trail travel across a flat plain of rocks, speckled with brilliant blue meltwater lakes. However, it's not entirely flat as you will need to lose, then gain 100 m (328 ft) to cross **Zig Zag Creek**. Try to hike through this area on a clear day so you can admire the views of the Garibaldi Neve and Lava Glacier to the north. After you've climbed up from the creek, arrive at the **Rampart Ponds campground**.

CAMPING AND HUT

ELFIN LAKES CAMPGROUND

The Elfin Lakes campground is on a slight rise to the north of the lakes, beside the Elfin Lakes Hut. All of the campsites are on wooden platforms to protect the fragile subalpine vegetation. Many of the sites have amazing views.

The trail up to The Gargoyles.

Campsites: 35 wooden tent platforms
Toilets: Pit toilets at either end of the campground or use the toilet building near the shelter
Water: Collect from the north Elfin Lake.
Food Storage: On pulley-operated food-hanging poles
Other Amenities: A cooking shelter with picnic tables

ELFIN LAKES HUT

This popular hut is often fully booked on weekends year-round despite being one of the biggest public backcountry huts in southwestern BC. It's a great option for hikers who want to avoid carrying a tent and stove and who prefer the extra warmth of staying indoors.

Hut Sleeps: 33, in 22 double bunks and 11 single bunks upstairs
Toilets: Adjacent building has 4 pit toilets
Water: Collect from north Elfin Lake.
Food Storage: On hooks on the ground floor
Other Amenities: The hut has benches, picnic tables, a propane heater, a propane lighting system, 2 propane stoves, a wash sink, and a bicycle rack.

RAMPART PONDS CAMPGROUND

BC Parks opened the Rampart Ponds campground in 2015 to replace the Mamquam Lake campground, which closed after Indigenous cultural artifacts were discovered in the area. The Rampart Ponds campground offers incredible views of the Garibaldi Neve, Lava Glacier, Mount Garibaldi, and Mamquam Mountain, but that openness makes it a poor choice in stormy weather. It's 10 km (6.2 mi) from Elfin Lakes.

Campsites: 12 gravel tent pads
Toilet: Pit toilet next to the tent pads
Water: Collect from the Rampart Ponds.
Food Storage: In metal food lockers

EXTENDING YOUR TRIP

Both Elfin Lakes and Rampart Ponds make a great base camp for day hikes.

The Gargoyles: This short hike to a pair of volcanic towers is a good afternoon objective if you're staying at Elfin Lakes. It's 5 km (3.1 mi) return with 350 m (1148 ft) of elevation gain. The trail starts just north of the Elfin Lakes Hut.

Diamond Head: Diamond Head is a 2056-m (6745-ft) pyramid-shaped summit on the flanks of Mount Garibaldi. An intermittent trail leads there from The Gargoyles and is for experienced off-trail hikers only due to tricky route-finding, persistent snowfields, loose rock, and some scrambling. From the summit, enjoy the close-up views of the Diamond Glacier and Atwell Peak, a sub-summit on the Garibaldi Massif. It's 11 km (6.8 mi) round trip with 580 m (1903 ft) of elevation gain.

Opal Cone: This extinct volcanic cinder cone provides great views of Garibaldi's volcanic and glacial features, including the Garibaldi Neve and Lava Glacier to the north and northeast, triangular Pyramid Mountain rising above Mamquam Lake to the west, and the expansive Mamquam Icefield, crowned by Mamquam Mountain to the southwest. You can climb Opal Cone as a 1-km (0.6-mi) detour from the main trail to Rampart Ponds. From Elfin Lakes, it's a 13-km (8.1-mi) round trip.

Mamquam Lake: From Rampart Ponds, it's a 3-km (1.9-mi) round trip to Mamquam Lake. The lake is 200 m (656 ft) lower than Rampart Ponds in a subalpine forest ecosystem with Pyramid Mountain towering above. The large lake is a great place to cool off on a hot day. Camping is no longer allowed here.

FURTHER RESOURCES

Garibaldi Provincial Park: info, fees, reservations http://bcparks.ca/explore/parkpgs/garibaldi/
Trail Map: Garibaldi Provincial Park Map by Clark Geomatics
Driving Map: Vancouver, Coast & Mountains BC Backroad Mapbook
NTS Maps: 092G14, 092G15

13
WATERSPRITE LAKE

Difficulty: ■
Duration: 2 days
Distance: 17 km (10.6 mi)

Elevation Gain: 660 m (2165 ft)
High Point: 1470 m (4823 ft)
Best Months: Mid-June to October

Fees and Reservations: Camping is free and all campsites are first-come, first-served. The hut is locked. Online reservations are required to get the hut access code. Hut fees are $20/person/night, also payable online. Book far in advance, as the hut is usually fully reserved.

Regulations: No fires. No dogs in the hut.

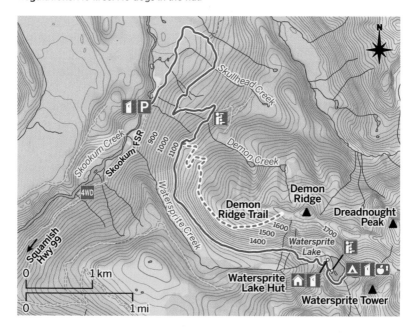

WATERSPRITE LAKE IS an Instagram sensation and it's easy to see why. It's a tiny ice-blue lake nestled against spires of rock and craggy cliffs. We can thank the British Columbia Mountaineering Club (BCMC) for discovering this area, building the trail, adding a campground, and building a backcountry hut. Enjoy the Milky Way overhead on a cloudless night, then rise early the next day to watch the sun rise over the shoulder of Watersprite Tower. Its location high in the Mamquam River watershed is remote, yet within easy reach of Squamish if you have a 4WD vehicle. Although this is a newer trail,

Watersprite Tower from the shore of Watersprite Lake.

it's already seeing a lot of use and the sensitive subalpine environment is suffering. Please practise your best Leave No Trace skills and consider hiking mid-week to reduce overcrowding.

GETTING THERE

To get to the trailhead, you'll have to drive 20 km (12.4 mi) of logging road, and the last few kilometres are quite rough; **4WD drive vehicles are recommended**. In Squamish just north of the Stawamus Chief, turn off Highway 99 onto the Mamquam River Forest Service Road.

Follow this bumpy and potholed road, avoiding any minor side roads. At 13 km (8.1 mi), turn left to cross a bridge over the Mamquam River, and then cross a bridge over Skookum Creek a few minutes later. After the second bridge, turn left onto the Skookum Forest Service Road at the signs for the Skookum Power Project. If you have a **2WD vehicle**, park here, 6.5 km (4 mi) away from the trailhead. Past this point, **4WD is required**. The road climbs very steeply for the next few kilometres.

Sixteen kilometres (9.9 mi) from the highway, go left at a junction with a large metal candy cane–shaped vent. The road flattens out through this section, but there is a very steep hill towards the end and a couple of very deep water bars. The road dead-ends at a parking lot in front of a metal gate. Park here. The trailhead is just up the hill past the gate, and there's a new outhouse thanks to volunteers from the BCMC.

TRAIL

Watersprite Lake is nestled between the summits of Martin Peak, Gibson Peak, Watersprite Tower, Dreadnought Peak, and Iron Duke Peak. The steep and rocky terrain holds snow late into the year, which melts and collects in Watersprite Lake. Fine particles of rock dust suspended in the water give the lake its unique turquoise colour. It's a popular photo spot, so don't forget your camera.

The first section of the trail is on old road, which allows for amazing views of the surrounding mountains, as well as the occasional wildflower soaking up the sun on the sides of the trail. However, the lack of tree cover means it is very exposed on sunny days. There are a few creeks in the first 4 km (2.5 mi), but no water sources after that, so fill up your bottles.

From the trailhead signboard, the path travels through a rocky area before merging with an old road. After about 1 km (0.6 mi), the route leaves the old road and heads steeply uphill on a newly cut trail for a few minutes before emerging on another old road. Turn right and follow this road as it contours along the side of the mountain, then heads up a few switchbacks. You'll start to get views across the valley of spectacular Mount Garibaldi (Nch'kay to the Squamish people) to the west. The best **viewpoint** is about 4 km (2.5 mi) from the trailhead.

Shortly after the viewpoint, the **Demon Ridge Trail** branches off to the left. Stay on the main trail as it trends southeast into the Watersprite Creek valley. At around 7.5 km (4.7 mi), the **road ends** at an old burn and the true trail begins. You will scramble across a talus slope, then through some dense alder. Follow a newly cut trail through old-growth forest, crossing a few damp sections on boardwalks.

The trail heads steeply up to the left of a boulder field before topping out in heathery meadows just above the lake. Take the side trail to the left to reach the **Watersprite Lake Hut**. Go straight to visit the lake. The trail to the **Watersprite Lake campground** heads right, hugging the southern shore of the lake and working its way through a tricky boulder field.

CAMPING AND HUT

CAMPGROUND

Newly completed in 2018, the Watersprite Lake campground is in a pretty meadow around the outwash of a creek on the opposite side of the lake from the hut.

Campsites: 10 wooden tent pads and several more gravel tent spots
Toilet: Outhouse slightly uphill from the tent pads
Water: Collect from the stream flowing through the campground.
Food Storage: In metal food lockers around the campground

BCMC WATERSPRITE LAKE HUT

Completed in 2017, the cozy two-level Watersprite Lake Hut provides a great alternative to camping.

Sleeps: 10 on the floor of the loft
Toilet: Outhouse behind the hut
Water: Collect from the lake or Watersprite Creek.
Food Storage: On hooks inside the cabin
Other Amenities: Benches, tables, and a wood stove

EXTENDING YOUR TRIP

Demon Ridge Trail: This rough route follows an overgrown logging road and then a flagged trail to the crest of Demon Ridge with spectacular views of the peaks surrounding Watersprite Lake. The trail starts at 4.7 km (2.9 mi) on the Watersprite Lake Trail. It's a 6-km (3.7-mi) round trip from the junction to the ridge, with 540 m (1772 ft) of elevation.

NATURE NOTE

Mount Garibaldi is a dormant stratovolcano. It is made of hardened lava and volcanic ash and began erupting on top of a large glacier about 250,000 years ago. The volcano also sent out a long tongue of liquid magma that flowed 20 km (12.4 mi) down the Ring Creek Valley. Look northwest from the viewpoint to trace the path of the Ring Creek lava flow descending the slope, recognizable as a brown-grey band of rocks amid the trees. As the glaciers melted, the rocky slopes of the volcano became unstable, sending numerous slides down the mountain into the creeks and rivers below. In the Squamish language, Nch'kay means "dirty place" or "grimy one," so named since the streams on its flanks are muddy and silty with volcanic debris.

Watersprite Lake Hut from the trail below the lake.

FURTHER RESOURCES
BCMC: hut info and reservations https://bcmc.ca
Watersprite Lake Facebook group: road and trail conditions https://www.facebook.com/groups/WaterspriteLakeConditions/
Driving Map: Vancouver, Coast & Mountains BC Backroad Mapbook
NTS Map: 092G10

SUNSHINE COAST

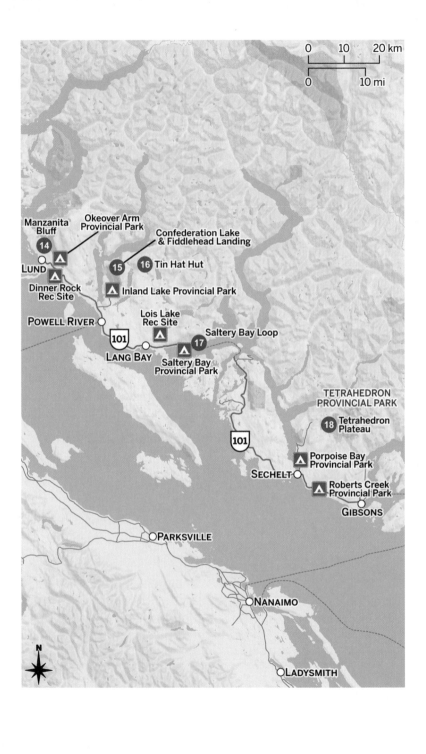

WHILE IT'S JUST a ferry ride away from Vancouver, the Sunshine Coast has a small population and quiet trails. Little towns dot the coast, but most of the landscape is dominated by lush rainforest, punctuated by rocky peaks. Along the trails you'll find pockets of old-growth forest, lakes hidden in wooded hollows, and lots of homey cabins.

The Sunshine Coast is part of British Columbia's mainland, but access is by ferry because no roads lead there. Jervis Inlet—another ferry ride—separates the Upper and Lower Sunshine Coasts. The Lower Sunshine Coast is centred on the town of Sechelt. Powell River is the regional hub for the Upper Sunshine Coast. This is an active logging area. Most of the forest service roads are 2WD accessible, but use a backroad map book or GPS to help you navigate the maze of intersections.

The 180-km-long (112 mi) Sunshine Coast Trail (SCT) stretches along the Upper Sunshine Coast from near Lund in the north to Saltery Bay in the south. This book includes four of the most scenic and easily accessible sections of this destination trail. Unlike the SCT, the hut-to-hut hiking in Tetrahedron Provincial Park on the Lower Sunshine Coast has remained a bit under the radar. With four volunteer-maintained cabins spread across a lake-speckled plateau, it's a great place to spend a few days.

The Sunshine Coast has a coastal temperate climate but is a bit warmer and drier than Vancouver, hence the name. Most of the local mountains are not that tall, which means many of the hikes are snow-free in spring and fall.

The Lower Sunshine Coast is the traditional territory of the Shíshálh (Sechelt). Visit the tems swiya Museum in Sechelt to learn more about their history, culture, and art. The Upper Sunshine Coast is the traditional territory of the Tla'amin (Sliammon), and they share the southern portion of their territory with the Shíshálh.

Supplies: On the Lower Sunshine Coast, Sechelt and Gibsons have grocery stores and gas stations. There are outdoor stores in Sechelt. Powell River on the Upper Sunshine Coast has outdoor stores, gas stations, and grocery stores.

Accommodation: Hotels and vacation rentals are located throughout the region. First-come, first-served campsites are available at Roberts Creek and Porpoise Bay Provincial Parks on the Lower Sunshine Coast. On the Upper Sunshine Coast, both Saltery Bay and Inland Lake Provincial Parks have a mix of reservable and first-come, first-served campsites. There are also first-come, first-served campsites at Lois Lake Rec Site near Lang Bay, and Okeover Arm Provincial Park and Dinner Rock Rec Site, both near Lund.

14
MANZANITA BLUFF

Difficulty: ●/■
Duration: 2 days
Distance: 7 to 16 km (4.3 to 9.9 mi)

Elevation Gain: 295 m (968 ft)
High Point: 365 m (1198 ft)
Best Months: March to November

Fees and Reservations: None, though donations are welcome. All huts and camping are first-come, first-served.

Regulations: Fires permitted in firepits only. Dogs permitted.

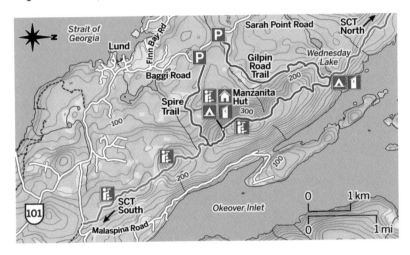

RAMBLE ALONG AN arbutus-covered ridge to a hut perched on the bluffs above the village of Lund. Thanks to the trail's low elevation, you can do this trip at almost any time of year. The northernmost of 14 huts along the 180-km-long (112 mi) Sunshine Coast Trail, Manzanita Hut sits on a rocky knoll surrounded by old-growth forest with patches of shiny-barked manzanita bushes. Gaze out the windows for commanding views of the Strait of Georgia and Vancouver Island. On warm afternoons, watch for eagles riding thermal air currents overhead.

There are several ways to hike to the hut. The most scenic option is via the Gilpin Road access trail to Wednesday Lake and then along the crest of the Gwendoline Hills. If you just want to reach the hut, there's also a short and direct route using the Spire Trail. Both are described below. If you're willing to walk 0.7 km (0.4 mi) of road, you can combine both routes to make a loop.

Arbutus trees and a view of the Strait of Georgia and Vancouver Island near Manzanita Hut.

GETTING THERE

SPIRE TRAILHEAD

From Powell River, drive north to Lund, then turn right on Finn Bay Road, which becomes gravel. After 0.6 km (0.4 mi), turn right onto Baggi Road. Continue for 0.4 km (0.2 mi), then turn left onto Sarah Point Road. Drive 1.1 km (0.7 mi) and look for an old logging road on the right with a sign for the Sunshine Coast Trail. Park on the shoulder.

GILPIN ROAD TRAILHEAD

To reach the Gilpin Road trailhead, follow the directions for the Spire trailhead above. Drive another 0.7 km (0.4 mi) and look for another old road on the right with an SCT sign. This is Gilpin Road and the trailhead. Park here on the shoulder.

TRAIL

SPIRE TRAIL

TRIP PLANNER

0 km (0 mi)	Trailhead
2 km (1.2 mi)	Junction with Spire Trail
3 km (1.9 mi)	Junction with SCT
3.5 km (2.2 mi)	Manzanita Bluff Hut and camping

If you want to make a beeline for the hut, take this 3.5-km-long (2.2 mi) direct route. From the trailhead on Sarah Point Road, follow the old gravel road gently uphill through tight thickets of young alder trees, watching for red trail markers. About 2 km (1.2 mi) from the start, reach a **junction**. Go left, following signs for the Spire Trail. Follow this trail more steeply uphill for 1 km (0.6 mi) to a **junction** with the Sunshine Coast Trail.

Turn left onto the Sunshine Coast Trail as it begins to switchback steeply up a rise through cedar forest, sprinkled with arbutus trees. The climbing here is strenuous but thankfully brief. Half a kilometre (0.3 mi) later, arrive at the **Manzanita Bluff Hut**.

GILPIN ROAD TRAIL

TRIP PLANNER

0 km (0 mi)	Gilpin Road trailhead
4 km (2.5 mi)	Wednesday Lake campground and junction with SCT
6 km (3.7 mi)	Hummingbird Bluff
8 km (5 mi)	Manzanita Bluff Hut and campground
13.3 km (8.3 mi)	Malaspina Road trailhead

The 8-km-long (5 mi) route to Manzanita Bluff Hut from the Gilpin Road trailhead is not as direct, but it travels across beautiful bluffs. From the trailhead, hike up the rough 4WD-only Gilpin Road. The old road climbs gently through a second-growth forest for about 1 km (0.6 mi) before reaching a swampy area. Follow a side trail to the right for a few minutes to circle around the swamp before rejoining the road again.

Past the swampy area, follow the sign for Wednesday Lake onto a trail leaving the road. About 4 km (2.5 mi) from the trailhead, reach the shores of Wednesday Lake. Follow the trail along the east shore to a junction where you join the SCT. Take a break to soak up the views from a well-sited bench, or strip off and plunge into the lake to cool off. If you want to camp here, head left for a few minutes to the **Wednesday Lake campground** on the north shore of the lake. The route to Manzanita Bluff heads right. If you're pressing on, fill up with water here or at the creek a few minutes down the trail as these are the last water sources before the hut.

Leaving Wednesday Lake, the trail climbs out of the Wednesday Creek valley. It quickly emerges onto the spine of the Gwendoline Hills. You'll follow this undulating ridge all the way to Manzanita Bluff Hut 4 km (2.5 mi) away and 250 m (820 ft) higher. The beginning of the trail is in the forest and incorporates a few ancient-looking moss-covered logging roads. About 2 km (1.2 mi) from the lake, you'll climb up onto **Hummingbird Bluff**. You can catch glimpses of the ocean from here, in between the curved branches of the arbutus trees.

The trail to the hut continues along the ridge crest through beautiful stands of old-growth forest. Top out at 365 m (1198 ft) above sea level on MacPherson Hill at 7.5 km (4.7 mi). Shortly afterwards, reach the **Manzanita Hut**. This welcoming shelter is nestled onto a rocky 300-m-high (984 ft) bluff with incredible views of the Strait of Georgia, sandy Savary Island, and the mountains of Vancouver Island's Strathcona Provincial Park beyond.

CAMPING AND HUT

MANZANITA HUT AND CAMPING

Built in 2011, the Manzanita Hut is a partially open shelter with an enclosed (but not bug- or rodent-proof) sleeping loft upstairs. Downstairs two sides of the shelter have half-height walls and the other two have full walls with large Plexiglas windows that afford incredible views to the west. A picnic table on a nearby bluff provides an even better vantage point.

Campsites: Space for 2 or 3 tents near the hut
Hut Sleeps: 10 on the loft floor
Toilet: Outhouse near the hut
Water: Haul in your own water from the trailhead, or top up at Wednesday Lake if you hike in from Gilpin Road.
Food Storage: Bring rope to hang your food in a tree, or bring a bear canister.
Other Amenities: A picnic table, a firepit, and benches outside the hut. A picnic table and cooking countertops inside the hut.

WEDNESDAY LAKE CAMPSITE

This small campsite is located on the north shore of Wednesday Lake, which supplies water for an oyster farm in Okeover Inlet. Take care to keep the water clean.

Campsites: Space for 2 or 3 tents
Toilet: Outhouse near the campsite
Water: Collect from the lake.

NATURE NOTE

The bluff is named for the hairy manzanita bushes that grow on its slopes. These evergreen bushes produce small blackish-red berries, which give the bush their name: *manzanita* means "little apple" in Spanish. Like their relatives the arbutus trees, manzanita bushes grow on sunny rock outcroppings at low elevations. You'll see plenty of both on this hike.

Beginning the climb to Manzanita Hut from the Spire Trail.

Food Storage: Bring rope to hang your food in a tree, or bring a bear canister.

Other Amenities: A bench with a view of the lake

EXTENDING YOUR TRIP

Start at Sarah Point: Hire a water taxi in Lund and get dropped off at Sarah Point, the official start point of the Sunshine Coast Trail. From there, it's 12 km (7.5 mi) to Wednesday Lake where you pick up the description above.

Traverse to Malaspina Road: If you arrange a shuttle, you can do a traverse from the Gilpin Road trailhead to another trailhead on Malaspina Road 5.3 km (3.3 mi) east of the hut. The route includes views from bluffs, some old-growth forest sections, and a rhododendron grove, but it travels past several clear-cuts.

Sunshine Coast Trail: You've just walked the northernmost section of the SCT. Why not continue south to complete more of the 180-km (112-mi) trail? The hike from Sarah Point to the Shinglemill Pub on the banks of the Powell River is a popular three- to four-day trip that covers 50 km (31.1 mi).

FURTHER RESOURCES

Sunshine Coast Trail: info and maps https://sunshinecoast-trail.com/

Sunshine Coast Trail donations: https://sunshinecoast-trail.com/prpaws/donate/

Sunshine Coast Trail Facebook Group: trail conditions and info https://www.facebook.com/groups/1454789984814708/

NTS Maps: 092K02, 092F15

15
CONFEDERATION LAKE
AND FIDDLEHEAD LANDING

Difficulty: ■/◆
Duration: 2 to 3 days
Distance: 15 to 30 km (9.3 to 18.6 mi)

Elevation Gain: 600 m (1969 ft)
High Point: 690 m (2264 ft)
Best Months: April to November

Fees and Reservations: None, though donations are welcome. All huts and camping are first-come, first-served.

Regulations: Fires permitted in firepits only. Dogs permitted on leash at Confederation Lake. No drones, smoking, vaping, or cannabis at Confederation Lake.

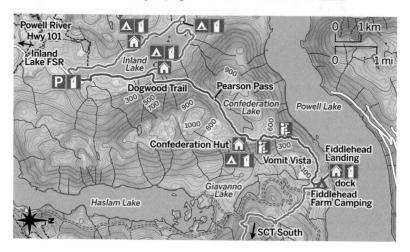

THIS LOW-ELEVATION SECTION of the Sunshine Coast Trail (SCT) in Inland Lake Provincial Park makes a great shoulder-season hike or an off-the-beaten-path destination at any time of year. With two huts to choose from, you can tailor the trip length and difficulty to your liking. Climb through thick old-growth forest to a hut on the shores of Confederation Lake. Swim in the lake or just enjoy the views from the nearby picnic table or the benches on the hut's porch. To extend your trip, descend steeply past numerous viewpoints to the shores of Powell Lake and the hut at Fiddlehead Landing. Stay at the waterfront hut or hike a few minutes farther inland to camp in a historical apple orchard. Hire a water taxi to return to Powell River if you don't want to retrace your route.

Climbing through the forest below Confederation Lake.

GETTING THERE

From downtown Powell River, go east on Alberni Street up the hill, then turn left at the stop sign onto Manson Avenue. Follow Manson for 1.4 km (0.9 mi), then turn right onto Cassiar. Make the next left onto Yukon, then follow Yukon for about 1 km (0.6 mi). Turn right onto Haslam, which quickly turns to gravel and becomes the 2WD-accessible Inland Lake Forest Service Road. Follow it for 6 km (3.7 mi) to reach Inland Lake Provincial Park. Park in the day-use parking lot near the boat launch. You can also reach Fiddlehead Landing by hiring a water taxi to ferry you up Powell Lake from a marina near Powell River.

TRAIL

TRIP PLANNER

0 km (0 mi)	Trailhead
3 km (1.9 mi)	Junction with Inland Lake Loop Trail (13-km/8.1-mi loop)
6.5 km (4 mi)	Confederation Lake
7.5 km (4.7 mi)	Confederation Lake Hut and campground
8.3 km (5.2 mi)	Vomit Vista
15 km (9.3 mi)	Fiddlehead Landing Hut and Fiddlehead Farm campground
25 km (15.5 mi)	Tin Hat Hut (see Trip 16)

From the parking lot, follow the trail north through the campground and past the swimming dock. The first section of the trail follows the shore of Inland Lake on a wide and flat trail that is wheelchair accessible. At about 3 km (1.9 mi), you'll reach a **junction** where you join the Sunshine Coast Trail. Turn right and hike uphill on the SCT, away from Inland Lake on a section of trail known as the Dogwood Trail. Hike here in spring to enjoy their white flowers. About 0.5 km (0.3 mi) later, turn left to follow an old road and continue climbing steadily in a rising traverse.

About 5 km (3.1 mi) from the start, cross a new bridge, pausing to admire a small waterfall in the creek. Shortly after the bridge, stay on the old road as it switchbacks uphill and becomes a trail with tight zigzags that leads you into a dark canyon. This is the steepest part of the climb. Follow the trail uphill to Pearson Pass. From here, continue gradually downhill to the south end of **Confederation Lake**. There's a short spur trail to a lakeside viewpoint. The main trail continues to the right above the lake, which is barely visible through the trees.

About 1 km (0.6 mi) of undulating trail later, arrive at the **Confederation Lake Hut** at the north end of the lake. Stop for the night here, or pause for a swim in the lake. Follow a short trail past the cabin along the shoreline to a tiny gravel beach.

If you are continuing on from Confederation Lake, follow the trail past the hut and the outhouse through thickets of blueberry and huckleberry bushes. A sign advertises **Vomit Vista** 0.8 km (0.5 mi) ahead. While the name doesn't sound appealing, the views of Powell Lake and nearby Tin Hat Mountain (Trip 16) from the rocky outcrop are incredible. (You will appreciate the name on your return trip as it's a steep climb to get here.)

From the viewpoint, the trail follows the spine of a ridge for the next 3.5 km (2.2 mi) as it descends towards Powell Lake. Pause at several lookouts along the way to enjoy views of Powell Lake below, Goat Lake on Goat Island, the Rainbow Peaks to the northeast, and Tin Hat Mountain to the east. As the grade lessens, the route passes through a stand of old-growth trees, then crosses a gravel road. Look carefully for trail markers to pick up the trail on the other side.

The final 1 km (0.6 mi) of trail to the Fiddlehead Landing Hut navigates a maze of logging roads of various ages and regenerating cutblocks. Keep your eye out for trail markers to stay on track. At a marked junction, take the spur trails to **Fiddlehead Landing** and the former Fiddlehead Farm, 15 km (9.3 mi) from the trailhead. The main SCT heads southeast to begin the ascent of Tin Hat Mountain.

CAMPING AND HUTS

CONFEDERATION LAKE HUT

The Confederation Lake Hut at the north end of Confederation Lake is fully winterized and even has a pellet stove for heat. (You'll need to bring your own pellets and look up instructions for operating it beforehand as it can be tricky.)

Campsites: A few small cleared areas in the brush near the hut. Or within the foundations of the old cabin.
Hut Sleeps: 10 on the loft floor
Toilet: Composting toilet north of the hut
Water: Collect from the lake outflow stream southeast of the hut.
Food Storage: On hooks inside the hut
Other Amenities: A picnic table, firepit, and benches outside the hut. A short trail leads to a swimming beach. Inside the hut are a picnic table, countertop, and pellet stove.

FIDDLEHEAD LANDING HUT

This hut is in a gorgeous spot on the shore of Powell Lake. It may seem remote, but several private float homes are within sight of the hut. And it is accessible by boat as well as trail, so you may share it with paddlers on the Powell Forest Canoe Route or motorboaters out for the weekend. Constructed in 2012, the hut has an enclosed upper storey for sleeping and a dirt-floored and open-sided lower level for cooking.

Campsites: None near the hut, though some have pitched small tents directly on the dock. Fiddlehead Farm a few minutes away has flat areas but no toilet, water source, or food storage. Use caution: both hikers and bears like the fruit in the elderly apple orchard.
Hut Sleeps: 6 on the loft floor
Toilet: Outhouse near the hut
Water: Collect from the lake.
Food Storage: On hooks inside the hut
Other Amenities: A picnic table in the open lower level of the hut. A firepit and dock nearby.

HISTORY

Powell River locals hiked through the area in 1971 and named the lake to commemorate British Columbia's 100th year in Confederation. For years an old BC Forest Service log cabin welcomed visitors to the site. In 2016 the Powell River Parks and Wilderness Society built a beautiful new hut next to the crumbling foundation of the old cabin.

The insulated Confederation Lake Hut is a warm refuge on cold and wet days.

EXTENDING YOUR TRIP

Inland Lake: Add a circuit of Inland Lake to your trip. A 13-km (8.1-mi) fully wheelchair-accessible trail loops all the way around the lake. Three backcountry cabins along the way, plus walk-in campsites on Anthony Island, provide options for an overnight stay.

Sunshine Coast Trail to Tin Hat Mountain: Continue along the SCT from Fiddlehead Landing up the gruelling climb to the top of Tin Hat Mountain (Trip 16). You'll gain over 1000 m (3281 ft) in less than 10 km (6.2 mi)! Together with this trip, you'll make a 30-km (18.6-mi) one-way traverse over three or four days.

FURTHER RESOURCES

Sunshine Coast Trail: info and maps https://sunshinecoast-trail.com/
Sunshine Coast Trail donations: https://sunshinecoast-trail.com/prpaws/donate/
Inland Lake Provincial Park: info http://bcparks.ca/explore/parkpgs/inland_lk/
Sunshine Coast Trail Facebook Group: trail conditions and info https://www.facebook.com/groups/145478998481470 8/
Water Taxi: Justin Behan 604-483-6527
Driving Map: Vancouver, Coast & Mountains BC Backroad Mapbook
NTS Map: 092F16

16
TIN HAT HUT

Difficulty: ◆

Duration: 2 days

Distance: 12 km (7.5 mi)

Elevation Gain: 700 m (2297 ft)

High Point: 1170 m (3839 ft)

Best Months: June to October

Fees and Reservations: None, though donations are welcome. The hut and camping are first-come, first-served.

Regulations: Fires permitted in firepits only. Dogs permitted.

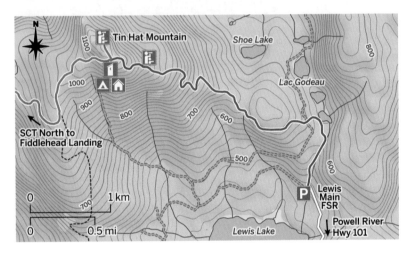

THE 360-DEGREE VIEW from the summit of Tin Hat Mountain is so spectacular that the peak was once home to a fire lookout station. Today there's an insulated hut near the summit and a few campsites, so you can catch both sunset and sunrise or just gaze down at expansive Powell Lake and the peaks of the Powell Divide to the north and west or the snowy summits of Strathcona Provincial Park on Vancouver Island across the Strait of Georgia to the southwest. Several trails lead up Tin Hat Mountain, but the one described here is the most scenic and provides the easiest access for 2WD vehicles.

GETTING THERE

From the Saltery Bay ferry terminal, follow the Sunshine Coast Highway 12.5 km (7.8 mi) north to Lang Bay. Turn right onto Dixon Road, opposite the Lang Bay store. Zero your odometer. Stay on Dixon Road as it becomes Goat Lake Main FSR and turns to gravel. The logging roads here are well signed but

Celebrating on the summit of Tin Hat Mountain.

can still be confusing. Bring a backroad map or GPS to avoid getting lost. The gravel roads are a bit bumpy but are 2WD accessible.

About 4 km (2.5 mi) from Lang Bay, reach a junction. Keep left as the road becomes one-way only. The right fork is your return route. Continue north on Goat Main FSR to another junction about 12 km (7.5 mi) from Lang Bay. The road becomes two-way again past here. Stay on Goat Main until a junction about 18 km (11.2 mi) from Lang Bay where you turn left onto Spring Lake Main. At 22 km (13.7 mi), turn right onto Lewis Main. Ignore the spur road to the Lewis Lake Rec Site. About 27 km (16.8 mi) from Lang Bay, cross a small bridge and look for SCT markers on both sides of the road. Drive a few metres down to a pullout on the left and park.

TRAIL

TRIP PLANNER

0 km (0 mi)	Trailhead
5.5 km (3.4 mi)	Viewpoints
6 km (3.7 mi)	Tin Hat Hut and campground
16 km (9.9 mi)	Fiddlehead Landing Hut (see Trip 15)

From the pullout, walk back down the road towards the bridge. Find the marked trail on the north side of the road, just west of the bridge. Follow it into the forest alongside the creek. This is the last surefire water source before the hut, so be sure to fill up here. The trail climbs gradually through the forest before curving to the left and crossing a new logging road. Pick up the trail on the other side of the road as it climbs up and around a small hill, remaining in the trees.

About 2.5 km (1.6 mi) from the start, you'll reach a saddle. From here, the steep climbing begins. You'll gain over 500 m (1640 ft) in the next 3.5 km (2.2 mi) to the summit. The trail switchbacks up the mountain, at times climbing very sharply. Watch for mushrooms on the sides of the trail, especially huge boletes in late summer and early fall. As you get towards the top, the forest cover thins out as blueberry and huckleberry bushes begin to dominate.

A few beautiful **viewpoints** on rocky outcrops may tempt you to stop. However, don't linger too long as the views from the peak are even better. From the viewpoints, it's only 0.5 km (0.3 mi) to the top as you make your way over granite bluffs. You'll spot the tall outhouse first, then the **Tin Hat Hut** just beyond, behind a clump of trees.

There are great views from near the hut, but for the best vista, follow the trail to the north for a few minutes to the true summit. A huge green radio tower detracts from the wilderness feel, but you can see in all directions.

CAMPING AND HUT

The fully winterized Tin Hat Hut is one of the most popular backcountry destinations on the Upper Sunshine Coast thanks to the incredible views. The Powell River Parks and Wilderness Society built the hut just below the summit of Tin Hat Mountain in 2011.

Campsites: No designated campsites, but some cleared flat spots near the hut
Hut Sleeps: 10 on the loft floor
Toilet: Composting toilet just east of the hut
Water: No water sources nearby. Haul your water up from the creek near the trailhead.

HISTORY

Tin Hat Mountain takes its name from the protective helmets early loggers wore. The history of the Sunshine Coast Trail is intertwined with logging since the trail sits on Crown land in a working forest. The Powell River Parks and Wilderness Society has worked collaboratively with local forestry companies to protect stands of old-growth and leave intact forest buffers along the SCT wherever possible—and to reroute the trail when it is not.

Tin Hat Hut near the summit of Tin Hat Mountain.

Food Storage: On hooks inside the hut
Other Amenities: The hut has a picnic table, counters, and a pellet stove. (You'll need to bring your own pellets and look up instructions for operating it beforehand as it can be tricky.) Outside the hut are a firepit and a picnic table.

EXTENDING YOUR TRIP
Sunshine Coast Trail to Fiddlehead Landing or Inland Lake: Combine this trip with Trip 15 for a longer outing. Continue along the SCT down to Powell Lake at Fiddlehead Landing, 10 km (6.2 mi) away. You can get a water taxi to Powell River from there or hike onwards to Confederation Lake and the trailhead at Inland Lake. Allow three to four days to cover the full 30 km (18.6 mi).

FURTHER RESOURCES
Sunshine Coast Trail: info and maps https://sunshinecoast-trail.com/
Sunshine Coast Trail donations: https://sunshinecoast-trail.com/prpaws/donate/
Sunshine Coast Trail Facebook Group: trail conditions and info https://www.facebook.com/groups/1454789984814708/
Driving Map: Vancouver, Coast & Mountains BC Backroad Mapbook
NTS Map: 092F16

17
SALTERY BAY LOOP

Difficulty: ■

Duration: 2 to 3 days

Distance: 18 km (11.2 mi) loop

Elevation Gain: 570 m (1870 ft)

High Point: 570 m (1870 ft)

Best Months: April to November

Fees and Reservations: None, though donations are welcome. All huts and camping are first-come, first-served.

Regulations: Fires permitted in firepits only. Dogs permitted.

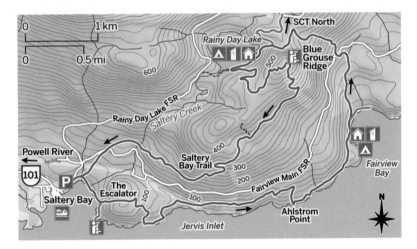

THIS LOOP TRIP on the southernmost section of the Sunshine Coast Trail begins with a ramble along scenic arbutus bluffs on the shores of Jervis Inlet. Stay overnight at sheltered Fairview Bay, the only oceanfront hut on the Sunshine Coast Trail. Continue your journey by climbing inland to the hut and campsite at cool, clear Rainy Day Lake, where you can enjoy a swim. The loop finishes with a gorgeous view of Hotham Sound, then a ramble downhill through the forest to the trailhead. This low-elevation trip is a great option for spring and fall. Or do the Fairview Bay portion all year long.

GETTING THERE
From the Saltery Bay ferry terminal, turn right onto Rainy Day Lake Road. Look for the Sunshine Coast Trail information kiosk and parking lot about 100 m (328 ft) after the turn. It's also possible to get to Saltery Bay on public transit. From Vancouver, take a TransLink bus to the Horseshoe Bay ferry

Arbutus trees along the shore of Jervis Inlet.

terminal. Take the ferry to Langdale on the Sunshine Coast. Next, take the Sunshine Coast Connector bus from the Langdale ferry terminal north to the Earls Cove ferry terminal. Take the ferry to Saltery Bay. Walk off the ferry, turn right onto Rainy Day Lake Road, and reach the trailhead 100 m (328 ft) later.

TRAIL

TRIP PLANNER

0 km (0 mi)	Trailhead
1.5 km (0.9 mi)	Pirates Cove
2.5 km (1.6 mi)	Power transmission towers
4.5 km (2.8 mi)	Ahlstrom Point
6 km (3.7 mi)	Fairview Hut and campground
7.5 km (4.7 mi)	Cross Fairview Main logging road
9 km (5.6 mi)	Rainy Day Lake Hut and campground
11 km (6.8 mi)	Blue Grouse Ridge viewpoint
18 km (11.2 mi)	Trailhead

Fairview Bay Hut nestled into the forest just inland from the water.

From the information kiosk, walk a few metres down the road, then turn right and follow signs for the SCT down a gravel track towards Rose Beach. The trail meets the beach, then immediately heads back into the forest. A short spur trail to the right leads out to Harbour Point. The main SCT heads left, steeply uphill on switchbacks. This section of the trail is nicknamed "The Escalator," as it gains 120 m (394 ft) of elevation in 0.5 km (0.3 mi).

There's a brief reprieve of flat trail at the top of The Escalator before the trail plunges back down to sea level again to reach **Pirates Cove**. Take a break here on the bluff to enjoy the twisted arbutus branches stretching out over Jervis Inlet. Shortly after leaving the cove, look through the trees to glimpse a floating fish farm anchored near the shore. The trail continues beside the ocean for another 0.5 km (0.3 mi) before climbing back up the bank and meeting an old road next to a power-line cut. Follow the old road for about 0.5 km (0.3 mi) until it ends at **power transmission towers**. These lines carry power to the Upper Sunshine Coast.

Follow the trail beneath the towers, then into the forest. The path weaves between ferns and undulates through the forest about 80 m (262 ft) above sea level before descending to the ocean at **Ahlstrom Point**. Beyond the point, the trail traverses rocky bluffs above the ocean on some lovely stretches of trail, thoughtfully improved with stairs and retaining walls by volunteers from the Powell River Parks and Wilderness Society. The trail briefly turns away from the ocean to climb over a small hill before descending to sea level again at Fairview Bay. You'll reach the tent spots in the trees first, then the **Fairview Bay Hut** across a wooden bridge. Camp here for the night, or push on to Rainy Day Lake Hut.

The SCT continues on the far side of the hut as it plunges back into the forest and starts to climb. Cross the gravel **Fairview Main logging road** about 1.5 km (0.9 mi) from the hut and continue ascending. You are now in an old-growth management area, so enjoy the lush forest and tall trees.

About 3 km (1.9 mi) from Fairview Bay, the trail begins to descend towards Rainy Day Lake. Reach a junction where the main SCT goes right towards Mount Troubridge and your route goes left to Rainy Day Lake. The campsite is a few metres along the lake. There's a swimming raft nearby as well. The **Rainy Day Lake Hut** is perched just above the lake on Hailstone Bluff.

To complete the loop, continue along the lakeshore, then turn left on the Saltery Bay Trail, an alternate branch of the SCT. The trail climbs steadily for the next 2 km (1.2 mi) to the top of **Blue Grouse Ridge**, the high point of your hike at 570 m (1870 ft). From the viewpoints at the top, you can see Jervis Inlet and Hotham Sound below you. There's also a great view of Freil Falls, which drops over 400 m (1312 ft) from Freil Lake into the ocean. The waterfall is also known as Harmony Falls after the nearby Harmony Islands. The cascade is at its fullest in spring and after heavy rains; it often dries up by late summer.

From the ridge, the trail descends steeply through regenerating forest below, joining a long-abandoned logging road. The route continues to descend before levelling out around 5.5 km (3.4 mi) from Rainy Day Lake. Shortly after, watch the trail markers carefully to find the bridge over Saltery Creek, built by the BOMB Squad (Bloody Old Men's Brigade), a volunteer group from Powell River that has constructed most of the infrastructure along the SCT.

After the bridge, the trail rejoins the old road. The final few kilometres back to Saltery Bay are a maze of new cutblocks and logging roads. However, local volunteers have done an excellent job of installing signage, so just keep following the trail markers. They will lead you back to the information kiosk and **trailhead** where you started.

CAMPING AND HUTS

FAIRVIEW BAY HUT AND CAMPSITE

Fairview Bay is a beautiful spot where the hut and campsite are right next to the ocean, set into a rocky cove. Several side trails lead down to the water and the cleared area in front of the hut boasts a great firepit. As the only oceanside

NATURE NOTE

If you're lucky, you'll spot grey whales feeding in Jervis Inlet. These huge cetaceans head north to their Arctic feeding grounds in the spring, passing by the Sunshine Coast. They come through the area again in the fall, on the way to Mexico's Baja Peninsula where they spend the winter breeding and giving birth.

hut in southwestern BC and the first hut built on the SCT, Fairview Bay is pretty special.

Campsites: Cleared area south of the hut with space for 2 to 3 tents
Hut Sleeps: 10 on the loft floor
Toilet: Composting outhouse just north of the hut
Water: Follow a trail north of the hut for 0.5 km (0.3 mi) to a creek that empties into Fairview Bay.
Food Storage: On hooks inside the hut
Other Amenities: A picnic table and firepit with benches in front of the hut. A picnic table and fire ring next to the camping area. A table, benches, and countertop inside the hut.

RAINY DAY LAKE HUT AND CAMPSITE
The Rainy Day Lake Hut sits on a bluff above the lake. Volunteers from the Powell River Parks and Wilderness Society and the Rotary Club of Powell River built the hut in 2010. It has an enclosed sleeping loft and an open lower floor with big Plexiglas windows on one side.

Campsites: Small clearings near the lake for 3 to 4 tents
Hut Sleeps: 10 on the loft floor
Toilet: Outhouse on the spur trail to the hut
Water: Collect from the lake.
Food Storage: The hut is not animal-proof, so bring rope to hang your food in a tree, or bring a bear canister.
Other Amenities: A picnic table and firepit with benches in front of hut. A picnic table near the lake. Swimming dock. A table, benches, and countertop inside the hut.

EXTENDING YOUR TRIP
Sunshine Coast Trail: Instead of returning to Saltery Bay on the Saltery Bay Trail, continue on the Sunshine Coast Trail for another 5 km (3.1 mi) towards Mount Troubridge (Trip 42). You could hike the entire 180-km-long (112 mi) trail or just the 40-km (24.9-mi) section from Saltery Bay to Lois Lake.

FURTHER RESOURCES
Sunshine Coast Trail: info and maps https://sunshinecoast-trail.com/
Sunshine Coast Trail donations: https://sunshinecoast-trail.com/prpaws/donate/
Sunshine Coast Trail Facebook Group: trail conditions and info https://www.facebook.com/groups/1454789984814708/
NTS Map: 092F16

18
TETRAHEDRON PLATEAU

Difficulty: ■

Duration: 2 to 3 days

Distance: 12 to 17 km (7.5 to 10.6 mi)

Elevation Gain: 280 to 680 m (919 to 2231 ft)

High Point: 1500 m (4921 ft)

Best Months: Mid-June to October

Fees and Reservations: Cabins are first-come, first served. Cabin fees are $15/person/night, payable online, in person, or by mail.

Regulations: No tent camping: you must stay in the huts. No dogs, no fires, no swimming. No drones. No smoking, vaping, or cannabis. The mosquitos can be thick in early summer. This trip is inside the watershed for the community of Sechelt and the greater Sunshine Coast Regional District. It's very important to respect the water protection rules in the park.

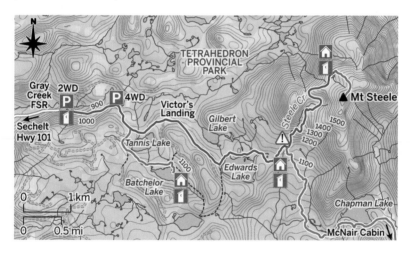

ALTHOUGH IT'S A short ferry ride from Vancouver, Tetrahedron Provincial Park near Sechelt doesn't see that much traffic. It's a rolling subalpine plateau with pockets of old-growth hemlock, Pacific silver fir, and yellow-cedar, dotted with lakes and criss-crossed by trails. Four snug backcountry log cabins were built in 1987 and have been maintained ever since by the volunteer-run Tetrahedron Outdoor Club. (Tenting in the park is not permitted.) This trip takes in some of the best scenery in the park, including an ascent of 1659-m-high (5443 ft) Mount Steele. It also makes a great winter backpacking trip on snowshoes. However, you'll need avalanche training to make the ascent to Mount Steele Cabin.

GETTING THERE

In Sechelt, go north on Wharf Road, then turn right a few blocks later at the four-way stop onto Porpoise Bay Road. Stay on Porpoise Bay Road, which becomes Sechelt Inlet Road, for about 10 km (6.2 mi). Cross a bridge over Gray Creek, then turn right onto the Sechelt-Gray Forest Service Road, which is also known as Gray Creek FSR. This gravel road is okay for experienced backroad drivers in 2WD vehicles, but it does have a few water bars that may be challenging. **AWD or 4WD vehicles are recommended.**

About 1 km (0.6 mi) from where you left the pavement, take the left fork to stay on the main road. The road climbs steadily for the next few kilometres and has some loose sections and bumps. After about 3 km (1.9 mi), the road starts to climb more gradually. At 7 km (4.3 mi), it crosses a bridge and starts to ascend more steeply. Reach an information kiosk and outhouse at 11 km (6.8 mi) and park here. This is the trailhead. If you have a **high-clearance 4WD**, take the right fork and drive another 1 km (0.6 mi) up the rough road to the upper parking lot.

TRAIL

TRIP PLANNER

0 km (0 mi)	Lower parking lot
1 km (0.6 mi)	Upper parking lot
1.5 km (0.9 mi)	Junction with Batchelor Lake Trail (1.5 km/0.9 mi to Batchelor Lake Cabin)
2.5 km (1.6 mi)	Victor's Landing
4 km (2.5 mi)	Edwards Lake
6 km (3.7 mi)	Edwards Lake Cabin
6.1 km (3.8 mi)	Junction with McNair Lake Trail (5.5 km/3.4 mi to McNair Lake Cabin)
9 km (5.6 mi)	Mount Steele Cabin
10 km (6.2 mi)	Mount Steele summit

From the lower parking lot, follow the right fork of the road steeply uphill for about 1 km (0.6 mi) to the upper lot. Past the parking lot, the trail continues along the old road, now closed to cars. After about 0.5 km (0.3 mi), reach a signposted **junction**. The easy trail to Batchelor Lake heads right, and your route towards Edwards Lake goes straight.

Keep hiking on the old road for another 1 km (0.6 mi) to **Victor's Landing**, where another old road heads right. Stay on the main road as it travels through regenerating clear-cuts. About 4 km (2.5 mi) from the trailhead, the

Tetrahedron Peak as seen from Mount Steele. Photo: Stephen Hui

trail leaves the old road and descends slightly towards **Edwards Lake** in unlogged forest.

The trail follows the northern edge of the lake, then begins to climb above the lake. You'll pass through a few boggy sections near small ponds before arriving at the **Edwards Lake Cabin**, about 280 m (919 ft) higher than your start. While the cabin is named for Edwards Lake, it's actually about 0.5 km (0.3 mi) away from the lakeshore. You can overnight here, or push onwards to Mount Steele Cabin.

Continue on the trail past the cabin to Steele Creek. Unfortunately, there is no bridge over this creek. In the middle of summer, you may be able to hop across on rocks. But early in the season or in times of high rainfall, the creek may run high and fast. There is a log to assist your crossing, but you should straddle it rather than walk across it. You can also remove your boots and carefully ford the creek.

Just after the creek crossing, reach a **junction**. The trail to Mount Steele goes left while the route to McNair Lake Cabin is to the right. Follow the trail to Mount Steele as it climbs steeply uphill with a few switchbacks. The route curves through the headwaters of Steele Creek, then climbs up the spine of a ridge to **Mount Steele Cabin**. The cabin sits near a small tarn in a rocky bowl, 680 m (2231 ft) higher than the trailhead.

CABINS

Tenting is not allowed in the park, so plan to stay in one of the cabins maintained by the Tetrahedron Outdoor Club. They are first-come, first-served, but guests can register on the club's Facebook group to get an idea of how busy the area will be.

EDWARDS LAKE CABIN

The Edwards Lake Cabin sits well above Edwards Lake in a clearing. It makes a great base camp for a day hike to Mount Steele or McNair Lake Cabin.

Sleeps: 10 to 12 on the loft floor
Toilet: Outhouse behind the hut
Water: Collect from Steele Creek just past the hut.
Food Storage: On hooks inside the hut
Other Amenities: A table and bench seats, countertop, wood stove with firewood, sink with grey-water bucket, mattresses

MOUNT STEELE CABIN

If you base yourself at Mount Steele Cabin, you'll put yourself in a great position to make the quick hike up to the peak to catch the sunrise or sunset. This cabin also has the most beautiful setting of any in the park.

Sleeps: 10 to 12 on the loft floor
Toilet: Outhouse near the hut
Water: Collect from the tarn east of the hut.
Food Storage: On hooks inside the hut
Other Amenities: A table and bench seats, countertop, wood stove with firewood, sink with grey-water bucket, mattresses

EXTENDING YOUR TRIP

Mount Steele Summit: To reach the peak from the Mount Steele Cabin, follow the trail as it heads northeast, then swings around to the south, following the top of an open ridge. Use caution here early in the season as snow lingers on the steep slopes. The 1659-m-high (5443 ft) summit is about 1 km (0.6 mi) from the cabin and about 150 m (492 ft) higher. The views from the top

NATURE NOTE

The park protects the habitat of the endangered marbled murrelet, a small brown-and-white bird. While they spend most of their life at sea, they come inland to old-growth forests to lay their eggs. Marbled murrelets don't built nests. Instead, they carefully place their eggs in a hollow of moss on a large tree branch. As old-growth forests have declined, marbled murrelet populations have as well, leading to their endangered status.

Mount Steele Cabin at sunset. Photo: Stephen Hui

are spectacular: look for Panther Peak to the southeast and Mount Elphinstone to the south. To the northeast you can see the summits of the Tantalus Range and Mount Garibaldi in Squamish. Gaze north for a view of Tetrahedron Peak, which gives the park its name. In 1956, an Alpine Club of Canada party, including UBC geology professor W.H. Matthews, climbed the peak. Matthews christened it "Tetrahedron" after its distinct four-faced profile.

McNair Lake Cabin: While Tetrahedron Provincial Park is rarely crowded, if you really want solitude, make the trek to seldom-visited McNair Lake. The route starts just past Edwards Lake Cabin and travels through rolling and sometimes boggy terrain. Cross a narrow and rickety bridge over Chapman Creek about 2.5 km (1.6 mi) from the cabin, then contour around the shore of Chapman Lake at the 4-km (2.5-mi) mark. You'll find the McNair Lake Cabin near McNair Lake, about 5.5 km (3.4 mi) from Edwards Lake Cabin. It has great views of Panther Peak and Mount Steele.

Batchelor Lake Cabin: If you want to break up the journey to Mount Steele or are looking for a beginner-friendly option, stay at the Batchelor Lake Cabin. It's a 1.5-km (0.9-mi) detour off the main trail, but it's flat and easy walking through a nice forest first on an old road, then on a trail. The cabin sits in the trees on a rise above Batchelor Lake.

FURTHER RESOURCES

Tetrahedron Provincial Park: info and maps http://bcparks.ca/explore/parkpgs/tetrahedron/

Tetrahedron Outdoor Club: info and cabin fees http://www.tetoutdoor.ca/

Tetrahedron Facebook Group: trail conditions https://www.facebook.com/groups/tetrahedronoutdoor/

Driving Map: Vancouver, Coast & Mountains BC Backroad Mapbook

NTS Map: 092G12

The view above Mount Steele Cabin. Photo: Stephen Hui

METRO VANCOUVER

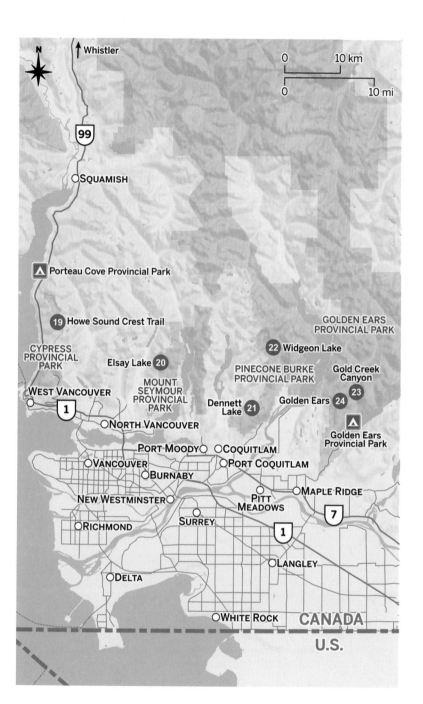

METRO VANCOUVER IS the most densely populated part of southwestern BC. However, the northern boundary of the city bumps right up against the wilderness. The area is characterized by rugged peaks with expansive views, old-growth trees, and bountiful berry bushes. When city life gets to be too much, I love that I can retreat to the solitude of nature in minutes. Listening to birdsong, feeling the wind in my hair, or swimming in a wilderness lake are great ways to recharge. While there are lots of places throughout the region to go for day hikes, backpacking is only permitted in a few areas: Vancouver's North Shore, the Burke Mountain region of Coquitlam, and Golden Ears Provincial Park in Maple Ridge. Access is very straightforward with paved roads reaching every trailhead.

The region has a temperate coastal climate, which means that it is often cold, wet, and cloudy in the mountains, even if it is sunny down below in the city. The mountains are steep and rugged, and trails in the area usually involve lots of elevation gain over very challenging terrain.

The area currently known as Vancouver's North Shore is the traditional territory of the səl̓ilwətaʔɬ təməxʷ (Tsleil-Waututh), Skwxwú7mesh-ulh Temíxw (Squamish), and xʷməθkʷəy̓əm (Musqueam) peoples. Visit the Musqueam Cultural Centre in Vancouver or the Squamish Líl'wat Cultural Centre in Whistler to learn more about their art, culture, and history. The Kwikwetlem and S'ólh Téméxw (Stó:lō) peoples have traditional territory in the Burke Mountain area of Coquitlam. And what is now Golden Ears Provincial Park is the traditional territory of the Katzie and Stó:lō peoples.

Supplies: The Metro Vancouver area has lots of grocery stores, gas stations, and outdoor stores.

Accommodations: Hotels are widely available throughout the region. However, there are few places to camp. The only real options are the reservable sites at Golden Ears Provincial Park or, if you're hiking the Howe Sound Crest Trail, the reservable sites at Porteau Cove Provincial Park near the north end of the trail.

19
HOWE SOUND CREST TRAIL

Difficulty: ◆◆	**Elevation Gain**: 660 m (2165 ft)
Duration: 2 to 4 days	**High Point**: 1548 m (5079 ft)
Distance: 31.7 km (19.7 mi) one way	**Best Months**: Mid-July to September

Fees and Reservations: Camping is free and all campsites are first-come, first-served.

Regulations: No fires. Dogs permitted on leash but not recommended due to the terrain. No drones. No smoking, vaping, or cannabis.

Caution: This is a very rugged trail with scrambling sections and exposure. In some areas, it is more of a marked route than a trail. This trip is recommended for fit and experienced hikers only. Do not attempt this trip in snowy conditions unless you have mountaineering skills and avalanche training.

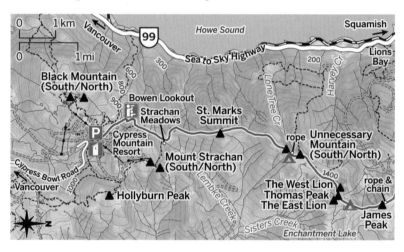

THE HOWE SOUND CREST TRAIL (HSCT) should be on any experienced hiker's bucket list. This rugged route climbs and dips like a roller coaster along the mountainous spine of Howe Sound's west side between Cypress Provincial Park and Porteau Cove. It's by far the most challenging trip in this book, as it takes in some rough terrain, scrambling sections, exposed climbing, and route-finding challenges. But hikers who are up for an arduous trek will be handsomely rewarded. There are awe-inspiring views of Howe Sound and the Sunshine Coast from high mountains and ridges, gorgeous alpine meadows, and jewel-blue lakes to swim in. You'll also climb up and over several mountain peaks. While the distances on this trail may seem short, the

At Unnecessary Mountain's south summit with The Lions in the background.

difficult terrain makes for very long travel times, so plan your trip accordingly. Very fast and fit parties could complete the trail in two very long days. However, spending three or even four days on the trail is more realistic (and more enjoyable) for most hikers.

GETTING THERE

The Howe Sound Crest Trail is usually hiked as a one-way traverse, so you'll need to arrange to have someone pick you up at the end, or park a second vehicle at the other trailhead. Hiking from south to north is more popular because it involves less overall elevation gain (660 m/2165 ft of net elevation gain and 1500 m/4921 ft of net descent). That's the direction described below. If you start in the north, you'll gain 1570 m (5151 ft) and lose 2405 m (7890 ft).

CYPRESS PROVINCIAL PARK TRAILHEAD

From Highway 1 in West Vancouver, take exit 8, signed for Cypress Bowl Road. Follow the road as it switchbacks up the mountain to the ski resort. Overnight parking is only permitted in the signed area of Lot 3B, about 0.6 km (0.4 mi) before the gate to the main parking lot at the downhill ski area.

PORTEAU COVE TRAILHEAD

Take the Porteau Road exit about 10 km (6.2 mi) past Lions Bay on Highway 99. If you reach Porteau Cove Provincial Park, you've gone too far. From the exit ramp, turn right and drive a few metres up the hill to the parking lot. Don't leave anything in your car here, as break-ins are common.

TRIP PLANNER

0 km (0 mi)	Cypress Provincial Park trailhead
1.7 km (1.1 mi)	Junction with Bowen Lookout Trail
2 km (1.2 mi)	Junction of HSCT East and HSCT West Trails
6.5 km (4 mi)	St. Marks Summit
10.25 km (6.4 mi)	Unnecessary Mountain informal camping
12.5 km (7.8 mi)	Junction with Lions-Binkert Trail
14 km (8.7 mi)	Thomas Peak informal camping
15.5 km (9.6 mi)	James Peak
16.75 km (10.4 mi)	David Peak
18.3 km (11.4 mi)	Harvey Pass
18.7 km (11.6 mi)	Magnesia Meadows informal camping
21 km (13 mi)	Junction with Brunswick Mountain Trail (1 km/o.6 mi to summit)
23 km (14.3 mi)	Brunswick Lake informal camping
24.3 km (15.1 mi)	Hanover Lake
25.6 km (15.9 mi)	Deeks Lake
26.6 km (16.5 mi)	Deeks Lake informal camping
28.6 km (17.8 mi)	Trail turns to old road
31.3 km (19.4 mi)	Junction with new bypass trail
32.3 km (20.1 mi)	Highway 99
32.7 km (20.3 mi)	Porteau Cove trailhead

Water can be a real challenge on the HSCT. In late summer, there may be no water between Cypress Bowl and Brunswick Lake. Notes in the trail description below indicate where you might be able to find water in this section. The most reliable spots are the tarns to the east of Unnecessary Mountain, a tarn north of East Lion near Thomas Peak, and in Magnesia Meadows.

The trailhead is at the west end of the Black Mountain Lodge. Follow signs for the HSCT heading up a gravel ski area access road and to a large green water tower 0.5 km (0.3 mi) from the trailhead. Take the trail to the left signed "HSCT West," then be sure to take the short spur trail to **Bowen Lookout**, which has a commanding view of Bowen Island, Gambier Island, and the mountains of the Sunshine Coast.

Reach another **junction** 2 km (1.2 mi) from the trailhead and go left to stay on the HSCT heading north. The next section contours across the side of the slope through pleasant old-growth forest, then crosses a small stream at an open area known as Strachan Meadows. This is the last reliable water source on the trail for many kilometres.

The trail climbs steadily from the meadows on a series of tight switchbacks. Trail work over the last decade has smoothed the path to a crushed gravel sidewalk. Eventually, you'll reach the end of the improved gravel section and continue on dirt criss-crossed with countless roots. About 4.5 km (2.8 mi) from the start, the trail reaches the crest of a ridge and turns north to follow it for about 2 km (1.2 mi).

After a few final switchbacks, arrive at a signpost marking **St. Marks Summit**. Drop your pack to take in the views of Howe Sound from several spur trails. There are a few murky seasonal ponds just south of the summit if you're short on water, but they are generally unappetizing.

From St. Marks Summit, the HSCT loses 155 m (509 ft) as it drops into a saddle. A sign marks the end of the improved and well-travelled trail, so expect to see few day trippers in the next section. The route you are walking now is the original rough trail to The Lions, built in the 1960s. Unnecessary Mountain got its name from the fact that going up and over the peak was seen as inconvenient if your objective was The Lions.

From the saddle, head up the steep trail through the forest over tree roots and through thickets of blueberry and black huckleberry bushes. You'll gain 345 m (1132 ft) as you ascend to the south summit of Unnecessary Mountain. At 1548 m (5079 ft), this is the highest point on the HSCT. A few scattered campsites make up the informal **Unnecessary Mountain camping area**, on the open and rocky summit ridge. The views of Howe Sound below you and The Lions to the north are spectacular. Take care to stick to the trail to avoid trampling the pink mountain heather and other subalpine plants that grow between the granite rocks.

Drop down from Unnecessary Mountain's south summit into a saddle 40 m (131 ft) lower. If you need water, an indistinct trail heads off to the right to some tarns. Climb to the north peak of Unnecessary Mountain through groves of western hemlock, passing the junction with the Unnecessary Mountain Trail coming up from Lions Bay on the left. The steep rope-assisted descent off the north side of the summit is exciting, and you can look forward to more fixed ropes in airy terrain farther along the HSCT.

INDIGENOUS KNOWLEDGE

To early European settlers, the peaks of The Lions looked like two lions sitting down and facing each other. But Indigenous peoples already had a name for them: the Twin Sisters, known as Ch'ich'iyúy to the Squamish. In their stories, the twin sisters were daughters of a chief. The sisters convinced their father to make peace with a tribe that had long been an enemy of the Squamish. The Great Spirit was so impressed by what the sisters had done that he turned them to stone, immortalizing them for all time.

Continue north along the crest of the granite ridge towards The Lions. Pass a search and rescue emergency cache, then arrive at a **junction with the Lions-Binkert Trail** coming up from the left. Head north from the junction on a rocky ridge speckled with yellow-green lichen that requires a few scrambly moves. The ridge tops out next to West Lion. Take a moment to enjoy the view, but stay back from the huge drop-offs on the north side.

From the base of the West Lion, the trail drops steeply into a loose gully following cairns and painted markers. The next section is one of the most exposed parts of the trail and requires some scrambling skills. Be careful. Cross the gully, then traverse the south face of West Lion on a series of grassy and rocky ledges. Do not attempt this section in wet or icy conditions as a fall here would be fatal.

After the ledges, climb steeply up to a notch between East and West Lion, then follow the route downhill along the narrow ridge of Thomas Peak. You'll need to do a bit of downclimbing through exposed terrain here, so use caution. Thomas Peak and nearby David Peak are named for the Wade brothers who perished when a landslide hit their home in Lions Bay in 1983. As the ridge flattens out, look for a large round tarn below to the right and a flattish plateau leading off the ridge. This is the **Thomas Peak camping area.** You can scramble down the slope to get water from the tarn.

From the plateau camping area, lose 150 m (492 ft) of elevation as you descend a steep and rocky slope with patches of deer ferns to the base of James Peak. Watch carefully for markers, tape, and cairns as you descend. Next, ascend **James Peak,** watching for markers and passing gnarled and windblown white pines and mountain hemlock. At the top, you'll face one of the HSCT's most infamous obstacles: an airy rock gap that you'll have to cross with the help of a fixed rope and chain. Once on the other side, you'll be on the true summit of James Peak, 170 m (558 ft) higher than the rocky saddle you just climbed out of.

Look for tape and cairns that mark the descent trail. Head downhill, losing 100 m (328 ft) of elevation, through open slopes of rock and heather to a grassy saddle. Traditionally, the HSCT headed downhill to the east, making a wide circuit around David Peak. However, that route travels through the restricted Capilano watershed and is now closed. What used to be an informal peakbaggers' trail up and over the summit of David Peak is now the official HSCT route.

From the saddle, head steeply up **David Peak,** gaining 145 m (476 ft) over a short distance as you scramble up the rocky slopes through patches of krummholz, small trees stunted by wind and harsh weather. Pause to enjoy the views and the red-tinged rocks at the peak. Plunge steeply down the north side of David, using a few handlines to assist you as you lose 150 m (492 ft)

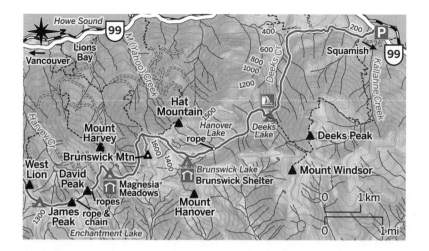

of elevation and scramble over lots of tree roots. After the grade eases off in a meadow, the trail heads northwest as it ascends through an old clear-cut with patches of bright pink fireweed. The blueberries and huckleberries in this section are tasty in August, but make lots of noise since the bears like them too.

Partway through the clear-cut, pass a junction with a rough trail heading downhill to the left, connecting with overgrown logging roads turned trails that lead to Lions Bay. Continue uphill through the old clear-cut to another junction at **Harvey Pass**. A rough climbers' trail continues to the left across the meadows to Mount Harvey. Turn right and stay on the HSCT as it descends gradually through subalpine heather meadows to a tarn and emergency shelter at the **Magnesia Meadows camping area**. The tarn gets muddy and dry in late summer, but it is one of the only water sources in the area so be sure to fill up.

Past Magnesia Meadows, the trail heads west on an undulating traverse around the slopes of Brunswick Mountain with a few meadows sprinkled with purple lupines and pale green false hellebore to distract you along the way. About 2.5 km (1.6 mi) from Magnesia Meadows, reach a **junction with the Brunswick Mountain Trail**. Turning left will lead you down to Lions Bay nearly 1600 m (5249 ft) below. Turn right to climb Brunswick, the highest peak in Vancouver's North Shore mountains at 1788 m (5866 ft).

Continuing past the Brunswick junction, reach Hat Pass between Hat and Brunswick Mountains. It's all downhill from here—literally. The rest of the trail descends to Porteau Cove, sometimes very steeply! You'll drop 285 m (935 ft) from Hat Pass to the shores of Brunswick Lake. Reach the Brunswick emergency shelter, then continue down the trail for a few more metres to

Camping on the plateau near Thomas Peak.

a junction near the lake. Turn right along the lakeshore to the **Brunswick Lake camping area**.

Cross a narrow arm of the lake on stepping stones. Early and late in the season, the lake level can be high enough that you'll need to take your boots off. Follow the trail gently downhill through hemlock, Douglas-fir, and bushes dripping in huge salmonberries for about 1 km (0.6 mi) to Hanover Falls. Use a fixed rope to help you down a steep section, then continue downhill for a few minutes to reach **Hanover Lake**. The trail follows the eastern shore of the turquoise lake before starting a descent beside Deeks Creek. Cross the creek about halfway down the slope. It's a rock-hop most of the year but may be more serious in times of high runoff.

Reach the southern end of **Deeks Lake**. Follow the trail as it works its way along the western shore of the lake for another 1 km (0.6 mi), passing clumps of yellow and orange chicken of the woods mushrooms. Carefully cross the lake outlet on a massive logjam. A trail to the right leads to the **Deeks Lake campground**.

Follow signs to locate the main trail heading northwest away from the lake. The trail descends rapidly through subalpine vegetation to the Douglas-fir and cedar dripping with old man's beard and witch's hair lichens more typical of the coastal rainforest. About 0.5 km (0.3 mi) from Deeks Lake, the trail swings close to Deeks Creek at Phi Alpha Falls. After the falls, the trail heads into the forest and begins a punishing descent towards Highway 99. Trekking poles are useful here to take some of the pressure off your knees on the steep and gnarly trail.

Roughly 2 km (1.2 mi) from the lake, the trail turns into an **old logging road**. At one time it was possible to drive up this road to the trailhead, but years of neglect and a dispute with a private landowner in the lower portions of the trail mean that you'll have to walk the whole way. About 2.7 km (1.7 mi) down the old road, turn left onto a **new trail**. Constructed in 2019, it bypasses the last portion of the road, which sits on private land. If you reach a junction on the right marked as the Kallahne Lake Trail, you've gone too far down the road. Follow the new trail for nearly 1 km (0.6 mi) as it switchbacks down the slope. The new trail emerges on the side of **Highway 99**, just south of the Porteau Road off-ramp. Walk north on the highway shoulder, up the off-ramp to the **parking lot** 0.4 km (0.2 mi) away.

CAMPING

There are no designated campsites or outhouses on the HSCT. However, several areas along the trail are commonly used as campsites. If you're just spending one night on the trail, plan to sleep at Magnesia Meadows. For a two-night trip, aim for the Thomas Peak camping area and Brunswick Lake. If you're out for three nights, camp at Unnecessary Mountain, Magnesia Meadows, and Deeks Lake.

UNNECESSARY MOUNTAIN CAMPING AREA

This is the closest camping to the southern trailhead. Many of the sites have incredible views.

Campsites: Space for about 5 tents scattered across the southern part of the summit ridge

Toilet: None. Dig a cat hole and use Leave No Trace toilet practices. Try to get well away from the trail and avoid the north peak area as it is directly above your water source.

Water: Collect from seasonal tarns below the north peak. In late summer, they may be dry. To reach the tarns, follow an indistinct trail heading east from the saddle between the north and south peaks of Unnecessary Mountain.

Food Storage: Bring rope to hang your food in one of the small trees on the ridge. A bear canister is a better option.

THOMAS PEAK CAMPING AREA

This campsite at the 14-km (8.7-mi) mark has a gorgeous view of the Capilano watershed to the east and north. To the south, you can see the lights of Vancouver. The campsite also has reliable water.

Campsites: Cleared sites for 5 or 6 tents along the plateau

Toilet: None. Dig a cat hole and use Leave No Trace toilet practices. Try to get well away from the trail and avoid the south side of the ridge as it is directly above your water source.

Water: Follow faint paths through the trees to the south, then scramble down a steep and rocky slope to the round tarn about 40 m (131 ft) below the plateau.

Food Storage: Bring rope to hang your food in a tree, or bring a bear canister.

MAGNESIA MEADOWS CAMPING AREA

The sloping meadows sit below a crumbling rocky ridge. If you approach from the south, you'll reach a shallow rocky tarn first. An emergency shelter is 50 m (164 ft) ahead through the trees.

Campsites: A few flat sites near the tarn and the shelter. The alpine vegetation is very fragile here, so please put your tent on a spot that is already clear of plants.

Shelter: The small A-frame shelter is designed for emergencies only. It will sleep 3 or 4 in a pinch but has no amenities.

Toilet: None. Dig a cat hole and use Leave No Trace toilet practices. Head off the trail to the west to distance yourself from the tarn water source.

Water: Collect from the tarn at the south end of the meadows. It gets shallow and stagnant late in the season, so use a water filter.

Food Storage: Hang inside the emergency shelter.

BRUNSWICK LAKE CAMPING AREA

Brunswick Lake, 23 km (14.3 mi) from the southern trailhead, is a gorgeous spot against the rocky slopes of Mount Hanover. On a hot day, it's a great place for a swim. An emergency shelter is situated on the slopes above the southwest side of the lake. To reach the main camping area, take a spur trail to the east along the lakeshore for a few minutes.

Campsites: A dozen campsites at the southeast end of the lake on a broad creek delta

Shelter: The small A-frame shelter is designed for emergencies only. It will sleep 3 or 4 in a pinch but has no amenities.

Toilet: None. Dig a cat hole and use Leave No Trace toilet practices. Avoid the area along the creek behind the campsite. Instead, walk back up the trail towards the emergency shelter and head into the forest.

Water: Collect from the stream flowing into the lake behind the campground. Beware of human waste contamination.

Food Storage: Hang it in the emergency shelter, which is a 10-minute walk away. Alternatively, bring rope to hang it in a tree, or bring a bear canister.

At the 26.5-km (16.5-mi) mark, Deeks Lake is the closest campsite to the northern trailhead. It's a large lake ringed with steep peaks. The main camping area is at the northwest end of the lake.

Campsites: Several great campsites in the trees near the logjam. More sites along the shoreline to the north as well.
Toilet: None. Dig a cat hole and use Leave No Trace toilet practices. Head into the forest to the north of the lake, avoiding the trail and Deeks Creek.
Water: Collect from the lake outlet stream near the logjam.
Food Storage: Bring a rope to hang your food, or bring a bear canister.

Using a fixed rope to scramble across the summit of James Peak.

EXTENDING YOUR TRIP
Brunswick Mountain: If you have time on your HSCT hike, drop your pack and make the quick side trip to this impressive peak. It's 2 km (1.2 mi) return from the junction, with 288 m (945 ft) of elevation gain. The route to the top is very steep and can feel exposed, but the views of the islands dotting Howe Sound are worth it.

FURTHER RESOURCES
Cypress Provincial Park: info http://bcparks.ca/explore/parkpgs/cypress/
Trail Map: North Shore Trail Map by Trail Ventures BC
NTS Maps: 092G06, 092G11

20
ELSAY LAKE

Difficulty: ◆◆
Duration: 2 days
Distance: 20 km (12.4 mi)

Elevation Gain: 575 m (1886 ft)
High Point: 1250 m (4101 ft)
Best Months: June to October

Fees and Reservations: No fees. Camping and the hut are first-come, first-served.

Regulations: No fires. Dogs permitted on leash only. No drones. No smoking, vaping, or cannabis.

Caution: The area is known for lots of mosquitos in June and early July, as well as ground wasp nests. BC Parks officially closes this area in winter due to avalanche danger.

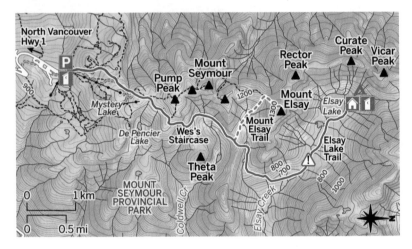

FROM THE SUMMIT of Mount Seymour, an unbroken sea of craggy granite peaks stretches away to the north. Leave the day trippers behind and hike into the backcountry of Mount Seymour Provincial Park to the sapphire-blue pool of Elsay Lake. It's nestled between rugged mountains but is still incredibly close to the city. Enjoy a refreshing swim, then spend the night at the lake. There's a hut here too. The stats make the trip to Elsay Lake sound easy, but it's actually one of the most challenging hikes in this book. The trail has 250 m (820 ft) of ascent, then 600 m (1969 ft) of descent, and finally 100 m (328 ft) more of ascent. That means that the return trip will be mostly uphill. As well, the trail is very rough with lots of technical terrain and boulders to scramble over. Give yourself plenty of time to take breaks and enjoy the views.

Reflections at Elsay Lake. Photo: Jaime Adams

GETTING THERE

From Mount Seymour Parkway in North Vancouver, turn onto Mount Seymour Road and follow it uphill to its end at the Mount Seymour ski resort. Park outside the yellow gate, either along the west shoulder of the road or in Lot 1 at the last switchback. The ski resort requests that you leave a note with emergency contact information and your trip dates on the dashboard of your vehicle.

TRAIL

TRIP PLANNER

0 km (0 mi)	Trailhead
3 km (1.9 mi)	Junction with Mount Seymour Trail
5 km (3.1 mi)	Junction with Mount Elsay Trail (2 km/1.2 mi to summit)
8 km (5 mi)	Elsay Creek
9.5 km (5.9 mi)	Elsay Lake
10 km (6.2 mi)	Elsay Lake Hut and campground

Find the trailhead at the north end of the ski area parking lot at a large information kiosk with trail maps and information. From the kiosk, follow the ski area gravel road north for a few metres, then turn left onto the signed "Mount Seymour Trail." The rocky trail climbs steadily and sometimes steeply up into the forest beside the ski runs. Within the first few minutes, you'll arrive at the Tim Jones Memorial.

After the memorial, ignore junctions with trails heading off to the left and remain on the main Mount Seymour Trail as it continues climbing. The trail emerges briefly onto a ski run at the 1.5-km (0.9-mi) mark, then turns left towards a pond before climbing up to Brockton Point. From there, it contours east around Mount Seymour, then climbs up its flank to a **junction** about 3 km (1.9 mi) from the trailhead. The trail to the left climbs to the peak of Mount Seymour. Go straight onto the rough and rugged Elsay Lake Trail, maintained by volunteers from the Vancouver Korean Hiking Club.

From the junction, the trail descends steeply down a rockslide on switchbacks known as Wes's Staircase. The path hugs the sheer north face of Mount Seymour. Each winter, water and snow build up in the cracks between the rocks. As the water freezes into ice, it expands, shattering the rocks and creating the scree slopes at the bottom of the cliff. After the switchbacks, the grade lessens and the path continues downhill as the trail heads north through more rockslides. From this point onwards, the trail can be quite overgrown with salmonberry and blueberry bushes. Look for orange flagging, trail markers, and rock cairns to help keep you on track.

About 5 km (3.1 mi) from the trailhead, you'll head into a section of forest and reach a **junction**. The trail to Mount Elsay heads left. Continue straight through the forest to remain on the Elsay Lake Trail. Past this point, the trail gets much rougher and less maintained. Over the next few kilometres, the trail crosses numerous creeks and scrambles through challenging boulder fields as it curls around the flank of Mount Elsay. You'll continue to descend slowly to a low point at 675 m (2215 ft). At this point, you are actually 345 m (1132 ft) lower than the parking lot, despite having climbed up over the shoulder of Mount Seymour to get here!

After the low point, you'll ascend gradually through old-growth forest to the lake. Cross **Elsay Creek**, which is an easy rock-hop or boots-off ford at the height of summer, but it can also turn into a raging torrent. Use caution and be prepared to turn back if the creek is running high. The remaining 2 km (1.2 mi) to the lake is through open forest that can be quite muddy. A few carefully placed planks keep you out of the worst of it. You'll reach the southern shore of **Elsay Lake** near the creek outlet. Follow the trail for another 0.5 km (0.3 mi) along the east side of the lake to the hut and campsites. The lake is

HISTORY

Tim Jones was the beloved leader of North Shore Rescue and a vocal advocate for wilderness safety. He passed away from an unexpected heart attack where his memorial now stands during a training exercise in January 2014. Pause to pay your respects. (And also to ensure you have the Ten Essentials. That's what Tim would have wanted.)

Looking across Elsay Lake to the hut and camping area. Photo: Stephen Hui

set in a bowl ringed with peaks: Mount Elsay rises to the south, and along a ridge to the west are Rector, Curate, and Vicar Peaks, named to go along with nearby Mount Bishop.

CAMPING AND HUT

The main hut and camping area are on the north shore of Elsay Lake. The basic A-frame hut is set just back from the lake. It's not in great shape, so most campers prefer to sleep in tents.

Hut Sleeps: 4 to 6 in the loft upstairs and another half dozen on the floor downstairs
Campsites: 4 or 5 tent sites just outside the cabin, plus a few more flat spots near where the trail meets the lake. However, the lake can flood the campsites in spring.
Toilet: Outhouse behind the cabin
Water: Collect from the creek near the hut.
Food Storage: On hooks inside the hut
Other Amenities: The hut has some old metal chairs and a falling-apart table.

EXTENDING YOUR TRIP

Mount Elsay: If you want to get up high into the surrounding mountains, add a trip to Mount Elsay to your hike. You can drop your packs and secure your food at the Mount Elsay junction, then climb the peak. It's only 4 km (2.5 mi) return, but you'll ascend 470 m (1542 ft) over very tough terrain including a huge boulder field. Allow at least 2.5 hours for the round trip.

FURTHER RESOURCES

Mount Seymour Provincial Park: info http://bcparks.ca/explore/parkpgs/mt_seymour/
Trail Map: North Shore Trail Map by Trail Ventures BC
NTS Map: 092G07

21
DENNETT LAKE

Difficulty: ■/♦
Duration: 2 to 3 days
Distance: 11.4 to 18 km
(7.1 to 11.2 mi)

Elevation Gain: 725 to 860 m
(2379 to 2822 ft)
High Point: 1075 m (3527 ft)
Best Months: July to October

Fees and Reservations: Camping is free and all campsites are first-come, first-served.

Regulations: No fires. No drones. No smoking, vaping, or cannabis. Dogs permitted on leash but not recommended.

Caution: This area has a very active black bear population. The mosquitos can be thick here, so bring insect repellent or a head net.

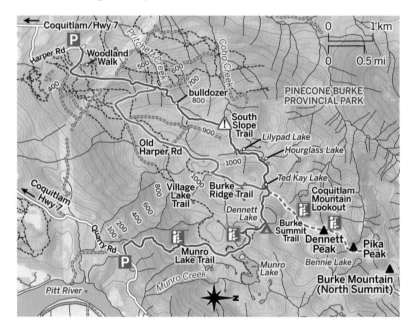

COQUITLAM MAY NOT be the first place that springs to mind when you think of backpacking. However, the extensive trail network in the Burke Mountain section of Pinecone Burke Provincial Park is a great place to backpack in the wilderness. The hike up to the summit of Burke Mountain and the surrounding subalpine lakes is too long for most people to complete in a day. By camping at Dennett Lake, a quiet spot set in a forested bowl against the

The southern shore of Dennett Lake.

shoulder of Burke Ridge, you can explore the area over a few days. Hike to tiny lakes, clamber along the spine of Burke Ridge to viewpoints, or summit seldom-visited Burke Mountain. You can access the area from two different trailheads, making a traverse possible.

GETTING THERE

HARPER ROAD TRAILHEAD

The South Slope Trail leaves from this trailhead. In Port Coquitlam, head north on Coast Meridian Road for 5 km (3.1 mi) into Coquitlam, then turn right onto Harper Road. Follow Harper as it curves through a switchback and turns to gravel. Ignore a gated road 0.3 km (0.2 mi) after the gravel begins. About 0.4 km (0.2 mi) later, park in a large pullout opposite a yellow gate. Don't continue straight to the road's end at a gated parking lot for a gun range.

MUNRO LAKE TRAILHEAD

The Munro Lake Trail departs from this trailhead. From Coast Meridian Road in Coquitlam, turn right onto Victoria Drive. Stay on Victoria for a little over 1 km (0.6 mi), then turn left to continue on Victoria Drive. Two kilometres

(1.2 mi) later, the road goes over a bridge and becomes Quarry Road. Follow Quarry Road past the entrance to Minnekhada Regional Park, where it turns to gravel. About 3 km (1.9 mi) past Minnekhada, look for a trail leaving the road on the left. Park in a pullout on the right where there is room for three or four cars. If you have trouble finding the trailhead, it's next to a white road marker with "12" printed on it.

TRAIL

The Burke Mountain area is criss-crossed with dozens of hiking routes, mountain bike trails, and gravel roads. A trail map is essential in this area to stay on track. Several possible routes lead to Dennett Lake. The two most scenic options are described below.

SOUTH SLOPE TRAIL

TRIP PLANNER

0 km (0 mi)	Harper Road trailhead
2.6 km (1.6 mi)	Junction with South Slope Trail
3.5 km (2.2 mi)	Bulldozer
5 km (3.1 mi)	Coho Creek crossing
6 km (3.7 mi)	Lilypad Lake
6.5 km (4 mi)	Hourglass Lake
8 km (5 mi)	Ted Kay Lake and junction with the Burke Ridge Trail South (8 km/5 mi to Harper Road trailhead)
8.1 km (5 mi)	Junction between Dennett Lake Trail and Burke Ridge Trail North (1 km/0.6 mi to viewpoint or 2 km/1.2 mi to Burke Mountain south summit)
8.6 km (5.3 mi)	Dennett Lake
9 km (5.6 mi)	Dennett Lake informal camping

At 9 km (5.6 mi) each way with 725 m (2379 ft) of elevation gain, the South Slope Trail is a longer option than the Munro Lake Trail with comparable

HISTORY

Volunteers with the Burke Mountain Naturalists (BMN) were instrumental in getting this area designated as a provincial park in 1995. They campaigned to save it from logging and built trails in the Burke Mountain area, as well as in the wilder northern section of the park that stretches all the way up to the boundary with Garibaldi Provincial Park. BMN volunteers have also stepped in to fill the gaps left by decades of inadequate BC Parks budgets, working hard to maintain trails and install signage.

elevation gain. However, it climbs much more gradually and passes by some pretty subalpine ponds on the way to Dennett Lake. It's also a much drier option.

From the Harper Road parking area, walk around the yellow gate and up the gravel road, a continuation of Harper Road. Stay on the road, ignoring mountain bike trails on both sides, and another gravel road branching to the left, signed "Woodland Walk." In the lower section of this trail, you'll be within audible range of the nearby gun club.

About 0.6 km (0.4 mi) from the gate, turn left up a gravel road to remain on Harper Road. Continue on the road, passing under some power lines. At 2.6 km (1.6 mi), turn left to take the **South Slope Trail** as it leaves Harper Road after a gate. This trail is sometimes signed as the South Slope Trail or as the Burke Summit Trail. On some maps, the upper parts of this trail are also called the Sterling Loop Trail.

The trail starts as a decommissioned road that is badly eroded. A few hundred metres after leaving Harper Road, cross a creek on a log. Immediately afterwards, ignore an old road branching to the left. Continue up the old road, then branch right following signs for Pritchett Creek Canyon. This short section of trail, built by the Burke Mountain Naturalists (BMN), heads through a beautiful little canyon with some small cascades.

After the canyon, the trail rejoins an old road. A huge decaying **bulldozer** is parked just off the trail to the left, a relic from the logging days. Near the 5-km (3.1-mi) mark, the trail leaves the old road and descends to cross **Coho Creek** near a small cascade. The next section follows the north side of the creek as it climbs upwards through an older forest. Pass by the aptly named **Lilypad Lake**, then carry on to **Hourglass Lake**, which is named for its shape. Watch for mushrooms, including vibrantly dark purple violet corts, lining the trail in this area.

Past Hourglass, the trail gains elevation and passes a few ponds. Arrive at **Ted Kay Lake**. At the north side of the lake, cross a stream, then meet the **Burke Ridge Trail** coming in from the right. Continue straight on the Burke Ridge Trail for a minute or so to another **junction**. Turn right onto the newer Dennett Lake Trail. The Burke Ridge Trail continues straight towards the summit of Burke Mountain.

Follow the Dennett Lake Trail through a wet and overgrown area. Watch carefully for flagging turning sharply to the left. From here the trail plunges steeply through a stand of hemlock, cedar, and fir as you lose 120 m (394 ft). Arrive at the southwest corner of the lake, then follow a faint trail along the marshy southern shoreline to the informal camping area at **Dennett Lake**.

Tiny Hourglass Lake on the South Slope Trail.

MUNRO LAKE TRAIL

TRIP PLANNER

0 km (0 mi)	Quarry Road trailhead
2.5 km (1.6 mi)	Junction with Viewpoint Loop
3.5 km (2.2 mi)	Junction with Village Lake Trail
4.2 km (2.6 mi)	Munro Lake
5 km (3.1 mi)	Junction with Munro Lake Lookout Trail
5.7 km (3.5 mi)	Dennett Lake camping
6.6 km (4.1 mi)	Junction with Burke Ridge Trail North (1 km/0.6 mi to viewpoint or 2 km/1.2 mi to Burke Mountain south summit)
6.7 km (4.2 mi)	Ted Kay Lake and junction with the Burke Ridge Trail South (8 km/5 mi to Harper Road trailhead) and South Slope Trail (8 km/5 mi to Harper Road)

Choose the Munro Lake Trail if you want a workout. This trail is steep, especially the first half. It's only 5.7 km (3.5 mi) to Dennett Lake, but you'll gain 860 m (2822 ft) over that distance. From the trailhead, the first few minutes of trail are on an old boulder-strewn logging road. Turn right off the road at a sign for Munro Lake and follow a trail uphill into the trees.

The trail in this section is unrelentingly steep with rocks and roots. There are red and orange markers on the trees, as well as flagging tape to keep you on track. The trail has several branches, which can be confusing. Choose the well-trodden forks marked with flagging tape.

About 2 km (1.2 mi) from the start, take a side path to the right for a great view of the farms along the banks of the Fraser and Pitt Rivers below you. After the viewpoint, the trail begins to switchback. Stay on the main trail rather than cutting straight up the middle, to prevent trail erosion. At the top of the switchbacks, follow a trail to the left signed "**Viewpoint Loop**." Walk a few minutes down the trail to a bluff with views of the Pitt River. Follow the other side of the loop from the top of the bluff back to the main trail, then go left to continue towards Munro Lake.

The grade eases a bit past here, but the footbed becomes more technical with lots of roots. At the 3.5-km (2.2-mi) mark, reach a major **junction** in the dark and mossy forest. You are at an elevation of 870 m (2854 ft), having climbed a staggering 780 m (2559 ft) already. The trail to the left, signed "Village Lake Trail," heads to the Harper Road trailhead. Continue straight towards Munro Lake.

About 0.7 km (0.4 mi) after the junction, reach an open area with a small pond on your left. This is actually part of **Munro Lake**. The lake was dammed in the early 20th century to provide water to a quarry and was much larger. Now that the dam has been partially dismantled, it is a series of ponds surrounded by wet marshes with a healthy frog population and a thriving mosquito presence. Follow a spur trail to the right if you want to visit the rest of the reedy lake. The lakeshore is mostly wet and marshy, so it's not a great place to camp.

Continue around the right side of the pond through a wet area, head back into the forest on a trail flagged with blue tape, then cross a creek on a fallen log. The next 1.5 km (0.9 mi) to Dennett Lake is rough and very muddy. It will take some work to keep your feet dry. About 0.6 km (0.4 mi) after leaving Munro Lake, a signed trail heads left to the **Munro Lake Lookout**, a few minutes away. You'll get a better sense of the fragmented nature of Munro Lake from up here and a great view of Golden Ears (Trip 24) and Mount Baker.

From the viewpoint junction, follow the trail for a few minutes to the shores of **Dennett Lake**. A faint trail to the left crosses a creek and then leads to some small informal campsites, as well as to the other end of the lake.

CAMPING

Burke Mountain has no designated or improved campsites anywhere in the park. The nicest and most environmentally responsible option is to camp at Dennett Lake.

Campsites: Cleared space for 3 or 4 tents on the south side of the lake
Toilet: None. Dig a cat hole and use Leave No Trace toilet practices. Head away from the lake to the south, avoiding the outlet stream.
Water: Collect from the lake.
Food Storage: Bring a rope to hang your food in a tree, or bring a bear canister.

EXTENDING YOUR TRIP

Burke Mountain Summit: From the junction at Ted Kay Lake, continue north along the Burke Ridge Trail. The Coquitlam Mountain overlook, 1 km (0.6 mi) away and 50 m (164 ft) higher, is a good turnaround point if you're low on energy. Otherwise, continue along the ridge for another 1 km (0.6 mi), gaining 90 m (295 ft) of elevation to the south summit of Burke Mountain, also known as Dennett Peak, at 1210 m (3970 ft). From the junction, it's a 4-km (2.5-mi) round trip with 140 m (459 ft) of elevation gain. Experienced hikers comfortable with route-finding and exposure can follow a rough flagged route through meadows and over sub-summits to the higher north summit of Burke Mountain (1270 m/4167 ft), 4 km (2.5 mi) away.

Burke Ridge Trail: Vary your return trip to the Harper Road trailhead by taking this trail instead of the South Slope Trail. From Ted Kay Lake, follow this trail south past the remains of an old ski resort from the 1960s, then back to the car on a gravel road. This route is the same distance and elevation gain as the South Slope Trail.

FURTHER RESOURCES

Pinecone Burke Provincial Park: info http://bcparks.ca/explore/parkpgs/pinecone/
Trail Maps: PoMo to PoCo Trail Map by Trail Ventures BC, Tri-Cities Trail Map by Canadian Map Makers
NTS Map: 092G07

22
WIDGEON LAKE

Difficulty: ♦

Duration: 2 to 3 days

Distance: 19 km (11.8 mi)

Elevation Gain: 800 m (2625 ft)

High Point: 800 m (2625 ft)

Best Months: Mid-June to October

Fees and Reservations: Camping is free and all campsites are first-come, first-served.

Regulations: No fires. No drones. No smoking, vaping, or cannabis. Dogs permitted on leash but not recommended.

Caution: This area has a very active black bear population.

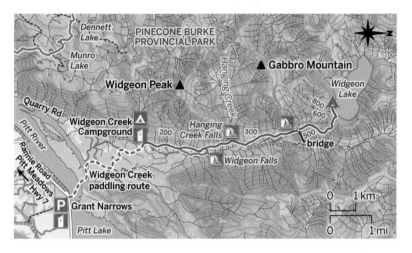

THE LONG TRIP to Widgeon Lake in Pinecone Burke Provincial Park is challenging, but the reward is a beautiful lake dotted with rocky islets and cradled in a bowl of granite peaks. Your adventure begins with a canoe trip across the narrowest part of Pitt Lake to the trailhead at the top of Widgeon Slough, the largest freshwater marsh in southwestern BC. Next you'll walk up a flat abandoned logging road, passing numerous waterfalls cascading down the slopes. Break up your journey with a side trip to visit Widgeon Falls as it tumbles over polished granite. The route culminates in a steep hike to the shores of Widgeon Lake, a hanging lake set high above the valley you just hiked through.

GETTING THERE
Go north at the traffic light onto Harris Road from Highway 7 in Pitt Meadows. One kilometre later (0.6 mi), turn right onto Old Dewdney Trunk Road.

Reflections in Widgeon Lake. Photo: Jaime Adams

Follow it for 3.4 km (2.1 mi), then turn left onto Neaves Road. Continue straight for 13 km (8.1 mi) as Neaves Road becomes Rannie Road and passes the Swaneset Bay Resort and Country Club. Drive through a gate into the Pitt-Addington Marsh Wildlife Management Area and arrive at a large parking area. The lot can fill up on weekends, so arrive early. Pay for parking with your credit card at the pay station, being sure to select the overnight parking option. Outhouses are located near the boat launch.

PADDLE

While Metro Vancouver Parks has proposed a new trail connecting Quarry Road in Coquitlam with the Widgeon Creek campground via the new Widgeon Marsh Regional Park, for the time being the only way to get to the trailhead is to paddle. Start your trip from the small-craft boat launch just past the parking lot. You can rent a canoe from the Katzie First Nation–owned Pitt Lake Canoe Adventures (cash only) next to the boat launch or bring your own.

Head straight across the outlet of Pitt Lake, aiming for an opening in the marsh. This is the most challenging part of the paddling trip as you will need to cope with wind, tides, and passing powerboats. Once you get across the channel and into Widgeon Slough, it's much easier to paddle. Follow the slough as it curves around, being careful to stay in the main channel. Later in the summer, water levels can drop drastically, so you may need to get out and pull your canoe through the shallow bits.

The slough and creek are named for widgeon ducks, which are common in the wetlands here. The males are easy to recognize: they have a green strip behind their eyes and a white patch on the top of their head. This area is protected as the Pitt-Addington Marsh Wildlife Management Area, an important migration and breeding habitat for dozens of bird species. Keep your binoculars handy as you paddle. About 5 km (3.1 mi) from the boat launch, look for a grassy landing area on your left. You've arrived at the **Widgeon Creek campground**. It takes most paddlers about 1.5 hours to get here. Pull your canoe up on the grass out of the way.

TRAIL

TRIP PLANNER

0 km (0 mi)	Widgeon Creek campground
1.5 km (0.9 mi)	Junction with Widgeon Falls Trail (2.5 km/1.6 mi to falls)
2.5 km (1.6 mi)	Junction with Widgeon Falls Trail (0.4 km/0.2 mi to falls)
5.6 km (3.5 mi)	Road turns to trail
6.2 km (3.9 mi)	Footbridge over Widgeon Creek
9 km (5.6 mi)	Widgeon Lake informal camping

The trailhead for Widgeon Lake begins on an old road at the northwest side of the **Widgeon Creek campground** near the outhouse. Walk up the old road for about 1.5 km (0.9 mi), then cross a large creek bed where the water has eroded the road. Shortly afterwards, arrive at a **junction**. Your route continues straight on the road, while the rough trail to the right leads down to Widgeon Creek, then along the creek to Widgeon Falls. At 2.5 km (1.6 mi), reach another **junction** where the Widgeon Falls Trail rejoins the old road.

Continue along the old road crossing a few creek beds. Take a break about 3.5 km (2.2 mi) from the trailhead to admire the cascade of Hanging Creek Falls. As the **road ends**, the trail begins.

The trail heads into the upper valley of Widgeon Creek and starts climbing steeply. Between here and the lake, you'll gain 560 m (1837 ft) over 3.6 km

NATURE NOTE

The old road is becoming overgrown with blueberries and salmonberries. These light pink or orange berries look like raspberries and taste a bit like them too. Salmonberries are an important food for Coastal First Nations people throughout BC. Along with the berries, they also eat the young shoots of the plant, often served with salmon. Black bears also love salmonberries, so make lots of noise on this hike.

(2.2 mi). Take your time: the footbed is very rough with lots of roots, boulders, and slippery sections that can be challenging to navigate with an overnight pack. Cross to the east side of the creek near a waterfall on a **footbridge**. Continue relentlessly upwards. The last kilometre to the lake is the steepest and slipperiest. Finally, crest a small rise and get your first glimpse of Widgeon Lake below you.

Follow the rough trail downhill to the west. Descend a granite outcropping (perhaps with the help of a fixed rope) to the lakeshore. The **Widgeon Lake campground** is just across the lake outlet stream on the south shore of the lake.

CAMPING

Most visitors to Widgeon Lake haul their backpacking gear up and spend the night. However, you could also camp at Widgeon Creek and make the long day trip to and from the lake.

WIDGEON CREEK CAMPSITE

The large and grassy Widgeon Creek campsite is 5 km (3.1 mi) up Widgeon Slough, at the trailhead for the Widgeon Lake Trail. The easy paddle to get there means most campers bring in luxurious camp set-ups. Partying and garbage can be common on weekends. Pack out what you pack in.

Campsites: 10 designated tent pads with lots of extra space for more tents on the grass
Toilet: Pit toilet at the north end of the campground
Water: Collect from Widgeon Creek.
Food Storage: In metal food storage lockers

WIDGEON LAKE CAMPSITE

The informal Widgeon Lake campsite is on the southern shore of Widgeon Lake near a small island. In early summer when the lake level is high, some of the shoreline sites are usually flooded.

NATURE NOTE

Widgeon Lake is surrounded by granite peaks on three sides. A glacier carved out the bowl that Widgeon Lake now occupies. At the same time, an even larger glacier stretched its tongue down the Widgeon Creek valley from the north, grinding away the rock directly south of the lake so that the present landscape drops away steeply. When the glaciers melted, the melting ice filled the rocky bowl left behind, creating a hanging lake. The water is held back only by the rock headwall you scrambled up on your way.

Paddling in Widgeon Slough.

Campsites: Space for 6 to 10 tents between the lake and a small pond to the south

Toilet: Very rudimentary open-air toilet on a spur trail before the main camping area. If this toilet is not being maintained, dig a cat hole and use Leave No Trace toilet practices. Head to the west along the lakeshore, then south away from the lake.

Water: Collect from the lake.

Food Storage: Bring a rope to hang your food in a tree, or bring a bear canister.

EXTENDING YOUR TRIP

Widgeon Falls: This multi-tiered granite waterfall is a popular destination for day hikers who have paddled to Widgeon Creek. The most direct way to the falls is via a side trail 2.5 km (1.6 mi) up the main trail to Widgeon Lake. From there, its 0.8 km (0.5 mi) return to the falls with 40 m (131 ft) of elevation loss. A more scenic route to the falls begins at a junction 1.5 km (0.9 mi) from the canoe takeout. A rough trail leads along the banks of Widgeon Creek to the falls 1.75 km (1.1 mi) away, then connects back to the main trail 0.4 km (0.2 mi) later.

FURTHER RESOURCES

Pinecone Burke Provincial Park: info http://bcparks.ca/explore/parkpgs/pinecone/

Pitt Lake Canoe Adventures: canoe rental prices and hours 604-836-7117

Trail Maps: PoMo to PoCo Trail Map by Trail Ventures BC, Tri-Cities Trail Map by Canadian Map Makers

NTS Map: 092G07

23
GOLD CREEK CANYON

Difficulty: ●

Duration: 2 days

Distance: 9.6 to 19.4 km (6 to 12 mi)

Elevation Gain: 170 to 275 m (558 to 902 ft)

High Point: 375 m (1230 ft)

Best Months: April to November

Fees and Reservations: Camping fees are $5/person/night, payable online. All campsites are first-come, first-served.

Regulations: No fires. No drones. No smoking, vaping, or cannabis. Dogs permitted on leash only.

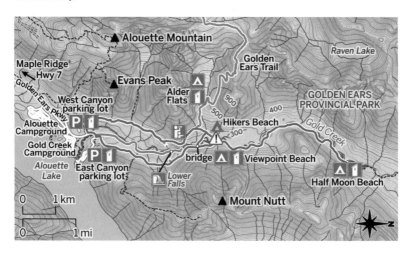

THIS EASY HIKE in Golden Ears Provincial Park is a great trip for families, beginners, or early season hikers. Trails on both sides of Gold Creek and a new bridge make a loop possible. Most campers will choose to stay at either Hikers Beach or Viewpoint Beach with its great views of Golden Ears' peaks high above. Both are a short distance from the trailhead. But if you're looking for solitude, trek the additional distance through rougher terrain to Half Moon Beach.

GETTING THERE

From Highway 7 in Maple Ridge, go north on Golden Ears Way North and stay on this road for 7.5 km (4.7 mi) as it becomes 128 Ave, then Abernethy Way. Turn left on 232 Street, then turn right at the roundabout 1.5 km (0.9 mi) later onto 132 Avenue, which becomes Fern Crescent. Continue on Fern

Broad and rocky Viewpoint Beach.

Crescent for 3.5 km (2.2 mi) to the entrance to Golden Ears Park. Continue on Golden Ears Parkway past the day-use area and campground entrances as the road turns to gravel. At the 11.5-km (7.1-mi) mark, reach a turnoff to the left for the West Canyon parking lot. To get to the East Canyon parking lot, continue down the road and cross a one-lane bridge over Gold Creek. At 13 km (8.1 mi), turn left into the parking lot.

TRAIL

With the addition of a bridge over Gold Creek in 2015, various loops in the Gold Creek Canyon are now possible. The route via the East Canyon Trail is shorter and flatter than the steeper and rougher West Canyon Trail, but the west-side route is more scenic. Both routes converge at the new bridge, and it's a short walk to either Viewpoint Beach or Hikers Beach from there.

WEST CANYON TRAIL

TRIP PLANNER

0 km (0 mi)	West Canyon trailhead
0.15 km (0.1 mi)	Junction with Menzies Trail to East Canyon trailhead
3 km (1.9 mi)	Junction with Lower Falls Trail (0.5 km/0.3 mi to falls viewpoint)
4 km (2.5 mi)	Gold Creek Lookout
4.75 km (3 mi)	Junction with Golden Ears Trail
5.15 km (3.2 mi)	Junction with Hikers Beach Trail (0.5 km/0.3 mi to Hikers Beach campground)
5.65 km (3.5 mi)	Bridge over Gold Creek
6.25 km (3.9 mi)	Viewpoint Beach campground
11.5 km (7.1 mi)	Half Moon Beach campground

Find the trailhead at the northwest corner of the parking lot near the outhouse. In the first few minutes, reach a **junction**. Your route goes straight, but if you wanted to get to the East Canyon parking lot from here, turn right and follow the Menzies Trail for 0.7 km (0.4 mi).

Continue on the West Canyon Trail as it crosses two rocky creek beds. The trail is an old logging railway grade from the 1920s, once part of the largest railway operation in British Columbia. A fire swept through this area in 1931, ending logging here. The trees you see today all reseeded after that historic fire. Since they are all the same age and have grown at the same rate, the forest canopy is too tight and dark for understory bushes to grow.

About 3 km (1.9 mi) from the parking lot, the old railway ends and an eroded and wet single-track trail begins. A steep spur trail near here heads down the hill to the right to a **viewpoint of Lower Falls** on Gold Creek.

Continue along the increasingly rough trail for another kilometre (0.6 mi) as it climbs to the slightly overgrown **Gold Creek Lookout**. From here you can look down to the rushing waters of Gold Creek and spot the new Gold Creek bridge in the distance. At 4.75 km (3 mi), cross a creek and reach a **junction**. The trail to Alder Flats campsite and Golden Ears (Trip 24) heads left and your route heads right. About 0.4 km (0.2 mi) later, reach another junction. Turning left will take you to Hikers Beach campsite whereas right heads to the bridge to the East Canyon Trail and then the Viewpoint Beach campsite.

If you're heading to Hikers Beach, turn left and immediately ford a creek. It can run deep and fast, so use caution. The **Hikers Beach campground** is 0.5 km (0.3 mi) from the junction. If the water is low enough, you can wade across Gold Creek to Viewpoint Beach from here.

To get to Viewpoint Beach, go right at the junction and walk 0.5 km (0.3 mi) to the new **bridge over Gold Creek**. After the bridge, turn left and walk 0.6 km (0.4 mi) past an outhouse to a junction. Go left for a few minutes to the **Viewpoint Beach campground**. There's a great view of the peaks of

HISTORY

In the 1970s three hanging cables connected the East and West Canyon Trails near the present-day bridge. Crossing the creek was reportedly both exhilarating and terrifying, as hikers tightrope-walked their way across on the bottom cable, using the other two waist-high cables as handrails. The Burma Bridge, as it was known, was dismantled in the late 1970s and the two routes were cut off from each other until recently. Today's Gold Creek bridge also has a historical connection. The concrete pillars supporting it date back to a 1920s-era bridge for logging trucks.

the Mount Blanshard massif: the twin summits of Golden Ears to the north, as well as Edge Peak, Blanshard Needle, and Alouette Mountain to the south. Hikers Beach is just across Gold Creek.

EAST CANYON TRAIL

TRIP PLANNER

0 km (0 mi)	East Canyon trailhead
2.6 km (1.6 mi)	Junction with route to Lower Falls (0.5 km/0.3 mi to falls)
3.8 km (2.4 mi)	Junction with trail to West Canyon and Hikers Beach campground (1 km/0.6 mi to beach)
4.5 km (2.8 mi)	Viewpoint Beach campground
9.7 km (6 mi)	Half Moon Beach campground

The trail starts at the northeast corner of the East Canyon parking lot. Follow the trail northeast for a few minutes, then turn left. The trail at this point is an old road, a remnant from decades of logging in the area. In a few places, time and weather have eroded it, but it is mostly easy walking. Watch for massive stumps along the way, the only sign of the huge old-growth cedars and hemlocks that dominated the forest a century ago. Look carefully for notches carved into the sides of the stumps. Loggers carved these grooves, then inserted boards to stand on so they could climb high enough to fell the tree above its flared base, where it was easier to cut with the handsaws used at the time.

About 2.5 km (1.6 mi) from the trailhead, cross a creek on a bridge made of a pair of huge parallel old logs. A minute later, reach a flagged **junction** where a rough trail descends steeply to join with the Lower Falls Trail deep in Gold Creek Canyon below you. Continue on the old road until you reach a **junction** at the 3.8-km (2.4-mi) mark.

To get to Hikers Beach, turn left and cross the **bridge over Gold Creek**, then walk 0.5 km (0.3 mi) up the trail to another **junction**. Go right here, ford the creek, and arrive at **Hikers Beach campground** 0.5 km (0.3 mi) later.

For Viewpoint Beach, continue straight from the junction for another 0.6 km (0.4 mi), then turn left onto a spur trail just after you pass an outhouse. Reach **Viewpoint Beach campground**.

If you're looking for a more isolated experience, continue up the trail past Viewpoint Beach. From the Viewpoint Beach junction, head north on the West Canyon Trail. It gets progressively overgrown the farther north you go. The trail is fairly flat and stays close to the edge of Gold Creek. You'll cross many feeder creeks that can run high and fast, so use caution, especially in the spring. Reach the **Half Moon Beach campground** 9.7 km (6 mi) from the trailhead.

Looking north from the bridge over Gold Creek.

Past Half Moon Beach, the East Canyon Trail continues all the way to Hector Ferguson Lake, 15 km (9.3 mi) from the trailhead. The trail is badly overgrown and includes many unbridged crossings of Gold Creek, so it is not recommended.

CAMPING

HIKERS BEACH AND VIEWPOINT BEACH CAMPGROUNDS

These two camping areas are located a few metres apart, separated by the usually shallow waters of Gold Creek. Hikers Beach is located on the west and Viewpoint Beach is on the east side. If the water is low, it's an easy wade across the creek between the two. But if you don't want to get your feet wet, it's a 1.7-km (1.1-mi) hike between the two over the Gold Creek bridge.

Campsites: Many spots on the sandbar on the Hikers Beach side. On the Viewpoint Beach side, there's space on the rocky beach and 3 cleared sites in the trees.

Toilet: Outhouse located 100 m (328 ft) from camp on the East Canyon Trail near the junction with the Viewpoint Beach Trail. If you're at Hikers Beach, ford Gold Creek to use the outhouse or dig a cat hole and use Leave No Trace toilet practices. Head into the trees away from Gold Creek to the north of camp.

Water: Collect from Gold Creek.

Food Storage: Bring a rope to hang your food in a tree, or bring a bear canister.

HALF MOON BEACH CAMPGROUND

This rocky beach is a lot less busy than other backcountry spots in Golden Ears Provincial Park. Gold Creek starts to meander in this area, creating gravel bars and large sunny openings in the forest.

Campsites: Space for lots of tents on the rocky beach
Toilet: Outhouse at the north end of the beach
Water: Collect from Gold Creek.
Food Storage: Bring a rope to hang your food in a tree, or bring a bear canister.

EXTENDING YOUR TRIP

Lower Falls from West Canyon Trail: If you're on the West Canyon Trail, you can make a short but steep side trip down the hill to view Lower Falls. It's 1 km (0.6 mi) return with 70 m (230 ft) of elevation gain.

Lower Falls Trail to East Canyon Trail: Instead of taking the East Canyon Trail for the first portion of your trip, start with a visit to Lower Falls. From the East Canyon parking lot, follow the easy and flat Lower Falls Trail for 2.6 km (1.6 mi) to the falls. Enjoy the falls, then find a steep and rough flagged connector trail and head uphill to meet up with the East Canyon Trail 70 m (230 ft) higher.

Golden Ears: Combine this hike with a trip to Golden Ears (Trip 24) by heading up to Alder Flats from the West Canyon Trail.

FURTHER RESOURCES

Golden Ears Provincial Park: info and fees http://bcparks.ca/explore/parkpgs/golden_ears/
Trail Map: Golden Ears Map by Canadian Map Makers
NTS Map: 092G08

24
GOLDEN EARS

Difficulty: ◆◆

Duration: 2 to 3 days

Distance: 21 km (13 mi)

Elevation Gain: 1180 m (3871 ft)

High Point: 1370 m (4495 ft)

Season: July to September

Fees and Reservations: Camping fees are $5/person/night, payable online. All campsites are first-come, first-served.

Regulations: No fires. No drones. No smoking, vaping, or cannabis. Dogs permitted on leash.

Caution: This is a rough and challenging trail with a lot of elevation gain.

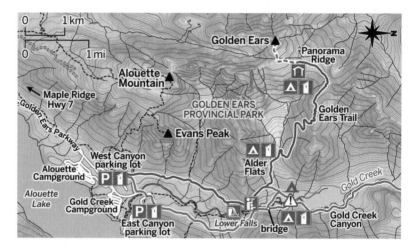

MOST VANCOUVERITES JUST gaze up at the lofty summit of Golden Ears. But if you make the challenging climb to the peak, you'll be rewarded with amazing views. Camp near the summit on Panorama Ridge to enjoy an incredible sunset or pitch your tent in Alder Flats and make the summit push with just a day pack. You'll need to work for the views though: along the way, you'll tackle a punishing 1180-m (3871-ft) ascent on steep and rough terrain. The upper section of the trail is particularly challenging. Thankfully, there are several smaller viewpoints along the trail to spur you on, plus lots of gorgeous subalpine terrain to ramble through once you break above the treeline. This trip is recommended for fit and experienced hikers only. Do not attempt this trip in snowy conditions unless you have mountaineering skills and avalanche training.

Looking north from the summit of Golden Ears to Raven Lake. Photo: Steve Ingold

GETTING THERE

From Highway 7 in Maple Ridge, go north on Golden Ears Way North and stay on this road for 7.5 km (4.7 mi) as it becomes 128 Avenue, then Abernethy Way. Turn left on 232 Street, then turn right at the roundabout 1.5 km (0.9 mi) later onto 132 Avenue, which becomes Fern Crescent. Continue on Fern Crescent for 3.5 km (2.2 mi) to the entrance to Golden Ears Park. Continue on Golden Ears Parkway past the day-use area and campground entrances as the road turns to gravel. At the 11.5-km (7.1-mi) mark, reach a turnoff to the left for the West Canyon parking lot.

TRAIL

TRIP PLANNER

0 km (0 mi)	West Canyon trailhead
3 km (1.9 mi)	Junction with Lower Falls Trail (0.5 km/0.3 mi to falls viewpoint)
4 km (2.5 mi)	Gold Creek Lookout
4.75 km (3 mi)	Junction with trail to Gold Creek bridge and East Canyon
5.85 km (3.6 mi)	Alder Flats campground
10.5 km (6.5 mi)	Panorama Ridge campground
12 km (7.5 mi)	Golden Ears summit

The trailhead is at the northwest corner of the parking lot next to an outhouse. Head up West Canyon Trail, ignoring junctions with the Menzies and

Viewpoint Trails within the first few minutes. For the first section, the trail is actually an old rail bed. You'll cross two rocky creek beds in this section.

The road transitions to a trail near the 3-km (1.9-mi) mark where a steep spur trail heads down the slope to a **viewpoint of Lower Falls** on Gold Creek. Past here, the single-track trail gets rougher and starts to climb. Next, arrive at **Gold Creek Lookout**. It's a bit brushed in, but you do get a view down to Gold Creek.

About 4.75 km (3 mi) from the trailhead, immediately after crossing a creek, arrive at a **junction**. Your route to Golden Ears heads uphill to the left. The West Canyon Trail continues downhill to the right, heading towards the bridge over Gold Creek and the campsites just upstream (Trip 23).

From the junction, the trail climbs uphill on bridges, stairs, and boardwalks beside a creek. Watch for a sign advising that there is no water past this point. If you need to fill your bottles, this is the best place to do it. After you cross all forks of the stream over to the north side, you'll start to notice small campsites next to the trail beside the often dry creek bed. Arrive at the main **Alder Flats campground**.

From here you still have the bulk of the elevation to ascend. You'll gain over 900 m (2953 ft) in the next 5 km (3.1 mi) to Panorama Ridge. After leaving Alder Flats, the trail immediately begins switchbacking upwards on a steep and rocky trail. The trail briefly breaks out of the trees just before the 6.5-km (4-mi) mark, giving you great views of Edge Peak, Blanshard Needle, Alouette Mountain, and Golden Ears.

Head back into the western hemlock forest as the trail gets steeper and rockier, requiring a bit of scrambling. A few flights of wooden stairs help your ascent as do some fixed ropes near 8 km (5 mi). As you climb higher and gain the crest of a ridge, the forest opens up and you'll pass more viewpoints. To the northeast, you can see the rocky flutes of Mount Robie Reid and the distinctive twin summit of Mount Judge Howay. To the south, you'll get views of Mount Baker's snow-capped cone. In the northwest, you'll see

HISTORY

While the twin peaks of Golden Ears do look like ears, the original name for the mountain was "Golden Eyries," meaning eagle's nests. The area was added to Garibaldi Provincial Park in 1933 to preserve its scenic mountains and lakes. After a failed attempt to establish the area as a national park, it was split off into its own park in 1967 and named Golden Ears Provincial Park after the prominent peaks. Today it protects 2875 km^2 (1110 mi^2) of wilderness, including the remote northern section of the park, which is home to the endangered Garibaldi-Pitt grizzly bear population unit and important winter mountain goat ranges.

Golden Ears Peak with the Panorama Ridge emergency shelter and campground in the fore-ground. Photo: Andy Gibb

Mount Garibaldi's rugged massif. You'll also get lots of views of Golden Ears ahead of you on the trail to the southwest.

The trail turns left and climbs onto the spine of Panorama Ridge and into subalpine terrain. The formerly thick forest slowly disappears as you walk, replaced by stunted trees, mats of pink mountain heather, and tufts of hardy brome grasses. At 10 km (6.2 mi), a wooden ladder helps you down a steep rock section. Shortly afterwards, the trees end as you emerge into the alpine. Follow orange markers amongst the granite rocks, being careful not to step on any fragile subalpine plants. Reach the **Panorama Ridge campground** and emergency shelter. Look down to Pitt Lake to the east or to Raven Lake to the north.

CAMPING

ALDER FLATS CAMPING AREA

Alder Flats is 5.85 km (3.6 mi) from the trailhead and 270 m (886 ft) higher. Many hikers choose to camp here to avoid carrying their backpacking gear up the steep and strenuous trail to Panorama Ridge. The campsite is located next to a slide path with lots of berry bushes, so be bear aware.

Campsites: Several cleared areas next to the trail near the outhouse and farther down the slope near the dry creek bed
Toilet: Outhouse to the right of the trail
Water: Collect from a creek at a bridge a few minutes before the campsite.
Food Storage: Bring a rope to hang your food in a tree, or bring a bear canister.

PANORAMA RIDGE CAMPING AREA

This campground is perched on the edge of Panorama Ridge, below the summit of Golden Ears. A small shelter here is for emergency use only, so do not plan to sleep in it.

Campsites: 6 wooden tent platforms next to the emergency shelter and a few small, rocky, and sloped sites for overflow camping
Toilet: A temporary toilet is flown in each summer, but be prepared to dig a cat hole and use Leave No Trace toilet practices. Head downhill from camp, away from water sources.
Water: Melt snow from lingering patches or collect water from a meltwater stream near camp that dries up in mid-summer.
Food Storage: On hooks in the emergency shelter

EXTENDING YOUR TRIP

Lower Falls: Drop your pack near the 3-km (1.9-mi) mark on the West Canyon Trail to make a side trip to Lower Falls. It's a short but steep hike down to Gold Creek. It's 1 km (0.6 mi) return with 70 m (230 ft) of elevation gain.
Golden Ears Summit: The steep route to the summit is only recommended for experienced hikers with mountaineering skills and an ice axe because there is a steep permanent snowfield to cross. It's a 3-km (1.9-mi) round trip to the peak with 345 m (1132 ft) of elevation gain. The rough and rocky route follows cairns and involves scrambling up rocks with some exposure, so use caution.

FURTHER RESOURCES

Golden Ears Provincial Park: info and fees http://bcparks.ca/explore/parkpgs/golden_ears/
Trail Map: Golden Ears Map by Canadian Map Makers
NTS Map: 092G08

FRASER VALLEY AND FRASER CANYON

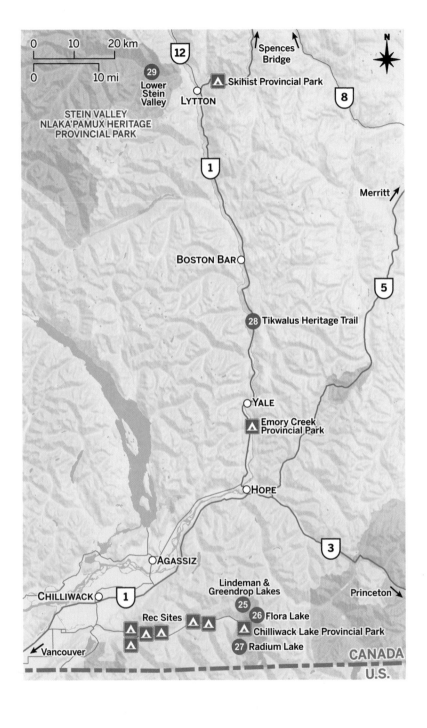

THE FRASER RIVER is the lifeblood of British Columbia, draining most of the southern part of the province. The Fraser Canyon is a tight gorge with mountains rising almost directly out of the river between Hope and Lytton. Hike in the footsteps of Indigenous travellers and historical fur traders high above the canyon on the Tikwalus Heritage Trail or in the nearby Stein River watershed, a tributary of the Fraser. Highway 1 parallels the Fraser River through the canyon, providing easy access.

West of Hope, the canyon opens up into the wide Fraser Valley, bordered on both sides by mountains. The Chilliwack River flows into the Fraser from the southeast. Here, sinuous trails follow rushing creeks upstream to mountain lakes, and sometimes beyond to peaks with impressive views. Getting there is simple thanks to a paved road along the length of the Chilliwack River valley.

The Fraser Valley is farther from the ocean than Metro Vancouver, so it can be a little bit colder and drier in the winter and warmer in the summer. However, as you travel north up the Fraser Canyon, the climate shifts to a drier Interior climate and the vegetation changes from lush coastal temperate rainforest to dry and open ponderosa pine forests. The climatic shift is complete by the time you reach Lytton, which often sets records for the hottest temperatures in BC in mid-summer.

The Fraser Valley and lower Fraser Canyon are the traditional territories of the S'ólh Téméxw (Stó:lō) and Nłeʔkepmx Tmíxʷ (Nlaka'pamux) peoples. The Nlaka'pamux also have traditional territory in the upper Fraser Canyon. The Stó:lō, like the other Indigenous groups near the ocean in southwestern BC, speak a Coast Salish language. But the Nlaka'pamux speak an Interior Salish language more closely related to other interior Indigenous groups than to their Stó:lō neighbours.

Supplies: The central Fraser Valley has lots of grocery stores, gas stations, and outdoor shops. However, there are no stores or gas stations in the Chilliwack River valley, so stock up before you make the drive. If you're headed to the Fraser Canyon, stop in Hope for groceries, gas, or outdoor supplies. Yale, Boston Bar, and Lytton have gas stations and small stores.

Accommodations: There are hotels in Chilliwack, Hope, and Lytton. In the Chilliwack River valley, you can reserve a site at Chilliwack Lake Provincial Park or choose from several first-come, first-served forest recreation campgrounds along the Chilliwack River: Tamihi Creek, Tamihi Rapids, Allison Pool, Thurston Meadows, Camp Foley, and Riverside. In the Fraser Canyon, camp at the first-come, first-served campsites at Emory Creek or Skihist Provincial Parks.

25
LINDEMAN AND GREENDROP LAKES

Difficulty: ●/■
Duration: 2 days
Distance: 3.4 to 11 km (2.1 to 6.8 mi)

Elevation Gain: 200 to 350 m
(656 to 1148 ft)
High Point: 990 m (3248 ft)
Best Months: May to October

Fees and Reservations: Camping fees are $5/person/night, payable online. All campsites are first-come, first-served.

Regulations: No fires. No drones. No smoking, vaping, or cannabis. Dogs permitted on leash only.

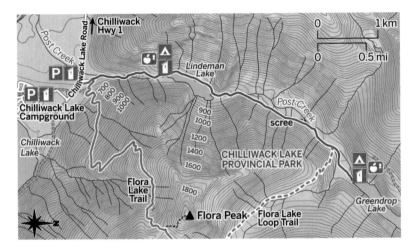

THE SHORT HIKE to photogenic Lindeman Lake in Chilliwack Lake Provincial Park is steep enough to offer a bit of a challenge but still easy enough for beginners and kids. This brilliant turquoise lake sits below a slope of rocky pinnacles and has a popular campground. Laze in the sun on the huge boulders that surround the lake or bring your rod and cast for trout. Hardier hikers can continue to Greendrop Lake to enjoy a bit of solitude away from the day-hiker crowds. The trail to get there isn't long or steep, but several boulder fields en route make for tricky footing and slow travel. Relax at the lakeshore and enjoy the views of the nearby waterfall across the lake.

GETTING THERE
In Chilliwack, head south on Vedder Road. Five kilometres (3.1 mi) from Highway 1, just before a bridge, go left at the roundabout onto Chilliwack

The blue waters of Lindeman Lake from the lake's north end.

Lake Road. Follow it for 36.5 km (22.7 mi), then turn left into a large parking lot. There's an outhouse here. Unfortunately, break-ins are common, so don't leave any valuables in your vehicle. If you're concerned about security, leave your car in the day-use area next to the campground in Chilliwack Provincial Park, 1 km (0.6 mi) away.

TRAIL

TRIP PLANNER

0 km (0 mi)	Trailhead
0.1 km (0.1 mi)	Junction with Flora Lake Trail (see Trip 26)
1.7 km (1.1 mi)	Lindeman Lake campground
2.8 km (1.7 mi)	North end of Lindeman Lake
5.5 km (3.4 mi)	Junction with Flora Lake Loop Trail (5 km/3.1 mi to lake)
6.5 km (4 mi)	Greendrop Lake campground

The trailhead is at the north end of the parking lot near an outhouse. The trail begins on an old gravel road. Reach a **junction** within the first few minutes. Your route to Lindeman and Greendrop Lakes continues straight ahead, while the trail to Flora Lake branches right.

Shortly after the junction, the old road ends and the trail begins to climb steeply beside Post Creek. The footbed is technical, with lots of rocks to clamber over. About 1 km (0.6 mi) from the trailhead, cross the creek on a large new bridge. It replaces an older log crossing that was daunting for some hikers. The trail continues climbing and is very steep in some places. As the grade eases, you'll start to see the lake through the trees. The trail arrives at the lake outlet 1.7 km (1.1 mi) from the parking lot and 200 m (656 ft) higher. You've reached the **Lindeman Lake campground**. The beautiful blue-green waters are named after Charles Lindeman, a reclusive trapper and prospector who lived on the shores of Chilliwack Lake in the 1920s when the only access to the area was on foot.

Past the campground, the trail works its way around the west side of Lindeman Lake through a boulder field. The footing can be tricky here, as well as in many sections on the way to Greendrop Lake. As you traverse around the lake, be sure to pause to admire the views of the rocky pinnacles, nicknamed The Gargoyles, on Flora Ridge across the lake. If you brought your fishing rod, the large boulders along the lake are a great place to cast for rainbow trout. The lake was stocked several decades ago.

Past the end of Lindeman Lake, the rocks continue through a section that can be wet in early season when Post Creek jumps its banks. The trail between Lindeman and Greendrop Lakes has been rerouted several times to cope with periodic flooding. Watch for trail markers to stay on track.

The trail alternates between forest and challenging scree slopes as you gain 150 m (492 ft) between the lakes. The steep slopes of Flora Ridge to the east and Goat Mountain to the west tower above the trail. Each winter avalanches crash down towards the trail, scouring the hills bare. Ice freezing in cracks in the rock high on the peaks expands, fracturing it into smaller chunks that also plummet towards the valley, forming the rockslides you will traverse in this section. You'll also cross branches of Post Creek on newer bridges.

About 5.5 km (3.4 mi) from the trailhead, arrive at a **junction** where the Flora Lake Trail comes in from the right. Continue straight for another kilometre (0.6 mi) to the **Greendrop Lake campground** on the brushy shores of the lake. While the scenery at Greendrop is not quite as postcard perfect as at Lindeman, the shallower water is a bit warmer and makes for better swimming. Greendrop also has an impressive waterfall, which is best viewed from the southeast corner of the lake. If you packed in gear, fishing for rainbow trout is a great way to while away the afternoon.

NATURE NOTE

Watch for patches of bright purple Davidson's penstemon clinging to clumps of soil on the talus slopes near Lindeman Lake. These wildflowers grow only in rocky soils in areas with winter snow cover. Hummingbirds love their nectar and if you are lucky, you may see some.

CAMPING

LINDEMAN LAKE CAMPGROUND
The very popular Lindeman Lake campground is set into a steep slope beside the lake. Arrive early to secure a spot.

Campsites: 6 wooden tent platforms and some cleared, very sloped spots on the ground
Toilet: New urine-diversion outhouse
Water: Collect from the lake or lake outlet stream.
Food Storage: On food-hanging wires near the tent pads
Other Amenities: A large wooden helicopter landing pad near the lake is a great place to hang out, but please don't camp on it.

GREENDROP LAKE CAMPGROUND
The main camping area is on the east side of the trail at the south end of the lake. The lakeshore itself is very brushy and prone to flooding, so the campsites are set back from the lake a bit.

Campsites: 6 compacted-dirt tent platforms near the lake, including one on the east side of the lake with a great view. The nearby open forest to the south has space for a dozen tents.
Toilet: Throne-style pit toilet south of the lake and east of the trail with very little privacy
Water: Collect from the lake.
Food Storage: In a metal food locker

EXTENDING YOUR TRIP
Flora Lake Loop: Experienced and fit hikers who are up for some bushwhacking can take on the Flora Lake Loop, combining the trip to Greendrop Lake with Flora Lake (Trip 26). Plan to spend two nights on the trail and hike the loop in a counterclockwise direction. The connector trail between Flora Lake camp and the Lindeman-Greendrop Trail is 5 km (3.1 mi) long and drops 420 m (1378 ft). It is very rough with many boulder sections and can be overgrown.

FURTHER RESOURCES
Chilliwack Lake Provincial Park: info and fees http://bcparks.ca/explore/parkpgs/chilliwack_lk/
Trail Map: Chilliwack East Map by Trail Ventures BC
NTS Map: 092H03

26
FLORA LAKE

Difficulty: ◆

Duration: 2 days

Distance: 14 km (8.7 mi)

Elevation Gain: 1060 m (3478 ft)

High Point: 1740 m (5709 ft)

Best Months: Mid-July to September

Fees and Reservations: Camping fees are $5/person/night, payable online. All campsites are first-come, first-served.

Regulations: No fires. No drones. No smoking, vaping, or cannabis. Dogs permitted on leash only.

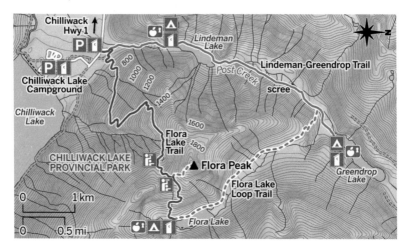

FLORA LAKE DOESN'T attract crowds like nearby Lindeman Lake (Trip 25), likely because this steep hike is uphill both ways. You'll gain over 1000 m (3281 ft) on the climb to Flora Pass, then drop down to your campsite on the tranquil shores of Flora Lake. And the return trip to your car involves nearly 400 m (1312 ft) of elevation gain back to the pass. But the effort is well worth the quiet, the incredible views down to Chilliwack Lake, and the wildflowers in the subalpine meadows at Flora Pass. Relax and enjoy the views from your lakeside campsite, try your hand at fishing, or plunge into the frigid waters on a hot day.

GETTING THERE

In Chilliwack, head south on Vedder Road. Five kilometres (3.1 mi) from Highway 1, just before a bridge, go left at the roundabout onto Chilliwack Lake Road. Follow it for 36.5 km (22.7 mi), then turn left into a large parking

The view of Chilliwack Lake from Flora Pass.

lot. There's an outhouse here. Unfortunately, break-ins are common, so don't leave any valuables in your vehicle. If you're concerned about security, leave your car in the day-use area next to the campground in Chilliwack Provincial Park, 1 km (0.6 mi) away.

TRAIL

TRIP PLANNER

0 km (0 mi)	Trailhead
0.1 km (0.1 mi)	Junction with Lindeman-Greendrop Lake Trail (see Trip 25)
2.5 km (1.6 mi)	Viewpoint
4 km (2.5 mi)	Avalanche path
6 km (3.7 mi)	Flora Pass and junction with Flora Peak Trail (0.6 km/0.4 mi to peak)
7 km (4.3 mi)	Flora Lake campground
12 km (7.5 mi)	Junction with Lindeman-Greendrop Trail (see Trip 25)

The trailhead is at the north end of the parking lot near an information board and outhouse. Walk a few minutes on an old gravel road to a **junction**. Turn right to head to Flora Lake. The trail to Lindeman and Greendrop Lakes (Trip 25) goes straight ahead. After the junction, the trail follows an old mossy road network for a few minutes before transitioning to single track and beginning to climb steeply in a wet forest of western hemlock trees cloaked in old man's beard and witch's hair lichens. The next few kilometres are a steady uphill climb with a couple of switchbacks. You'll cross a few small creeks along the way, which may be dry later in the year. This is the only opportunity to get water until close to Flora Lake.

After 2.5 km (1.6 mi), reach a **viewpoint** at the end of a switchback. This is your first view down to Chilliwack Lake and the mountains to the south. Take a break here to gather your strength. You've already ascended 465 m (1526 ft).

Continue steeply uphill from the viewpoint through more switchbacks. Around the 4-km (2.5-mi) mark, the switchbacks end and the trail starts making a rising traverse to the northeast across the slope. You'll break out of the trees into an open **avalanche path** with amazing views of Chilliwack Lake. Snow slides scour this hillside every winter, stripping it of trees. The trail is cut into the side of the steep hillside and drops off sharply in some places. Use caution if snow is still present since a slip could be fatal.

The grade eases a little through a flat section before getting a bit steeper a kilometre (0.6 mi) later as the trail goes back into the forest. Continue climbing through patches of mountain hemlock and more open subalpine meadows. Watch for wildflowers near the pass in mid-summer, especially pink mountain heather, yellow arnica, and the tall stalks of white Sitka valerian.

Reach **Flora Pass**, the most beautiful spot on the trail. Look down to Flora Lake below you and south to Chilliwack Lake. A faint spur trail leads across the ridge to the south to an even better viewpoint. **Flora Peak** towers above you to the north and an unmarked side trail leads to the summit from here.

When you've finished soaking up the views, follow the trail as it leaves the meadow and plunges a staggering 370 m (1214 ft) through the trees to

NATURE NOTE

From Flora Pass you'll have a great view of Chilliwack Lake and the surrounding mountains. Chilliwack comes from the word Tcil'Qe'uk in the Halkomelem language of the Coast Salish people and translates as "valley of many streams" or "head of the valley." Before European settlers arrived, a string of nine Stó:lō village sites stretched the length of the Chilliwack River, connected by a trail from the Fraser River in the northwest to Chilliwack Lake in the southeast. The Chilliwack River watershed encompasses about 1230 km² (475 mi²) of steep mountain peaks stretching from northern Washington to the Fraser Valley. Looking south from Flora Pass, gaze down the length of Chilliwack to the river's headwaters in Washington's North Cascades National Park.

Flora Lake in the next 1 km (0.6 mi). About halfway down, the trail briefly flattens out as it traverses to the south to cross a creek and avalanche chute, then continues relentlessly downhill again. Near the bottom, the trail swings north to cross a creek before arriving at the shores of Flora Lake and the **campground**. Across the lake, scree slopes tumble down into the water from Mount Wittenberg.

Although the lake has not been stocked recently, it is home to a thriving population of cutthroat and rainbow trout. They are easy to spot in the crystal-clear waters. The rocks along the shoreline make a good fishing spot. Brave swimmers may wish to jump into the cold water here too.

CAMPING

The small campground at Flora Lake is set amongst some trees at the southwest corner of the lake. Although it is not usually busy, plan to arrive early to ensure you get a campsite.

Campsites: 3 wooden tent pads
Toilet: Throne-style pit toilet in the trees nearby
Water: Collect from the lake or a nearby stream flowing into the lake.
Food Storage: In a metal food locker

EXTENDING YOUR TRIP

Flora Peak: Make a side trip on the unmarked and sometimes faint trail north from Flora Pass to the top of 1953-m-tall (6407 ft) Flora Peak. The steep trail gains 215 m (705 ft) as it climbs upwards through meadows and rocks to the summit, 0.66 km (0.4 mi) from the pass.

Flora Lake Loop: Experienced and fit hikers who are up for some bushwhacking can take on the Flora Lake Loop, combining this trip with one to Greendrop and Lindeman Lakes (Trip 25). Plan to spend two nights on the trail and hike the loop in a counterclockwise direction. The connector trail between Flora Lake camp and the Lindeman-Greendrop Trail is 5 km (3.1 mi) long and drops 420 m (1378 ft). It is very rough with many boulder sections and can be overgrown.

FURTHER RESOURCES

Chilliwack Lake Provincial Park: info and fees http://bcparks.ca/explore/parkpgs/chilliwack_lk/
Trail Map: Chilliwack East Map by Trail Ventures BC
NTS Map: 092H03

Difficulty: ◆

Duration: 2 to 3 days

Distance: 19 km (11.8 mi)

Elevation Gain: 900 m (2953 ft)

High Point: 1515 m (4970 ft)

Best Months: July to September

Fees and Reservations: Camping fees are $5/person/night, payable online. All campsites are first-come, first-served.

Regulations: No fires. No drones. No smoking, vaping, or cannabis. Dogs permitted on leash only.

Caution: Mosquitos can be a problem here, so pack repellent or a head net.

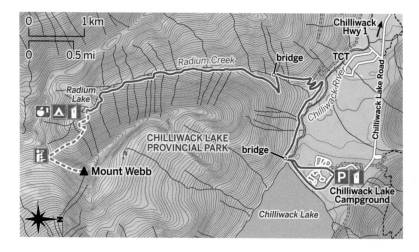

THE HIKE TO Radium Lake climbs beside a creek through a beautiful and verdant temperate rainforest in Chilliwack Lake Provincial Park. While you'll gain a lot of elevation, the path is usually not too steep. The lake itself is a bit underwhelming: a marsh-edged pond set in a rocky bowl. But the real reason to hike here sits just above the lake. Drop your pack at the campground and follow a flagged route high into the alpine. You can summit Mount Webb or just gaze down at the incredible views of the Chilliwack Lake area.

GETTING THERE

In Chilliwack, head south on Vedder Road. Five kilometres (3.1 mi) from Highway 1, just before a bridge, go left at the roundabout onto Chilliwack Lake Road. Follow it for 40 km (24.9 mi), then turn right into Chilliwack

The campground at Radium Lake.

Lake Provincial Park just before the road turns to gravel. Drive past the gate-house and campground, and park in the day-use area. There are outhouses here.

TRAIL

From the parking area, follow the shoreline trail or the Trans Canada Trail through the campground for 1 km (0.6 mi). The two trails converge at a **bridge** over the outlet of Chilliwack Lake. Pause to enjoy the view down the length of Chilliwack Lake. Across the bridge, follow an old roadbed downstream on the banks of the Chilliwack River. This short section of your route is shared with the Trans Canada Trail, also known as the Great Trail. It's a 24,000-km (14,913-mi) walking and cycling route that stretches across Canada from the Pacific to the Atlantic and up to the Arctic.

About 2.75 km (1.7 mi) from the trailhead, go left at a **junction** and uphill on a few switchbacks. Reach another **junction** 0.6 km (0.4 mi) later. Your route to Radium Lake heads uphill to the left. The Trans Canada Trail continues to the right, heading west along the Chilliwack River. Climb upwards through lush western hemlock forest, first on the remains of an old logging road, then on a single-track trail. The fronds of huge sword ferns drape across the path and devil's club, huckleberry, and salmonberry bushes crowd between the trees.

Reach a **suspension bridge** over Radium Creek. About 1.5 km (0.9 mi) later, descend to Radium Creek again and cross to the other side on a **log bridge**. A clearing here makes a great place to take a break. Just 0.5 km (0.3 mi) later, recross the creek on another **bridge**. There's a picturesque small waterfall just upstream here. Keep slogging uphill. The forest opens up a few minutes later as you cross a few brushy sections at the bottom of avalanche slide paths. If you're wearing shorts, watch for stinging nettles and devil's club.

Continue hiking steadily uphill through lush forest. Cross a small wet meadow, then arrive on the eastern shore of **Radium Lake**. The lake doesn't contain radium and isn't radioactive. Instead, the green waters of the lake reminded the first settlers of the green glow emitted from the luminous (and dangerous) radium paint used on watch dials in the early 20th century.

CAMPING

The small campsite at Radium Lake sits in a slightly sloping open forest. Several informal spur trails give access to the marshy lake edge. The crumbling remains of an old Forest Service log cabin sit nearby.

Campsites: 2 wooden tent platforms, 1 nice flat tent spot, and space to squeeze a few more tents in on sloping ground

NATURE NOTE

Stiff hairs along the leaves and stems of stinging nettles cause itching, blistering, and stinging if you touch them. Some Coast Salish First Nations gathered the shoots in the spring, then boiled and ate them like spinach. Thankfully, cooking neutralizes the stinging properties. Nettles are a popular wild food in BC's foraging community. There is even an annual Nettlefest on Galiano Island.

Crossing Radium Creek.

Toilet: Throne-style pit toilet uphill of the campsite on a short spur trail
Water: Collect from the lake.
Food Storage: In a metal food locker behind the campsite

EXTENDING YOUR TRIP

Mount Webb: From the campground, follow a flagged trail uphill in the trees. Arrive at the open col between Mount Webb and Macdonald Peak after gaining about 400 m (1312 ft) of elevation. The views down to Chilliwack Lake and back to your camp at Radium Lake are incredible from here, and you may wish to make this your turnaround point. To reach the 2159-m (7083-ft) summit of Mount Webb and even better views of Paleface Mountain, Mount Meroniuk, and a sea of additional peaks across Chilliwack Lake, turn left and scramble up the ridge for 0.7 km (0.4 mi), gaining another 250 m (820 ft) of elevation. It's quite steep and loose in places with no formal trail, so this route is best for experienced hikers.

FURTHER RESOURCES

Chilliwack Lake Provincial Park: info and fees http://bcparks.ca/explore/parkpgs/chilliwack_lk/
Trail Map: Chilliwack East Map by Trail Ventures BC
NTS Map: 092H03

28
TIKWALUS HERITAGE TRAIL

Difficulty: ◆

Duration: 2 days

Distance: 13 km (8.1 mi)

Elevation Gain: 790 m (2592 ft)

High Point: 910 m (2986 ft)

Best Months: May to October

Fees and Reservations: Camping is free and all campsites are first-come, first-served.

Regulations: Dogs permitted.

Caution: Ticks are common here, especially in the spring and early summer.

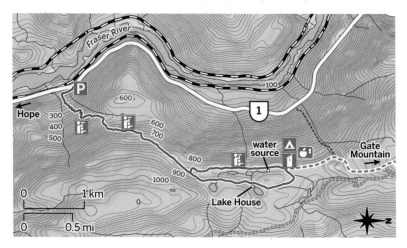

FOLLOW AN OLD Nlaka'pamux path turned fur-trading route high into the mountains above the Fraser Canyon. In the late 1840s, Nlaka'pamux guides led early traders from the Hudson's Bay Company and their horses along this trail to bypass the dangerous Hells Canyon portion of the Fraser River and cross the Cascade Mountains to Fort Kamloops. Recently, volunteers from the Hope Mountain Centre for Outdoor Learning and the Spuzzum First Nation have restored and renamed the old First Brigade Trail. The trail is now named for a former Nlaka'pamux village near the trailhead, and information signs along the route help explain First Nations and settler history. Camp up near the summit of Lake Mountain to enjoy beautiful views of the Fraser Canyon.

GETTING THERE
From Hope, head north on Highway 1 through the Fraser Canyon past Yale. About 2 km (1.2 mi) after the highway crosses the bridge from the west to

The view down to the Fraser Canyon from near the campground.

the east bank of the Fraser River, look for a pullout and parking area on the right-hand side. It has a large signboard with information about the trail and the history of the region.

TRAIL

BLUFFS ROUTE

TRIP PLANNER

0 km (0 mi)	Trailhead
1.2 km (0.7 mi)	A.C. Anderson Viewpoint
2.8 km (1.7 mi)	Chief Pahallak Viewpoint
4.2 km (2.6 mi)	Junction with Lakes Route Trail
5.2 km (3.2 mi)	Black Canyon Viewpoint
5.5 km (3.4 mi)	Junction with water access trail
6.2 km (3.9 mi)	Campground

From the trailhead next to the information sign, the trail climbs briefly away from the road before flattening out as it heads south and crosses a creek on a beautiful new bridge. This is likely the only water source you'll see for most of the hike. Shortly after the bridge, the trail bends left and begins a long and steep ascent with many switchbacks. You'll gain 600 m (1969 ft) in 3 km (1.9 mi). Pause to catch your breath at the A.C. Anderson and Chief Pahallak Viewpoints on the way up. They both have interpretive panels with great information on the First Nations and fur-trade history of the trail. Peer through the trees to the Fraser River far below you, with cars and trains threading their way along either side of the rushing waters.

Around the 4-km (2.5-mi) mark, the trail starts to flatten out as you pass through a grove of culturally modified cedar trees. First Nations people harvested cedar bark to roof lodges or weave into baskets and hats. By taking only a strip of bark from each tree, the cedar continues to grow even though its missing bark will never regenerate. Reach a **junction** at 4.2 km (2.6 mi). Left is the 2-km-long (1.2 mi) Bluffs Route and right is the 2.5-km-long (1.6 mi) Lakes Route. They meet again at the campsite.

The Bluffs Route follows the edge of a ridge high above the Fraser Canyon through terrain that is more open thanks to a forest fire that swept through the area several years ago. Look for the round, drooping blooms of yellow tiger lily, also called Columbia lily. Take a break at the **Black Canyon Viewpoint** about halfway along to enjoy the spectacular view over the roiling waters below.

A few minutes after the viewpoint, look for a trail heading off to the right in the trees. It leads down to a **small lake where you can get water**. From the water-access trail, it's another 0.5 km (0.3 mi) to the **campsite**. The Bluffs Route is shorter than the Lakes Route, but it has many small ups and downs that can make it feel a bit more challenging.

LAKES ROUTE

TRIP PLANNER

0 km (0 mi)	Trailhead
1.2 km (0.7 mi)	A.C. Anderson Viewpoint
2.8 km (1.7 mi)	Chief Pahallak Viewpoint
4.2 km (2.6 mi)	Junction with Bluffs Route Trail
5.5 km (3.4 mi)	Lake House site
6.7 km (4.2 mi)	Campground

NATURE NOTE

Watch for brightly coloured western tanagers in the open forest along the Bluffs Route. These insect-eating birds are slightly smaller than a robin. With their yellow body, black wings, and red head, you might mistake them for a tropical species, but the western tanager is most at home in coniferous forests from California to the Yukon.

From the junction, the Lakes Route continues climbing slightly to the trail's high point at 910 m (2986 ft). The trail passes between several lakes, each just out of view in the trees. Be sure to stop to read the interpretive sign at the site of the fur trade–era **Lake House site**. Between 1859 and 1860, a one-room wooden cabin provided meals and bunkbed accommodation for travellers here until a judge ordered it burned down for illegally serving liquor.

A few minutes past the Lake House site, reach a grove of small yew trees. First Nations people carved the durable wood of the yew into many useful tools, including bows, spears, sewing needles, frames for fishing dip-nets, and spoons. The **campground** is about 0.5 km (0.3 mi) past the yew grove.

CAMPING

The well-designed campsite is on a flattish bluff in an area of open forest. Informal trails lead to excellent viewpoints over the Fraser Canyon far below.

Campsites: Cleared spots to fit at least 10 tents
Toilet: Outhouse near the fire ring
Water: Collect from the lake on the Bluffs Route about 0.5 km (0.3 mi) away from the campsite.
Food Storage: In a metal food locker
Other Amenities: A picnic table, a large fire ring with benches, and a sign-board with historical information about the trail

EXTENDING YOUR TRIP

Gate Mountain: A rough trail continues north past the campground along the historic fur-trade route. However, it's not as well signed or maintained as the Tikwalus Heritage Trail. Follow the trail for 0.5 km (0.3 mi) to reach a viewpoint. At the 1-km (0.6-mi) mark, you'll reach a junction. Left descends steeply to Highway 1 on the 17 Mile Creek Mule Trail. The trail to the right leads to Gate Mountain, a hike of roughly 6 km (3.7 mi) one way with 600 m (1969 ft) of elevation gain.

FURTHER RESOURCES

Hope Mountain Centre for Outdoor Learning: info and maps http://hopemountain.org/trails/tikwalus-heritage-trail/
NTS Map: 092H11

29
LOWER STEIN VALLEY

Difficulty: ●
Duration: 2 days
Distance: 4 to 26 km (2.5 to 16.2 mi)

Elevation Gain: 30 to 350 m
(98 to 1148 ft)
High Point: 600 m (1969 ft)
Best Months: April to October

Fees and Reservations: Camping is free and all campsites are first-come, first-served.

Regulations: No fires. Dogs permitted on leash but not recommended. No drones. No smoking, vaping, or cannabis.

Caution: Ticks are common here, especially in the spring. The local black bear and grizzly bear population is high, so use caution. Temperatures around 40°C (104°F) are common in summer. Hike early in the day and drink lots of water.

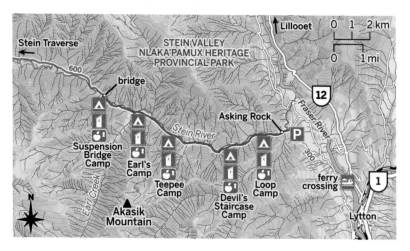

THE STEIN VALLEY is a special place. Known to the Nlaka'pamux people as Stagyn, which means "hidden place," the valley is their spiritual home and has some important First Nations pictographs and culturally modified trees. It's also southern BC's only intact watershed, and after years of community protest it was finally protected from logging in the 1980s. Today, the Stein Valley Nlaka'pamux Heritage Park attracts visitors most of the year. The dry ponderosa pine forest in the eastern part of the park sees little snow but gets fiery hot in the middle of summer. It's a great spring and fall option for all backpackers. And the flat and easy low-elevation trails in this section make this trip especially good for beginners and kids.

Looking upriver from near Earl's Cabin Camp.

GETTING THERE

From Hope, follow Highway 1 through the Fraser Canyon to Lytton. In Lytton, turn left onto Highway 12 and follow it across the bridge. Make the first left onto Lytton Ferry Road. Take the reaction ferry over the Fraser River and follow the signs for the Stein Valley for about 5 km (3.1 mi) on gravel roads through the Lytton First Nation reserve. The last kilometre (0.6 mi) is bumpy, but it's fine for 2WD vehicles. There's a large parking lot with picnic tables, a shelter, and an outhouse at the trailhead. Note: the reaction ferry doesn't run at times of very high river volume, which usually happens in late May.

TRAIL

TRIP PLANNER

0 km (0 mi)	Trailhead
0.3 km (0.2 mi)	Asking Rock
2 km (1.2 mi)	Loop Camp
4 km (2.5 mi)	Devil's Staircase Camp
8 km (5 mi)	Teepee Camp
10.5 km (6.5 mi)	Earl's Cabin Camp
13 km (8.1 mi)	Suspension Bridge Camp

The trail begins with a short descent from the parking lot to river level. Within a few minutes, you'll cross a long wooden bridge and arrive at a prominent rock outcropping. This is **Asking Rock**, an important spiritual place for the Nlaka'pamux people. They ask the spirits for permission to enter the sacred Stein Valley and leave offerings in hope of ensuring safe passage.

Past the Asking Rock, stroll along the flat trail and pass over a flat rock slab at the river's edge. Soon you'll reach **Loop Camp**, the first campsite on the trail. The trail continues along the flat benches of the old river bed, a bit higher than the current level. Look carefully at the trees as you walk. The jigsaw-puzzle shape of the thick ponderosa pine bark is designed to resist fire, a helpful attribute in this hot and dry climate.

About 4 km (2.5 mi) from the trailhead, watch for the turnoff to **Devil's Staircase Camp**. The main trail climbs to the left, switchbacking upwards on the Devil's Staircase, the biggest ascent in the Lower Stein. At the top of the switchbacks, cross a few talus fields and then follow the narrow trail as it traverses bluffs high above the river. Eventually, the trail descends steeply on tight switchbacks.

The next few kilometres of trail stay relatively close to river level. You will pass through stands of black cottonwood, aspen, and birch, which thrive in the wet environment of the floodplain. After crossing a small talus field, arrive at **Teepee Camp**. Past the campground, the trail follows a river bench again before plunging into a beautiful and shady cedar grove at Teaspoon Creek. Next, reach **Earl's Cabin Camp** beside the remains of a log cabin. Fred Earl, who lived in Lytton, trapped and prospected in the area in the early 20th century and built this cabin.

Past Earl's Cabin, cross the narrow bridge over Earl Creek and follow the trail back towards the river. The next section of trail is fairly flat until you reach a point where the rock bluffs nearly reach the river. Cross a small rock field, then head into the forest before you emerge into a clearing at **Suspension Bridge Camp**. A trail heads directly to the bridge from the middle of the campsite.

CAMPING

There are five campgrounds to choose from in the Lower Stein Valley spaced at regular intervals to suit backpackers of various abilities.

LOOP CAMP

Also called Easy Camp, Loop Camp is in a broad clearing on the riverbank.

Campsites: Space for 6 to 8 tents
Toilet: Outhouse on the main trail
Water: Collect from the river.
Food Storage: In a large metal food locker

DEVIL'S STAIRCASE CAMP

Located at the base of Devil's Staircase, this campground is nestled amongst large trees and huge boulders. It's a shady spot that is a bit chilly in spring and fall, but nice and cool on hot summer days.

Campsites: Space for 6 to 8 tents
Toilet: Outhouse towards the back of the campground
Water: Collect from the river.
Food Storage: In a large metal food locker

TEEPEE CAMP

Named for a teepee that once stood here, Teepee Camp is the largest and most popular campground in the Lower Stein Valley.

Campsites: Space for 10 to 12 tents. The prime spots are on a flat, grassy area above the water.
Toilet: Outhouse located inland from the campsite on a short and rocky spur trail
Water: Collect from the river.
Food Storage: In a large metal food locker

EARL'S CABIN CAMP

The centrepiece is the remains of Earl's Cabin. Just past the cabin, a clearing is a great place to watch for mountain goats on the cliffs across the river.

Campsites: 5 or 6 tent sites around the cabin, all very close to the trail or in dense forest
Toilet: Outhouse located behind the cabin
Water: Collect from the river.
Food Storage: In a large metal food locker

INDIGENOUS KNOWLEDGE

With dozens of rock-art sites throughout the park, the Stein River watershed has one of Canada's largest concentrations of pictographs. The Nlaka'pamux people created these rock paintings as part of spiritual rituals or to record history in the pre-contact era, making them hundreds of years old. If you look carefully as you hike, you may spot some along the trail, often where the river runs close to large cliffs or boulders, causing the sound of the river to reverberate. If you visit these places during the spring flood and feel the roar of the river rumble in your chest, you may understand why they hold so much power. The pictographs are made from a mixture of rock dust, red ochre clay, tree sap, and water that is very vulnerable to damage. Please do not touch them as the oils from your hands will degrade the paint.

Crossing a rockslide on the Devil's Staircase.

SUSPENSION BRIDGE CAMP

This campground is set amongst the trees on a gentle slope near the bridge.

Campsites: 6 tents, most on slightly sloping sites
Toilet: Outhouse on the far side of the campground
Water: Collect from the river.
Food Storage: In a large metal food locker

EXTENDING YOUR TRIP

Stein Valley Trail: If you have extra time in the Lower Stein Valley, day hike upstream as far as you like before turning back towards the trailhead. The lower valley up to the suspension bridge is the most scenic, but the mid-valley does have some lightly used campsites in forested terrain. If you're up for an epic adventure, tackle the entire 75-km-long (46.6 mi) Stein Traverse, which leads from the mouth of the Stein to the headwaters, and then over the divide towards Lizzie Lake and the shores of Lillooet Lake.

FURTHER RESOURCES

Stein Valley Nlaka'pamux Heritage Park: info http://bcparks.ca/explore/parkpgs/stein_val/
Lytton Reaction Ferry: info http://www.drivebc.com/
Trail Map: Stein to Joffre Trail Map by Trail Ventures BC
NTS Map: 092I05

COQUIHALLA

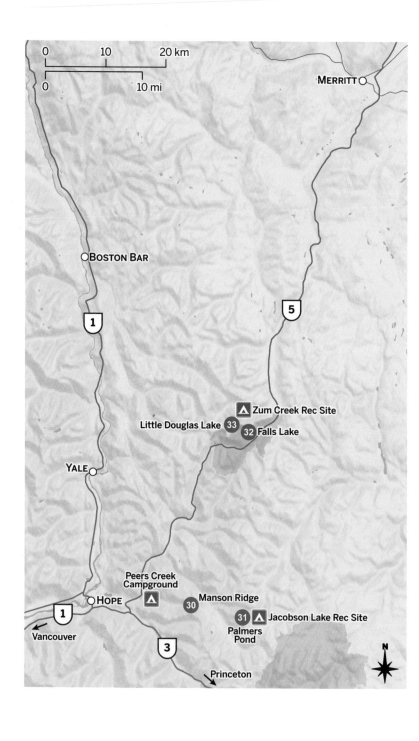

WHILE MOST VISITORS to the Coquihalla region speed through on the busy highway that links Hope with Merritt, backpackers who linger can explore the region's wilderness treasures. Gaze up at granite peaks polished smooth by glaciers, from lakeside campgrounds near Coquihalla Pass. Or venture south of the highway into the mountainous headwaters of the Tulameen River. The historic fur trade–era Hudson's Bay Company Heritage Trail (HBC Heritage Trail) runs through this area from near Hope in the west to Tulameen in the east. This book includes two of the most scenic and easily accessible sections of the trail that take you through lush forest, to mountaintop vistas, and into wildflower meadows in the heart of endangered grizzly bear habitat.

The area around Coquihalla Pass is characterized by mountains with craggy, exposed granite peaks, the product of millennia of glaciation. The region gets lots of snow in the winter and wildly changeable weather year-round. It sits at the apex of the Cascade Mountains, so clouds moving in from the Pacific Coast push up against the mountain range, dumping lots of precipitation. The west side of Coquihalla Pass has typical temperate forest vegetation, but the east side gradually transitions into a drier Interior forest.

The west side of Coquihalla Pass is the traditional territory of the Nłeʔkepmx Tmíxʷ (Nlaka'pamux) and S'ólh Téméxw (Stó:lō) peoples. Nlaka'pamux traditional territory continues on the east side of the pass, which they share with the Syilx tmixʷ (Okanagan) people. The Coquihalla River and Highway take their name from Kw'ikw'iya:la in the Halq'emeylem language of the Stó:lō. The name referred to a rock near the mouth of what is now the Coquihalla River that was a favourite place for Stó:lō people to spear salmon.

Supplies: No shops or services are available on the Coquihalla, so stop in Hope or Merritt for groceries, gas, or outdoor gear.

Accommodations: If you want to stay in a hotel, book one in Hope or Merritt. Camping is also limited: small campgrounds are found near a few trailheads. If you're heading to Manson Ridge, camp at the small site at the Peers Creek trailhead. The Jacobson Lake Rec Site is next to the trailhead for Palmers Pond. And the Zum Creek Rec Site is at the trailhead for Little Douglas Lake.

30
MANSON RIDGE

Difficulty: ● to ◆
Duration: 2 to 3 days
Distance: 12 to 15.5 km (7.5 to 9.6 mi)

Elevation Gain: 200 to 600 m
(656 to 1969 ft)
High Point: 950 m (3117 ft)
Best Months: June to October

Fees and Reservations: Camping is free and all campsites are first-come, first-served.

Regulations: Dogs permitted.

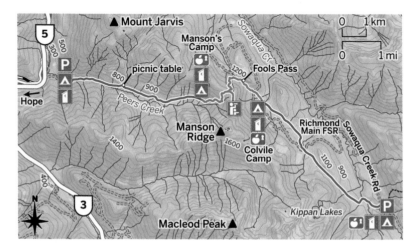

STEP BACK IN TIME and follow in the footsteps of fur traders from the 1840s and '50s. The historic Hudson's Bay Brigade Trail was part of a series of trails between Fort Langley and Fort Kamloops. After a failed attempt to navigate the bluffs above the Fraser Canyon on what is now the Tikwalus Heritage Trail (Trip 28), the Hudson's Bay Company (HBC) switched to a traditional hunting and trade route across the Cascade Divide brought to their attention by Chief Blackeye of the Similkameen First Nation. In 2016 the Hope Mountain Centre for Outdoor Learning officially reopened this historic trail as the HBC Heritage Trail. This trip takes in the first segment of that traditional path and includes impressive views from Manson Ridge.

Two routes to the top of Manson Ridge are possible: you can follow in the footsteps of the original fur traders and approach on the challenging and steep trail from Peers Creek in the west, camping at historic Manson's Camp. Or choose the easier and flatter backdoor route from Sowaqua Creek

Western columbine on the slopes of Manson Ridge.

in the east, staying overnight at Colvile Camp. From either camp, shoulder a day pack and make the stiff climb up to the top of 1450-m (4757-ft) Manson Ridge to enjoy incredible views of Mount Dewdney and the surrounding peaks. With two cars, a challenging one-way 18.75-km (11.7-mi) traverse over the summit of Manson Ridge is possible. Both options are described below.

GETTING THERE

PEERS CREEK TRAILHEAD

Take exit 183 off the Coquihalla Highway (Highway 5) just after Hope. Turn right from the off-ramp, then turn left almost immediately onto a wooden single-lane bridge over the Coquihalla River. You are now on Peers Creek Road. Stay on it for another 1.5 km (0.9 mi), ignoring any side roads as it climbs gradually. The gravel road is narrow and bumpy, but it is fine for 2WD vehicles. It ends in a large parking lot at the trailhead. There's an outhouse here as well as an information sign.

SOWAQUA CREEK TRAILHEAD

From the Coquihalla Highway (Highway 5), take exit 192. This rough gravel road has some steep sections with huge drop-offs and is prone to slides and rockfall. When it is in good condition, it is 2WD accessible with careful driving, but an AWD or 4WD vehicle is recommended. Immediately after leaving the pavement, ignore a downhill spur to the right. The first kilometre (0.6 mi) is the roughest and steepest. At the 16.25-km (10.1-mi) marker stay right. Go left at 16.7 km (10.4 mi) following a sign for Mount Davis. (The right branch is Richmond Main FSR, which will get you closer to your campsite but is suitable for high-clearance 4WD vehicles only.) Reach the parking area and campsite with information kiosk, outhouse, and bear cache at 20 km (12.4 mi). The trailhead is 75 m (246 ft) back along the road.

TRAIL

PEERS CREEK TRAIL

TRIP PLANNER

0 km (0 mi)	Peers Creek trailhead
6 km (3.7 mi)	Manson's Camp
8 km (5 mi)	Manson Ridge
9 km (5.6 mi)	Fools Pass
10.5 km (6.5 mi)	Cross logging road
11 km (6.8 mi)	Colvile Camp
18.75 km (11.7 mi)	Sowaqua Creek Camp

The original trail to Manson's Camp is on an old road used for logging in the 1960s, '70s, and '80s. As of the time of writing, the road was being reactivated so that logging can recommence. The Hope Mountain Centre plans to build a new trail in 2021. It will be located on the south side of Peers Creek and will be protected by a forested buffer. The new trail will rejoin the old trail at Manson's Camp. Until the new trail is complete in late 2021 or 2022, hikers can continue to use the logging road but should expect to encounter workers and industrial equipment.

The old trail along the road gains 600 m (1969 ft) in 6 km (3.7 mi) on its way to Manson's Camp. From the parking lot, cross a new logging road bridge over Peers Creek. The first few kilometres climb fairly steeply. Young alder and maple line the sides of the old road, taking advantage of the sunlight. Upslope, stands of tightly packed second-growth spruce, fir, and hemlock crowd together. Take care through a short section where the bluff is crumbling above the trail. About 2.5 km (1.6 mi) from the start, take a break at a picnic table beside a small creek with a rushing waterfall. Past here the trail continues climbing, but much less sharply.

About 5 km (3.1 mi) along, the grade kicks up again. In early summer, watch for columbine and other wildflowers blooming in the wet areas before you reach **Manson's Camp** and the end of the old logging road.

TRIP PLANNER

0 km (0 mi)	Sowaqua Road campground and trailhead
0.4 km (0.2 mi)	Cross Sowaqua Creek
4.5 km (2.8 mi)	Cross Richmond Main FSR
7.75 km (4.8 mi)	Colvile Camp
8.75 km (5.4 mi)	Crossing logging road
9.75 km (6.1 mi)	Fools Pass
10.75 km (6.7 mi)	Manson Ridge
12.75 km (7.9 mi)	Manson's Camp
18.75 km (11.7 mi)	Peers Creek trailhead

The trail from Sowaqua Road Camp to Colvile Camp covers 7.75 km (4.8 mi) with just 200 m (656 ft) of elevation gain, making it an easier approach to Manson Ridge than the Peers Creek route. From the parking area and campground, walk 75 m (246 ft) back along the road to the north to find the HBC Heritage Trail crossing the road. Turn left (west) and head into the trees. The forest is carpeted in trailing bunchberry, which is also known as dwarf dogwood. Like its relative the dogwood tree (BC's official provincial flower), it produces white blossoms in the spring and bright red berries in the fall.

Follow the trail downhill to cross **Sowaqua Creek**, then continue through wet coastal forest northwest through the Sowaqua valley. Western red cedar, hemlock, and amabilis fir dominate the landscape. Groves of old-growth are interspersed with younger trees, thanks to a 1930s wildfire sparked by lightning.

Your route contours the side of Mount Hatfield, crossing numerous creeks and several boggy sections. In the wet areas the coniferous forest gives way to devil's club and skunk cabbage. Watch for signs of digging and uprooted skunk cabbages along the trail. Their roots are a favourite early summer food

NATURE NOTE

The eastern slopes of Mount Davis are home to the mountain beaver. A distant relative of the North American beaver, mountain beavers are a fraction of their size, rarely weighing more than a kilogram (2.2 lbs). While they share a name and fondness for eating trees with their larger cousins, they live in complexes of burrows and tunnels in the moist forest, instead of building lodges and dams in lakes and streams. In addition to munching on branches, mountain beavers also bring ferns and leaves from young shrubs back to their burrows for snacking and to use as nesting material.

The welcoming sign at Colvile Camp. Photo: Stephen Hui

for black bears. These marshy areas used to be much wetter in the early fur-trade days, miring laden horses in the mud. Look carefully as you walk to spot historical drainage ditches constructed to improve the trail.

Cross the **Richmond Main FSR** and Richmond Creek soon after. Your trail follows a narrow buffer of older mossy forest between a patchwork of newer cutblocks. The path descends slightly to cross the south branch of Colvile Creek, and then arrives at **Colvile Camp**.

CAMPING

MANSON'S CAMP

Manson's Camp is a small site in a flat clearing on the side of a steep hillside. Traditionally, it was the first camp for fur brigades leaving Hope. The tent pads and table are set very close together. There are pleasant views of the Peers Creek valley from the camp.

Campsites: 3 small gravel tent pads
Toilet: Throne-style pit toilet slightly uphill from the campsite
Water: Collect from a seasonal creek nearby. If it's dry, continue east from camp to a side trail marked "water" and descend steeply half a kilometre (0.3 mi) to Peers Creek to fetch water.
Food Storage: In a metal food locker
Other Amenities: A fire ring, benches, a table, and a signboard with historical information

COLVILE CAMP

This campsite is nestled into a mossy old-growth forest between two branches of Colvile Creek. While the camp was not historically a stopping place on the HBC Heritage Trail, its namesake, Eden Colvile, was the governor of Rupert's Land and the Hudson's Bay Company. Colvile walked the trail and recommended many improvements that endure today, such as drainage in marshy areas and clover growing near campsites to feed the pack horses.

Campsites: 3 tent pads
Toilet: Throne-style pit toilet on a marked spur trail
Water: Collect from Colvile Creek.
Food Storage: In a metal food locker
Other Amenities: A fire ring, benches, 2 tables, and a signboard with historical information

EXTENDING YOUR TRIP

Manson Ridge: Continue along the HBC Heritage Trail from either Manson's Camp or Colvile Camp to the top of Manson Ridge. From Manson's Camp, it's a steep climb marked with 170-year-old axe blazes, gaining 500 m (1640 ft) in just 2 km (1.2 mi). As you ascend the ridge, imagine what it must have been like to walk this trail during the fur trade, laden with supplies and leading dozens of horses through steep and treacherous terrain. From Colvile Camp, you'll climb to Fools Pass, then up the east flank of Manson Ridge through groves of old-growth yellow cedar, hemlock, and fir, gaining 530 m (1739 ft) in 3 km (1.9 mi). From either approach, follow a short spur trail at the top of the ridge to the south for a few hundred metres. The views are spectacular. You can see Mount Dewdney to the southeast and Tulameen Mountain to the northeast. The HBC Heritage Trail threads in between them.

HBC Heritage Trail: This trip encompasses a small section of the much longer HBC Heritage Trail. You could walk the entire 74-km-long (46 mi) trail from Hope to Tulameen in about a week. If you don't have enough time for that, connect the hike from Peers Creek to Sowaqua Road with Trip 31 (Palmers Pond) to finish at Jacobson Lake, for a challenging 28-km (17.4-mi) one-way traverse over three days.

FURTHER RESOURCES

Hope Mountain Centre for Outdoor Learning: info http://hopemountain. org/trails/hbc-heritage-trail/
Trail Map: HBC Trail Map by Hope Mountain Centre and Clark Geomatics
NTS Map: 092H06

31
PALMERS POND

Difficulty: ●
Duration: 2 days
Distance: 6 to 12 km (3.7 to 7.5 mi)

Elevation Gain: 190 to 385 m
(623 to 1263 ft)
High Point: 1855 m (6086 ft)
Best Months: July to September

Fees and Reservations: Camping is free and all campsites are first-come, first-served.

Regulations: Dogs permitted.

Caution: This is grizzly bear habitat. Hike in groups, leash your dog, and keep a clean camp.

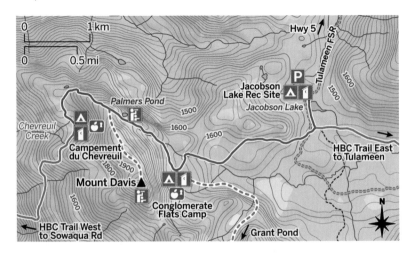

THIS BACKPACKING TRIP lets you enjoy the scenic middle section of the HBC Heritage Trail, a historic fur-trade route that has been reinvigorated as a modern hiking trail stretching from Hope to Tulameen. You'll stroll through subalpine terrain past picturesque Palmers Pond and cross the Cascade Divide on the shoulder of Mount Davis. In summer, the meadows erupt in flowers and the bushes drip with ripe huckleberries, blueberries, and salmonberries. You might be tempted to gorge on them, but leave them for the bears. This area is one of the rare chunks of endangered grizzly bear habitat in southwestern BC.

GETTING THERE
Take exit 228 off the Coquihalla Highway (Highway 5). Turn right onto Coquihalla Lakes Road, then almost immediately take the left fork onto the

Picturesque Palmers Pond.

Tulameen Forest Service Road. Stay on the Tulameen FSR for 46 km (28.6 mi), ignoring all side roads. It's a gravel road, but it is quite smooth and travel for 2WD vehicles is easy. Watch for the Jacobson Lake Rec Site on the left and park. It has toilets, camping, and a signboard with historical information about the trail.

TRAIL

TRIP PLANNER

0 km (0 mi)	Trailhead
0.3 km (0.2 mi)	Junction with HBC Heritage Trail
0.4 km (0.2 mi)	Cross Tulameen Forest Service Road
3 km (1.9 mi)	Conglomerate Flats Camp
4 km (2.5 mi)	Palmers Pond
6 km (3.7 mi)	Campement du Chevreuil (Deer Camp)
9.75 km (6.1 mi)	Sowaqua Road Camp (see Trip 30)

Find the trailhead for the Vuich Trail at the south end of the campsite. Follow this muddy and grassy trail for a few minutes to a **junction** with the HBC Heritage Trail and turn right. The trail crosses the **Tulameen Forest Service Road** and climbs gradually for the first kilometre (0.6 mi) as it meanders through the dry forest of pine and spruce, occasionally breaking out into small clearings with clumps of blueberry bushes. Next it heads downhill slightly, before climbing steeply next to a creek through a spruce forest covered in witch's hair lichen.

At the top of the climb, the forest opens up into a damp meadow at the foot of Mount Davis. You'll find **Conglomerate Flats Camp** here, 190 m (623 ft) higher than the trailhead. The camp is named for the conglomerate rock in the area, formed when the rounded stones of riverbeds and beaches were buried and compressed over millennia into solid rock. Watch for marmots scurrying between their burrows amongst the large boulders. Grizzly bears and elk are often sighted here too.

Continue on the main HBC Heritage Trail past the camp. The trail climbs a grassy draw, speckled with wildflowers in the summer. Look for purple lupines, red paintbrush, and the huge green leaves of false hellebore. There's even a small waterfall along the way. As you contour around the shoulder of Mount Davis, you'll arrive at **Palmers Pond**, named for Henry S. Palmer, a British Army engineer and surveyor who helped create the historic trail.

This idyllic pond is actually a tarn, formed by long-departed glaciers. It is perched on the edge of a steep cliff, with only a few boulders holding back the water. Take the short side trail around the edge of the pond to admire the view on the north side, but use care near the cliff edge. Tulameen Mountain is nearby to the northwest and the peaks of the Coquihalla Range rise up to the north. Palmers Pond is an ecologically fragile area without much flat ground, so there's no camping here. On a hot day, a swim can be refreshing, but be sure to remove any sunscreen or bug spray first to protect the salamanders that live in the pond.

Keep heading west on the HBC Heritage Trail as it curves around Mount Davis and gains a bit more elevation. A few minutes past the pond you'll reach the trail's high point at 1855 m (6086 ft). This is the Cascade Divide, which separates the headwaters of the Fraser River from the headwaters of the Columbia River.

From the divide, the trail follows the ridgeline as it descends, then curves around into open meadows that erupt in the bright colours of arnica, lupine,

INDIGENOUS KNOWLEDGE

The Cascade Divide is also the boundary between the traditional territories of the Stó:lō and Similkameen peoples, who shared this area with the Nlaka'pamux. Originally, this trail was called Chief Blackeye's Trail, after a Similkameen Chief who shared his people's traditional hunting route with the HBC fur traders and guided them through the mountains.

A carpet of wildflowers on the slopes above Palmers Pond.

glacier lily, columbine, paintbrush, and countless other wildflowers in early summer. You'll find **Campement du Chevreuil (Deer Camp)** here.

CAMPING

CONGLOMERATE FLATS CAMP

This campsite is a good destination if you're short on time or energy. It's also a great place to base yourself for a day hike to Palmers Pond or the off-trail scramble to the summit of Mount Davis.

Campsites: 3 wooden tent platforms amongst the shrubs
Toilet: Throne-style outhouse in the trees on the north side of the main trail
Water: Collect from the creek. The area near camp can be marshy, so walk west on the trail for better access.
Food Storage: In a metal food locker
Amenities: A fire ring and benches

CAMPEMENT DU CHEVREUIL (DEER CAMP)

This camp's French name comes from the French voyageurs who were an important part of the fur trade. The camp sits in a pretty meadow, a product of a 1930s wildfire, and is popular with deer. Head a few minutes uphill for fantastic views of Macleod Peak and Mount Hatfield to the southwest and Mount Outram to the south.

The HBC Heritage Trail winds through Conglomerate Flats.

Campsites: 3 wooden tent platforms
Toilet: Throne-style toilet with incredible mountain views through the trees
Water: Collect from Chevreuil Creek, which runs through the camp.
Food Storage: In a metal food locker
Other Amenities: A fire ring, benches, a table, and a signboard with historical information about the trail

EXTENDING YOUR TRIP

Grant Pond: The 4-km (2.5-mi) round trip is a pleasant side trip from Conglomerate Flats Camp. However, the trail is not as well marked or well travelled as the HBC Heritage Trail, so be sure to bring a map.

Mount Davis: No official trail leads to the top of 2012-m-high (6601 ft) Mount Davis, but it's a straightforward scramble up the ridge from the trail's high point just west of Palmers Pond.

HBC Heritage Trail: This trip encompasses a small section of the much longer HBC Heritage Trail. You could walk the entire 74-km-long (46 mi) trail from Hope to Tulameen in about a week. If you don't have enough time for that, combine this trip with Trip 30 (Manson Ridge) for a 28-km (17.4-mi) one-way traverse over three days.

FURTHER RESOURCES

Hope Mountain Centre for Outdoor Learning: info http://hopemountain.org/trails/hbc-heritage-trail/
Trail Map: HBC Trail Map by Hope Mountain Centre and Clark Geomatics
Driving Map: Vancouver, Coast & Mountains BC Backroad Mapbook
NTS Map: 092HO

32
FALLS LAKE

Difficulty: ●
Duration: 2 days
Distance: 2 km (1.2 mi)

Elevation Gain: 50 m (164 ft)
High Point: 1300 m (4265 ft)
Best Months: July to September

Fees and Reservations: Camping is free and all campsites are first-come, first-served.

Regulations: No fires. Dogs permitted on leash only. No drones. No smoking, vaping, or cannabis.

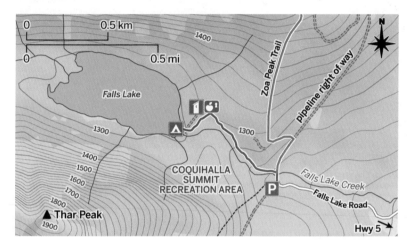

THIS SHORT AND EASY backpacking trip in the Coquihalla Summit Recreation Area is perfect for families or as a shakedown hike for testing new gear. Hike through lush forest to the shores of a subalpine lake ringed by granite peaks. Bring your rod to cast for rainbow trout at the lake outlet, or brave the chilly waters for a refreshing swim on a hot day. Bring your day packs to add on a hike to the top of nearby Zoa Peak. With paved access to the trailhead from the nearby Coquihalla Highway, getting here is simple year-round. It's also a great spot to try out winter camping.

GETTING THERE
On the Coquihalla Highway (Highway 5), take exit 221, signed for Falls Lake. Turn left under the highway, then turn left again on the westbound on-ramp. Before merging back onto the highway, go right onto the paved Falls Lake access road. Follow the road uphill for about 1 km (0.6 mi) until it ends at a

Reflections at Falls Lake on a misty morning.

parking area. Unfortunately, break-ins are common here, so don't leave anything of value in your car.

TRAIL

TRIP PLANNER

0 km (0 mi)	Trailhead and junction with Zoa Peak Trail (4 km/2.5 mi to summit)
0.25 km (0.2 mi)	Bridge
1 km (0.6 mi)	Falls Lake camping

At the north end of the parking lot, look for a BC Parks trail sign. Your route to Falls Lake heads left while the trail to Zoa Peak heads down the old gravel road to your right. For the first few minutes, the trail climbs uphill with the help of a few stairs. After about 0.25 km (0.2 mi), reach a wooden **bridge** over a small creek.

After about 20 minutes of walking, the trail descends slightly to reach the shores of **Falls Lake** and the campground. The lake stretches away to the north for nearly a kilometre (0.6 mi). To the west you can see the spiny granite ridge of Thar Peak high above, creating the prominent scree slopes. On your right, the rounded ridge of Zoa Peak rises above the eastern shore of the lake. Local mountaineer Philip Kubik named the peaks in this region for mountain ungulates from around the world. More commonly spelled "tahr," thars are Himalayan wild goats. A zoa is the female offspring of a male cow and a female yak.

The lake's outlet is to your left, blocked by a logjam. A dip in the chilly lake is a great way to cool off on a hot day. But be careful not to trample the wildflowers that grow along the shore. In July, look for clumps of bright yellow large-leaved avens.

CAMPING

The small campground has incredible views of the lake and the surrounding mountains. Be prepared for chilly nights when the wind picks up across the lake.

Campsites: 2 large wooden tent platforms, 2 small cleared flat tent sites in the brush near the creek, and a large cleared area on a slope near the lakeshore
Toilet: Throne-style pit toilet on a path uphill to the east of the campground
Water: Collect from the lake or the outlet stream.
Food Storage: In a metal food locker on the path to the toilet

EXTENDING YOUR TRIP

Zoa Peak: The moderate hike to 1872-m-tall (6142 ft) Zoa Peak is a great add-on to this backpacking trip. The 8-km (5-mi) return trip to the peak leaves from the Falls Lake parking lot. It gains 600 m (1969 ft) along the way to the summit, travelling up through open forest and gorgeous subalpine meadows. From the top, look out at the surrounding peaks and back down to your campsite far below at Falls Lake.

NATURE NOTE

The hike meanders through a temperate Douglas-fir forest, the trees dripping with long, lacy tufts of old man's beard and witch's hair lichen. First Nations people traditionally used these lichens for dye and as a substitute for hair on dance masks. Old man's beard and witch's hair are also very sensitive to air pollution. When the air contains high concentrations of sulphur dioxide, they stop growing or die. When the air is clean, they can grow to be 10 to 20 cm (4 to 8 in.) long. Falls Lake sits near the Coquihalla Summit, which separates the wet and temperate Cascade Mountains from the dry Interior of British Columbia. That means you won't find these moisture-loving plants once you travel just a few kilometres east.

Old man's beard and witch's hair lichens along the trail to Falls Lake.

FURTHER RESOURCES

BC Parks Coquihalla Summit Recreation Area: info http://bcparks.ca/ explore/parkpgs/coquihalla_smt/

NTS Map: 092H11

33
LITTLE DOUGLAS LAKE

Difficulty: ●

Duration: 2 days

Distance: 3.5 km (2.2 mi)

Elevation Gain: 100 m (328 ft)

High Point: 1330 m (4364 ft)

Best Months: Late June to October

Fees and Reservations: Camping is free and all campsites are first-come, first-served.

Regulations: Dogs permitted.

LITTLE DOUGLAS LAKE is a hidden gem. It's a quick drive on 2WD-accessible gravel roads from the Coquihalla Highway, but it sees very little traffic. The quick and flat hike is great for families or beginners, and the views of the granite peaks surrounding the lake will appeal to everyone. As the sun goes down, watch for the resident beavers to emerge from their lodge in search of food. In the early morning, the reflections of the rocky summits in the glassy waters of the lake are sublime.

GETTING THERE

Take exit 228 on the Coquihalla Highway (Highway 5) and turn left at the intersection onto Upper Coldwater Road. Follow it onto an overpass over the highway, then go straight to stay on Upper Coldwater Road as it crosses a wooden single-lane bridge. Stay on the main road as it passes a road maintenance yard and soon turns into a gravel road called the Upper Coldwater Forest Service Road.

From here the gravel road is bumpy but fine for 2WD vehicles. Stay on the main Upper Coldwater FSR for 6.5 km (4 mi) from where it turns to gravel, ignoring all minor spur roads. As the road starts to curve around a hairpin bend, look for a small sign for the trailhead on the left side. Park in the pullout here. A few metres down the road is the Zum Peak Rec Site.

TRAIL

TRIP PLANNER

0 km (0 mi)	Trailhead
0.6 km (0.4 mi)	Ford creek
1.75 km (1.1 mi)	Little Douglas Lake camping

The trail starts by crossing a small bridge over a ditch, then heading into a regenerating forest. Soon you will reach a marshy area with boardwalk installed as part of a 2016 trail maintenance project by Recreation Sites and Trails BC. The boardwalk doesn't cover the entire area though, so be prepared to get your boots a little muddy.

After the marshy section, the trail heads into the forest and reaches a wide **creek**. In late summer, it's a straightforward rock-hop across. At other times of the year, you may need to take your boots off and wade.

Past the creek, the trail climbs gently through spruce forest and crosses a small creek, this time on a bridge. As you near the lake, the path descends slightly to reach the **campground**. Walk through the campground and out onto the shore of Little Douglas Lake. In mid-summer, admire the brilliant red paintbrush wildflowers growing amongst the grass.

Gaze down the valley at the smooth granite of Zopkios Peak. The forested ridge of Zum Peak rises to your right while Zoa Peak is on your left. Like the peaks near Falls Lake (Trip 32), the three here continue the mountain ungulate theme: they are named for the progeny of a male cow and female yak. These mountains are scoured each year by avalanches, leaving them bare of trees and shrubs. Yak Peak is the most striking example: it is the stark granite face that rises steeply from the north side of the highway near Coquihalla Pass.

NATURE NOTE

Resident beavers have dammed the lake outlet, so the grassy shoreline occasionally floods. Keep an eye out at dusk and dawn for your best chance of spotting them when they venture out to gather food. Their favourites are the leaves, bark, and branches of deciduous trees like aspen, alder, birch, and cottonwood.

Gazing across to Zopkios Peak at the far end of Little Douglas Lake.

CAMPING

Recreation Sites and Trails BC has recently improved this campground and installed tent pads right by the lake so you can get a great view from your sleeping bag without damaging the fragile vegetation.

Campsites: 2 wooden tent platforms in the forest, 4 more on the lakeshore
Toilet: Outhouse beside the trail just before the campsites
Water: Collect from the lake.
Food Storage: In metal food lockers
Other Amenities: A metal fire ring with benches by the lakeshore. A stone fire ring with benches in the forest.

FURTHER RESOURCES

Recreation Sites and Trails BC: info http://www.sitesandtrailsbc.ca/search/search-result.aspx?site=REC1846&type=Trail
Driving Map: Vancouver, Coast & Mountains BC Backroad Mapbook
NTS Map: 092H11

Paintbrush wildflowers on the shores of Little Douglas Lake.

SKAGIT
AND
SIMILKAMEEN

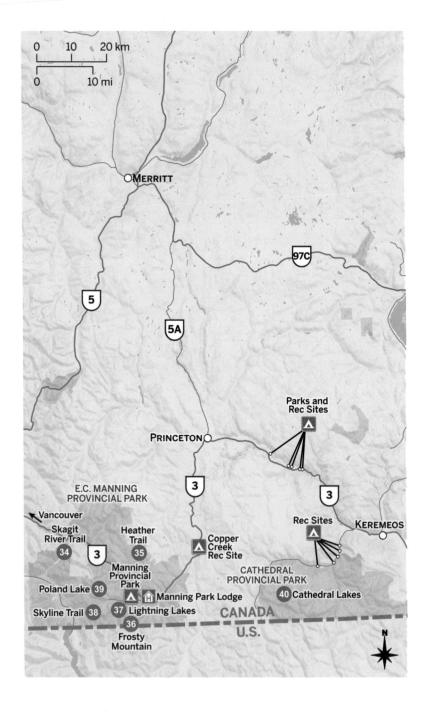

0   10   20 km

0   10 mi

○MERRITT

97C

5

5A

Parks and
Rec Sites

PRINCETON ○

3

E.C. MANNING
PROVINCIAL PARK

3

← Vancouver

Skagit
River Trail
34

3

Heather
Trail
35

Rec Sites

KEREMEOS ○

Copper
Creek
Rec Site

Poland Lake 39

Manning
Provincial
Park

CATHEDRAL
PROVINCIAL PARK

40 Cathedral Lakes

Skyline Trail 38

🏕 🏠 Manning Park Lodge

37 Lightning Lakes

CANADA

36

U.S.

Frosty
Mountain

N

HIGH-ELEVATION WILDFLOWER MEADOWS, easily accessible peaks, a warm, dry climate, and hundreds of kilometres of trails make the Skagit and Similkameen region a paradise for backpackers. When it's raining on the coast, I often head east on the Crowsnest Highway (Highway 3) to hike. E.C. Manning and Skagit Valley Provincial Parks stretch much of the way between the towns of Hope and Princeton, and trail networks on both sides of the highway travel from lush valley bottom to treeless alpine.

Farther east, tributaries of the Ashnola River trickle down the mountainsides, eventually draining into the Similkameen. In the heart of those mountains is Cathedral Provincial Park, a vast wilderness of sparkling lakes, high peaks, and a well-maintained network of trails to incredible viewpoints.

Allison Pass in E.C. Manning Provincial Park marks the transition zone between the temperate coastal climate and the drier Interior climate. On the west side of the pass, the Skagit River drains into Puget Sound at Bellingham, while on the east side, the Similkameen eventually joins the Okanagan River. The weather on the west side of the pass is wetter, with heavier snowfall, but on the east side of the pass the climate is drier and the snowpack melts sooner.

The traditional territory of the S'ólh Téméxw (Stó:lō) people extends from the southern coast and the Fraser River valley to Allison Pass. The traditional territory of the Syilx tmixʷ (Okanagan) people stretches east from the pass all the way to the Kootenays. The Similkameen River is named for the Similkameigh people, a subgroup of the Okanagan Nation. The vast territory of the Nłeʔkepmx Tmíxʷ (Nlaka'pamux) people extends on both sides of the pass.

Supplies: The Skagit and Similkameen Valleys have few shops or services, so stop in Hope, Princeton, or Keremeos for groceries, gas, or outdoor gear. Manning Park Lodge has a restaurant and also sells basic camping supplies and groceries. There is also a gas station on the eastern border of the park. Cathedral Lakes Lodge serves meals and snacks to campers.

Accommodation: Hope and Princeton have hotels or book a cabin at Manning Park Lodge. E.C. Manning Provincial Park has hundreds of reservable and first-come, first-served campsites spread across four campgrounds. East of Manning Park, Bromley Rock and Stemwinder Provincial Parks have reservable campsites and Copper Creek Rec Site has first-come, first-served campsites. If you're heading to Cathedral Lakes, a string of first-come, first-served Forest Service Rec sites lie along the Ashnola River Road: Red Bridge, Tunnel, Horseshoe Canyon, and Ashnola River. There is also a small campsite at the Cathedral Lakes trailhead.

34
SKAGIT RIVER TRAIL

Difficulty: ●
Duration: 2 days
Distance: 8 km (5 mi)

Elevation Gain: 75 m (246 ft)
High Point: 670 m (2198 ft)
Best Months: April to November

Fees and Reservations: Camping is free and all campsites are first-come, first-served.

Regulations: No fires. No drones. No smoking, vaping, or cannabis. Dogs permitted on leash.

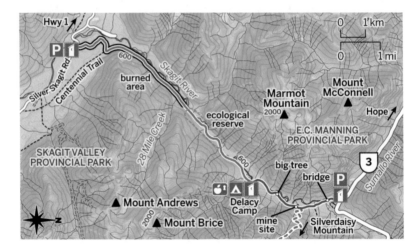

THIS LEVEL HIKE follows the banks of the Skagit River downstream through a lush rainforest. The trail was originally a First Nations trade route, linking coastal and Interior communities. During the gold rush in the 1850s, Colonel Walter de Lacy of the American army blazed an overland route called the Whatcom Trail through this valley. Today it's a much quieter place, protected for its ecological importance. Located at the divide between BC's coast and Interior forests, this valley is home to some special trees including a huge stand of black cottonwoods and lots of old-growth cedar and Douglas-fir. It's also very popular with flyfishers thanks to the healthy population of trout. This trip is a perfect overnight for beginners or families, and its low elevation makes it a great option for early or late in the season.

Camping next to the Skagit River at Delacy Camp.

GETTING THERE

Follow Highway 3 (Crowsnest Highway) to the entrance to E.C. Manning Provincial Park. About 10 km (6.2 mi) into the park, turn right into the Sumallo Grove day-use area. There is an outhouse here and a short interpretive trail through the old-growth cedars.

TRAIL

TRIP PLANNER

0 km (0 mi)	Trailhead
0.2 km (0.1 mi)	Bridge over Skagit River
1.5 km (0.9 mi)	Junction with Silverdaisy Mountain Trail (9 km/5.6 mi to summit)
1.6 km (1 mi)	Junction with spur trail to old mine
4 km (2.5 mi)	Delacy Camp
6.5 km (4 mi)	North boundary of Ecological Reserve
9 km (5.6 mi)	South boundary of Ecological Reserve and start of burned area
15.75 km (9.8 mi)	Silver Skagit Road trailhead

The Skagit River Trail extends from Sumallo Grove in E.C. Manning Provincial Park to Silver Skagit Road in Skagit Valley Provincial Park. The entire trail is 15.75 km (9.8 mi) long and is usually hiked as a traverse, leaving a car at each trailhead. However, forest fires in 2018 devastated the southern end of the trail and that portion is currently closed. Until the trail is reopened and restored, you can hike the first 4 km (2.5 mi) and stay at Delacy Camp, then day hike farther into the valley.

This section of the Skagit River is a special place. It is a wonderful example of an intact coastal rainforest and you can spot dozens of endemic plant species without leaving the trail. Western red cedar and Douglas-fir trees tower over the trail. Thorny devil's club, red huckleberry, and ferns dominate the understory. Along the ground, look for carpets of moss, the white flowers of bunchberry, spiny-leaved Oregon grape, and leathery mountain boxwood. The pink stalks of Western coralroot spring up in shady spots and tiny white western starflowers bloom where the forest is more open.

From the trailhead at Sumallo Grove, walk down the trail for a minute to a large **bridge**. This is the confluence of the Sumallo River, which you've been following alongside Highway 3 since Sunshine Village, and the Skagit River, which originates at Allison Pass near Manning Park Lodge. The name Sumallo is Nlaka'pamux for "Dolly Varden fish numerous here" while Skagit comes from the Skagit people who live at the mouth of the river in present-day Washington State.

Cross the bridge and start up the trail, barely recognizable as a former road used to access a mine from the 1920s. About 1.5 km (0.9 mi) from the trailhead, pass the **trailhead for Silverdaisy Mountain** on the left. A few minutes later, follow an unmarked trail to the left for a minute through a stand of cedars with no undergrowth. It leads to an **old mine** on Silverdaisy Creek. All that is left are the remains of a collapsed shack, a boarded-up mineshaft, and a fully intact truck parked amongst the trees. The waterfall next to the mine shaft is impressive during the spring melt.

After leaving the mine site, the trail traverses below a moss-covered talus slope and becomes single track. At 3 km (1.9 mi), follow markers and flagging tape carefully through a huge slide in a creek valley. As you scramble across the muddy rocks, you may notice that the trail markers are next to your feet rather than above your head. In spring 2020, the swollen creek carried rocks, trees, and mud down the slope, scouring out the stream bed and leaving a huge pile of debris in its wake, some of it 2 m (6.6 ft) deep.

From the slide, the trail heads downhill to follow the banks of the river more closely, passing through a grove of tall cedars, recognizable by their

NATURE NOTE

Watch for Harlequin ducks on the river. The showy males with their broad white stripes and blue and orange patches are only around in the spring, but the grey/brown females with the trademark white spot behind their eye can be seen all summer. Harlequin ducks breed and hatch their eggs near fast-flowing mountain streams like the Skagit River.

stringy bark. Huge Douglas-firs with deeply furrowed bark are also speckled through the forest here. Many of them are pocked with woodpecker holes. Watch and listen carefully for pileated woodpeckers tapping away at tree trunks in search of tasty insects.

About 4 km (2.5 mi) from the trailhead, pass a few flat camping areas next to the river and a No Fires sign. The silty ground here is evidence that this area is prone to flooding in the spring. Carry on for another 150 m (492 ft) to reach the main area of **Delacy Camp**, passing a few more informal camp-sites along the way.

CAMPING

Delacy Camp is 4.75 km (3 mi) from the trailhead near a bend in the river that creates a deep pool for fishing.

Campsites: Lots of cleared flat space in the main campsite, 2 packed-dirt tent platforms just up the hill from the main campsite, and more informal tent sites along the riverbank for a few hundred metres to the east of camp
Toilet: Throne-style toilet on a signed spur trail up the hill from the main camping area
Water: Collect from the Skagit River.
Food Storage: In a metal food locker
Other Amenities: A picnic table at the main camping area

EXTENDING YOUR TRIP

Skagit River Cottonwoods Ecological Reserve: Be sure to trek 1.75 km (1.1 mi) south from Delacy Camp to the Ecological Reserve. You can follow the trail through to the other side of the reserve, about 9 km (5.6 mi) from the trailhead. Past here, fire damage makes the trail impassable. The reserve con-tains stands of beautiful mature Douglas-firs and western red cedars. It also protects a grove of ecologically important alluvial black cottonwoods. These tall deciduous trees can grow up to 50 m (164 ft) tall. You can recognize them by their deeply furrowed, dark grey bark; shiny, heart-shaped leaves; and the cottony white hairs on their seed pods in spring and early summer.
Silverdaisy Mountain: Find the trailhead for this challenging hike at the 1.5-km (0.9-mi) mark. The route to the peak gains 1460 m (4790 ft) over 9 km (5.6 mi) and is not regularly maintained, so be prepared for some bush-whacking and route-finding. Silverdaisy Mountain is located in the middle of the "donut hole," an area of unprotected Crown land surrounded completely by E.C. Manning and Skagit Valley Provincial Parks. In 2019, the provincial government agreed to stop logging inside the donut hole, but mining is still permitted and continues to threaten wildlife populations and ecosystems in the adjacent parks.

A huge Douglas-fir along the Skagit River Trail.

FURTHER RESOURCES

Skagit Valley Provincial Park: info http://bcparks.ca/explore/parkpgs/skagit/
Trail Map: Manning Park and Skagit Valley by Clark Geomatics
NTS Map: 092H03

35
HEATHER TRAIL

Difficulty: ■
Duration: 2 to 5 days
Distance: 10 to 45 km (6.2 to 28 mi)

Elevation Gain: 320 m (1050 ft)
High Point: 2120 m (6955 ft)
Best Months: July to mid-September

Fees and Reservations: Camping fees are $5/person/night, payable online. All campsites are first-come, first-served.

Regulations: No fires at Buckhorn and Kicking Horse Camps. No drones. No smoking, vaping, or cannabis. Dogs permitted on leash.

Caution: Bring insect repellent as the mosquitos can be thick in the campgrounds in early summer.

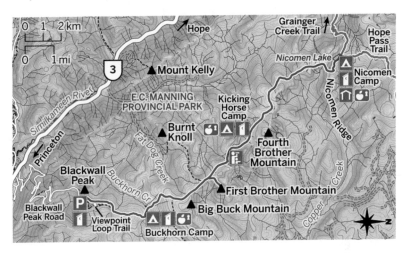

THE HEATHER TRAIL is E.C. Manning Provincial Park's signature trail, and a must-do for every backpacker. With its trailhead high in the subalpine meadows, the Heather Trail lets you enjoy the beauty of Manning Park's wildflower meadows for its entire length. Stop along the way to enjoy the incredible views of snow-capped mountains in all directions, clamber up to the peak of First Brother Mountain, or stay out past dark for superlative summer stargazing. Choose from two meadow-side subalpine campsites or camp at the trail's end at Nicomen Lake, a popular place for fishing or a bracing swim. During peak wildflower bloom from mid-July through mid-August, the trail can be very busy, so tread lightly to protect this special place.

GETTING THERE

Take Highway 3 into Manning Park. At the flashing yellow light just past Manning Park Lodge, turn left onto a service road, then immediately turn left again onto Blackwall Road. Follow this road as it switchbacks up into the subalpine, turning to gravel partway along. The road is usually well graded and is suitable for all vehicles. About 14 km (8.7 mi) from the highway, park at a pullout on the left side next to the trailhead for the Heather Trail.

TRAIL

TRIP PLANNER

0 km (0 mi)	Blackwall Peak trailhead
1 km (0.6 mi)	Junction with Viewpoint Loop Trail
2 km (1.2 mi)	Junction with Viewpoint Loop Trail
5 km (3.1 mi)	Buckhorn Camp
6.85 km (4.3 mi)	Junction with Bonnevier Trail
9.5 km (5.9 mi)	Junction with First Brother Trail (1 km/0.6 mi to summit)
13.5 km (8.4 mi)	Kicking Horse Camp
20.5 km (12.7 mi)	Nicomen Ridge
22.5 km (14 mi)	Nicomen Lake Camp and junction with Hope Pass–Grainger Creek Trail (see Trip 45)
39 km (24.2 mi)	Cayuse Flats trailhead for the Hope Pass Trail

From the trailhead, the path heads downhill to the north on an old fire service road through forest interspersed with meadowy slopes. In the first 2 km (1.2 mi), you'll pass two different **junctions** with the Viewpoint Trail on the right. Both trails lead to Blackwall Peak, slightly higher up the road from where you parked.

Reach **Buckhorn Camp** at the 5-km (3.1-mi) mark, 135 m (443 mi) lower than the parking lot. Walk through the campsite, which is named for a historic mining camp in this area, and cross a small stream on a bridge. Fill up on water here on a hot day. It's one of the last reliable water sources for a while, though in hot years it may run dry in late August. Take the path uphill to the right to continue onwards. The spur trail heading left along the creek leads to more campsites.

In the next few kilometres, the trail climbs first through the forest, then through open subalpine meadow interspersed with bleached dead trees. These trees are the result of a forest fire in 1945 that ignited from a single cigarette.

At 6.85 km (4.3 mi), the **Bonnevier Trail** joins from the right. Continue straight to stay on the Heather Trail as it continues to climb to the top of a

Alpine meadows along the Heather Trail.

broad ridge with views opening up in all directions. This is the original part of the park, which was established in 1931 as the Three Brothers Preserve to protect the meadows from being overgrazed by sheep. Just ahead of you are the triple peaks of the Three Brothers. To the south, you can see the dark, rocky ridge of Frosty Mountain (Trip 36), the highest mountain in E.C. Manning Provincial Park. The sheer twin summits of Hozomeen Mountain stand tall in the southeast, just across the American border.

At the 9-km (5.6-mi) mark, reach a small pond. In late summer, it will likely be dry, but earlier in the year it could be a welcome water source, provided you've packed a filter for the murky water. Just past the pond, descend to Windy Gap, then head uphill for a minute to a junction. The spur trail to the summit of **First Brother** heads right, while your route continues straight ahead. This is the highest point on the Heather Trail.

The path contours around the side of Second and Third Brother Mountains, crossing several seasonal streams on a gradual and undulating descent. Make note of which of these streams are running, as you may need to hike back here to fetch water if the source at camp is dry. Reach the turnoff to **Kicking Horse Camp** 13.5 km (8.4 mi) from the trailhead.

Past Kicking Horse Camp, the trail rises and falls through meadows for the next 4 km (2.5 mi) along the shoulder of Fourth Brother Mountain and its adjoining ridge. About 17.5 km (10.9 mi) from the car, the trail drops 80 m (262 ft) into a forested draw thick with subalpine fir. Climbing up out of the

Late-season wildflowers.

draw back into the meadows, the trail gains 145 m (476 ft) of elevation. Pass several ponds that fill with snowmelt in the early season, then dry up quickly. You soon top out on **Nicomen Ridge** and get your first views of Nicomen Lake below.

Over the next 2 km (1.2 mi), you'll drop down 235 m (771 ft) to the lake. From the rocky top, the slope looks shockingly sheer, but the descent is fairly easy on well-constructed switchbacks through subalpine fir and Engelmann spruce. At the bottom, the trail crosses a wet meadow beside a stream, then reaches the southeast corner of the lake. The **Nicomen Lake Camp** is 0.4 km (0.2 mi) away on the northeastern shore. The shallow water near the shoreline gets a little less icy cold in the afternoon sun, making this a great place to swim. Nicomen Lake is also popular with anglers, as it is stocked with rainbow trout.

CAMPING

Fit and fast groups could hike the Heather Trail as a two-day trip, camping at Nicomen Lake. However, it would be a shame to rush through the beautiful alpine scenery, especially if the wildflowers are blooming. A better option is a three-day trip: hike to Kicking Horse on the first day, day hike to Nicomen Lake on the second day, then head back on the third day. If you really want to savour the experience, plan for even more days on the trail. If you're short on time or stamina, plan an out-and-back trip to Buckhorn Camp, with a day hike to First Brother Mountain.

BUCKHORN CAMP

This busy campsite is in a meadow next to a stream.

Campsites: 10 wooden tent platforms on both sides of the creek, including on a spur trail to the left. Lots of flat spots on the ground provide overflow campsites.
Toilets: 2 outhouses
Water: Collect from the creek that runs through camp.
Food Storage: In a metal food locker
Other Amenities: A wooden picnic table

KICKING HORSE CAMP

The campsites are in a clump of subalpine fir on a spur trail down the slope from the main trail.

Campsites: 9 wooden tent pads, plus a few more informal flat spots for overflow camping
Toilet: Outhouse uphill from the tent platforms
Water: Collect from the stream running through the camp. If it is dry, hike back along the Heather Trail to the east to reliable water sources 500 m (0.3 mi) and 1 km (0.6 mi) away.
Food Storage: In a metal food locker

NICOMEN LAKE CAMP

The campsite at Nicomen Lake is on the northeast side of the lake. A small dirt-floored, lean-to shelter can be used as a cooking shelter, but it is showing its age.

Campsites: 4 wooden tent platforms along the lake as well as several flat dirt sites for overflow camping
Toilet: Outhouse on the north side of the trail
Water: Collect from the lake.
Food Storage: In a metal food locker

NATURE NOTE

If possible, time your hike with the peak wildflower bloom in late July and early August. The slopes along the whole trail light up in colour: red paintbrush, white western anemone, yellow asters and buttercup-like cinquefoil, blue lupines, and more. Bring a plant guide to help identify dozens of species. Although it can be tempting to go exploring, stay on the trail. These fragile alpine plants live in a harsh climate with a short growing season, so they can take several years to produce a flower. A careless bootprint can kill them.

Descending the switchbacks to Nicomen Lake.

EXTENDING YOUR TRIP

First Brother Mountain: Just past the 9-km (5.6-mi) mark, take the rocky spur trail to the summit of First Brother. It's a 2-km (1.2-mi) round trip to the 2272-m-high (7454 ft) peak. Along the way, you'll gain 250 m (820 ft).

Traverse to Cayuse Flats: If you leave one car at the Blackwall Peak parking lot and another at Cayuse Flats on Highway 3, you can make a one-way traverse over three or four days instead of an out-and-back trip. Hike the Heather Trail to Nicomen Lake, then continue on the Grainger Creek and Hope Pass Trails (Trip 45) down to Cayuse Flats for a total of 39 km (24.2 mi) of hiking.

FURTHER RESOURCES

E.C. Manning Provincial Park: info and fees http://bcparks.ca/explore/parkpgs/ecmanning/
Trail Map: Manning Park and Skagit Valley by Clark Geomatics
NTS Map: 092HO2

36
FROSTY MOUNTAIN

Difficulty: ■

Duration: 2 to 3 days

Distance: 14 km (8.7 mi)

Elevation Gain: 670 m (2198 ft)

High Point: 1910 m (6266 ft)

Best Months: July to early October

Fees and Reservations: Camping fees are $5/person/night, payable online. All campsites are first-come, first-served.

Regulations: No drones. No smoking, vaping, or cannabis. Dogs permitted on leash.

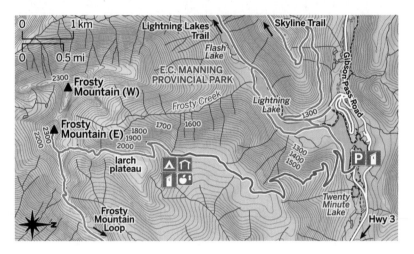

THE ASCENT OF Frosty Mountain, the highest mountain in Manning Park, is less challenging if you break up the trip over two days and gives you more time to savour the views. Visit in the fall to see the green needles of the larch trees turn gold and then drop to the forest floor. Carry on above the treeline to reach the peak and its unique alpine tundra landscape. In the last few minutes of the ascent, you'll pick your way across jagged rocks, sculpted by centuries of freezing and thawing. From the 2409-m (7904-ft) summit, admire the vistas of jagged, snow-capped peaks on both sides of the border.

GETTING THERE

Just past Manning Park Lodge on Highway 3, turn right onto Gibson Pass Road at the flashing yellow light. Follow this road for 3 km (1.9 mi), then take the left fork into the Lightning Lake day-use area. Park at the east end of the parking lot near the outhouses.

The view of the larch plateau in fall colour from the summit of Frosty Mountain.

TRAIL

From the parking lot, walk towards Lightning Lake, then go left to follow the trail around the east end of the lake to a **junction**. Your route to Frosty Mountain heads left up the rocky hill while the route around Lightning Lakes (Trip 37) goes right. The first 5 km (3.1 mi) of trail are a steady ascent on a series of long switchbacks as you gain about 600 m (1969 ft). Watch for red kilometre markers in the trees to track your progress. A few peekaboo views through the trees look down to Lightning Lake and across to prominent Silvertip Mountain to the northwest and the twin summits of Hozomeen Mountain to the southwest.

After the switchbacks end, the trail levels off for a few kilometres as it heads north through more open forest. In mid-summer, watch for wildflowers in the clearings. Reach the **Frosty Creek campground**, 670 m (2198 ft) higher than the trailhead.

CAMPING

The campsite at Frosty Creek is the only place on the trail to find running water reliably (at least until late August). Be prepared to pack water in if it's been a dry summer. The rough, dirt-floored cabin is best used as a kitchen shelter, as it is far from weather-tight.

Campsites: 3 flattish tent spots
Toilet: Outhouse
Water: Collect from the creek.
Food Storage: In a metal food locker

EXTENDING YOUR TRIP

Larch Plateau: The larch plateau is between the 8- and 9-km (5- and 5.6-mi) marks on the trail, 150 m (492 ft) higher than the campground. This open meadow offers views of Frosty Mountain and makes a worthwhile trip at any time of year.

Frosty Mountain Summit: To get to the top of Frosty Mountain, continue past the larch plateau and follow markers up switchbacks on the rocky north slope to a trail junction on the ridgetop. Snow stays late on this side of the mountain, so take care if the trail is icy. From here it's another 0.5 km (0.3 mi) to the cairn atop the 2409-m-high (7904 ft) east summit of Frosty Mountain (the west peak is a loose scramble that's not recommended). Watch for pink moss campion hanging onto the rocks. This rare plant grows only on high and rocky peaks. From the campsite, it's an 8-km (5-mi) round trip with 500 m (1640 ft) of elevation gain.

Frosty Mountain Loop: Make this trip into a loop by heading up to the summit ridge of Frosty Mountain, then using the Frosty Mountain East, Pacific Crest, Windy Joe, and Little Muddy Trails to return to your car. From the

NATURE NOTE

Try to time your visit for late September or early October when the larch trees in the plateau above the campground turn from green to brilliant gold and then drop their needles. These unique conifers live only at high elevations in rocky soil and they grow very slowly. The smallest trees can be hundreds of years old and some of the larger ones have lived for thousands of years.

Larch needles turning gold in fall.

campsite back to your car, this route is 20.5 km (12.7 mi) long. To break up the trip over two days, camp at Pacific Crest Trail Camp. This site is 0.5 km (0.3 mi) southwest of Windy Joe Mountain junction and has a pit toilet, fire ring, space for four tents, and a good stream for water.

FURTHER RESOURCES
E.C. Manning Provincial Park: info and fees http://bcparks.ca/explore/parkpgs/ecmanning/
Trail Map: Manning Park and Skagit Valley by Clark Geomatics
NTS Map: 092H02

37
LIGHTNING LAKES

Difficulty: ●

Duration: 2 days

Distance: 13 km (8.1 mi)

Elevation Gain: none

High Point: 1250 m (4101 ft)

Best Months: June to October

Fees and Reservations: Camping fees are $5/person/night, payable online. All campsites are first-come, first-served.

Regulations: No drones. No smoking, vaping, or cannabis. Dogs permitted on leash.

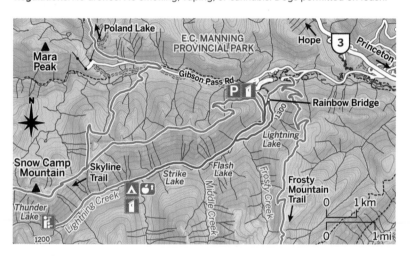

IN THE SUMMER, the waters of Lightning Lake teem with canoeists and the trails are full of day hikers from the popular campground nearby. But follow the flat former trapper's trail along a chain of lakes to the backcountry campsite near Strike Lake and you'll leave the crowds behind. Along the way keep an eye out for wildflowers and pause at Flash Lake to see if you can spot beavers near their impressive lodge. If you fish, all of the lakes along the trail hold impressively large rainbow trout. It's an easy trip for beginners or families and its low elevation makes it one of the earliest snow-free destinations in Manning Park.

GETTING THERE

Just past Manning Park Lodge on Highway 3, turn right onto Gibson Pass Road at the flashing yellow light. Three kilometres (1.9 mi) down that road, keep right at the fork. Two kilometres (1.2 mi) later, turn left into the

Lightning Lake campground. Just before the campground gatehouse, turn right and follow a short spur road to the Spruce Bay day-use parking lot.

TRAIL

From the parking lot, follow an old fire access road towards Lightning Lake. About 0.5 km (0.3 mi) from the trailhead, reach a **junction**. Turn right to head south on the Lightning Lakes Chain Trail towards Strike Lake. (Left leads to Lightning Lake Loop.) On your hike to Strike Lake Camp, you'll be following Lightning Creek downhill as it flows southwest, eventually emptying into Ross Lake in Washington's North Cascades National Park. The water in this glaciated valley used to flow east into the Similkameen River, but centuries of erosion near Thunder Lake reversed the flow. With the addition of a dam on Lightning Lake in 1968, the lakes currently drain to both the east and west.

Continue for 0.5 km (0.3 mi) until you reach another **junction**. Your route continues straight, while the Skyline Trail (Trip 38) ascends the slope to the right.

Follow the trail along the north shore of Lightning Lake. A canopy of Engelmann spruce, lodgepole pine, and subalpine fir creates shade on hot days. About 2 km (1.2 mi) from the start, arrive at the end of the lake and another **junction**. Stay to the right to continue on the Lightning Lakes Chain Trail to Strike Lake, ignoring the Lightning Lake Loop Trail to the left and

NATURE NOTE

In early July, watch for wildflowers all along the trail. The showy drooping blooms of red columbine and yellow tiger lily are particularly spectacular here. The Coast Salish people steamed the roots of tiger lilies and used them as a peppery flavouring for food.

Looking south down Lightning Lake.

a junction with the overgrown and closed Flash Lake Trail. Hike through a marshy section in the trees before arriving on the **northern shore of Flash Lake**.

As you hike along the shoreline of the lake past a few rockslides, watch for a beaver lodge on the far side of the lake. Dawn and dusk are the best times to spot these busy rodents swimming or foraging along the shoreline. Flash Lake is shallower and grassier than the other lakes in the chain thanks to the beaver dam at the southern outlet of the lake.

Reach the **south end of Flash Lake** about 4 km (2.5 mi) from the car and ignore a junction with the closed Flash Lake Trail. Head through the forest, following the banks of Lightning Creek and skirting a marshy section. Arrive at the east end of **Strike Lake**, then walk another kilometre (0.6 mi) along the banks of the lake. You'll pass through a few brushy sections overgrown with thimbleberry bushes and the huge white flowers of cow parsnip where avalanches sweep down the steep slopes in the winter. Avoid touching the cow parsnip as its sap can cause severe skin rashes and blisters, especially when combined with sun exposure. Continue past the end of Strike Lake for another 0.5 km (0.3 mi) to reach the **campground**.

CAMPING

The Strike Lake campground is on Lightning Creek, not right on the lake. It sits in a grove of Engelmann spruce trees.

Hiking beside Flash Lake.

Campsites: Lots of flat cleared areas with room for at least 8 tents
Toilet: Outhouse on the east side of the campground
Water: Collect from Lightning Creek.
Food Storage: In a metal food locker
Other Amenities: 4 metal fire rings and several wooden benches

EXTENDING YOUR TRIP

Lightning Lake Loop: Instead of making a beeline for the campsite at Strike Lake, incorporate the Lightning Lake Loop into your trip. You can park at the Lightning Lake day-use area, then take the eastern part of the Lightning Lake Loop trail to either Rainbow Bridge or the south end of Lightning Lake to meet up with the route described above. This will add an extra 1 to 1.5 km (0.6 to 0.9 mi) to your trip.

Thunder Lake: From the Strike Lake campsite, continue down the Lightning Lakes Chain Trail for 3 km (1.9 mi) to Thunder Lake, the fourth lake in the chain. This portion of the trail passes through some rocky sections and can be overgrown. The trail ends at a rocky viewpoint, high above the waters of the lake.

FURTHER RESOURCES

E.C. Manning Provincial Park: info and fees http://bcparks.ca/explore/parkpgs/ecmanning/
Trail Map: Manning Park and Skagit Valley by Clark Geomatics
NTS Map: 092H02

38
SKYLINE TRAIL

Difficulty: ■

Duration: 2 days

Distance: 25 km (15.5 mi)

Elevation Gain: 520 m (1706 ft)

High Point: 1890 m (6201 ft)

Best Months: July to September

Fees and Reservations: Camping fees are $5/person/night, payable online. All campsites are first-come, first-served.

Regulations: No drones. No smoking, vaping, or cannabis. Dogs permitted on leash.

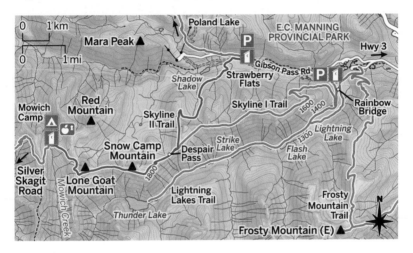

CLIMB UP TO a ridge high above Lightning Lakes in E.C. Manning Provincial Park, then undulate through subalpine meadows that overflow with wildflowers in mid-summer. Your destination for the night is Mowich Camp, a favourite hangout for mule deer who love to graze on the blueberry bushes nearby. Most groups will want to take the direct Skyline II Trail to the campsite, but hikers with more time and energy can opt for several alternate routes, including a start on Skyline I Trail from Lightning Lake.

GETTING THERE

Just past the Manning Park Lodge on Highway 3, turn right onto Gibson Pass Road at the flashing yellow light and continue for 8.5 km (5.3 mi). In the summer, the road is gated at this point at an area called Strawberry Flats. Park on the wide shoulder. The trailhead is on the south side of the road near an outhouse.

A blanket of wildflowers and views across to the mountains in Washington's Pasayten Wilderness.

TRAIL

From the trailhead, go right onto the flat and wide Three Falls Trail, a former fire access road. Follow it for 0.8 km (0.5 mi), being careful to stay on the trail to avoid trampling the strawberry blossoms and lupines that grow right up to the trail's edge. Reach a **junction** and turn left onto the Skyline I Trail. The first few metres of the trail are flat and easy, but it soon starts climbing up through a tight forest of Engelmann spruce and subalpine fir. About 3.7 km (2.3 mi) from the trailhead, emerge briefly into a small sloping meadow. You can spot lots of wildflowers here, including western anemone, lupine, arnica, and cow parsnip, but press on as the best meadows are yet to come.

Just past the meadow, the trail climbs steeply through an old burn for a few minutes on to the crest of a ridge. Follow the path as it swings around to head due south. The grade lessens for the next kilometre (0.6 mi) as you sidehill along a slope. About 6 km (3.7 mi) from the trailhead, reach a **junction above Despair Pass**. The continuation of Skyline I Trail heads left here along the crest of a ridge towards Lightning Lake. Your route to Mowich Camp is to the right along the Skyline II Trail. Take your pack off here for a snack break and enjoy the views. You can see Thunder Lake far below you and Hozomeen Mountain to the southwest.

Next, drop down into Despair Pass. You'll lose 100 m (328 ft) within a few minutes, then gain it all back (and then some) climbing up the other side. If your pack feels heavy at this point, you'll understand why Despair Pass got its name. As you ascend from the pass, you'll emerge from the trees into meadows on the flank of **Snow Camp Mountain**. For the next 3 km (1.9 mi), you'll ramble through meadows and traverse the steep slopes of Snow Camp and Lone Goat Mountains. Your route is high above Thunder Lake and Lightning Creek, which you can sometimes see far below. Take care on the narrow trail as a slip could be catastrophic. The views south to the peaks in Washington's Pasayten Wilderness are spectacular.

About 11.5 km (7.1 mi) from the start, the trail starts to descend and transitions from meadows to open subalpine forest. Hike another 1 km (0.6 mi) to reach **Mowich Camp** and its thickets of blueberry bushes.

CAMPING

Mowich Camp is in a small grassy depression between Lone Goat Mountain and Hozomeen Ridge. In Chinook jargon, a 19th-century Indigenous trading language, *mowich* means "deer," and the meadows near camp are a great place to spot them. Mowich Creek originates nearby and trickles through the camp. However, by August or in dry periods, the creek may dry up. Follow it downhill and you will likely find some water bubbling up in small pools.

Campsites: Cleared sites for 4 tents
Toilet: Outhouse
Water: Collect from Mowich Creek.
Food Storage: In a metal food locker

NATURE NOTE

The wildflower meadows here are some of the best in Manning Park. You may want to bring along a wildflower guide to help you identify the dozens of species you will spot. In early season, look for yellow glacier lilies and white avalanche lilies blooming at the edge of melting snowbanks. Later in the summer, look for purple lupines, white partridgefoot, yellow arnica, and the broad green leaves of false hellebore.

Hiking along a ridgetop on the Skyline I Trail.

Other Amenities: A metal fire ring and benches and a partially dismantled wooden lean-to-style shelter that seems to be used as a woodshed

EXTENDING YOUR TRIP

Skyline II Traverse: From Mowich Camp, continue on the somewhat overgrown Skyline II Trail all the way to Skagit Valley Provincial Park. Leave a car at each trailhead to set up a one-way traverse. The trailhead on Silver Skagit Road is 13 km (8.1 mi) of solid downhill from Mowich Camp. Trekking poles will help your knees endure the punishing 1310-m (4298-ft) descent. This route follows a historic trading route used to connect coastal and Interior Indigenous groups and offers spectacular views of the twin summits of Hozomeen Mountain and vast Ross Lake stretching across the border.

Skyline I to Spruce Bay: If you have the energy, add on the eastern section of the Skyline I Trail by starting at the Spruce Bay day-use area. This option adds 4 km (2.5 mi) of distance, but the incredible meadows along the way are worth it.

FURTHER RESOURCES

E.C. Manning Provincial Park: info and fees http://bcparks.ca/explore/parkpgs/ecmanning/
Trail Map: Manning Park and Skagit Valley by Clark Geomatics
NTS Map: 092H02

39
POLAND LAKE

Difficulty: ■

Duration: 2 days

Distance: 16 km (9.9 mi)

Elevation Gain: 465 m (1526 ft)

High Point: 1835 m (6020 ft)

Best Months: July to September

Fees and Reservations: Camping fees are $5/person/night, payable online. All campsites are first-come, first-served.

Regulations: No drones. No smoking, vaping, or cannabis. Dogs permitted on leash. Bikes and horses are permitted on the first 7 km (4.3 mi) of the trail only.

Caution: Bring insect repellent or a head net as the mosquitos can be persistent.

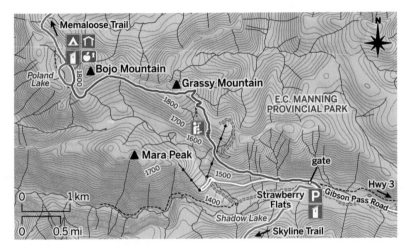

POLAND LAKE IS one of Manning Park's least-visited destinations in the summer, which is too bad because it's beautifully situated in a bowl at treeline and is a great place for a refreshingly icy dip on a hot day. If you're willing to pack in a rod, fly-fishing along the eastern shoreline may land you a rainbow trout. Along the way, you'll pass through wildflower meadows and viewpoints of the surrounding mountains. Wildflower lovers will further rejoice at the variety of blooms in the grassy meadows near the campsite.

GETTING THERE

Just past the Manning Park Lodge on Highway 3, turn right onto Gibson Pass Road at the flashing yellow light and continue for 8.5 km (5.3 mi). In the summer, the road is gated at this point at an area called Strawberry Flats. Park on the wide shoulder. The trailhead is on the north side of the road. There is an outhouse on the south side of the road.

TRAIL

From the trailhead on the north side of the road, turn left and follow the old fire access road west towards the ski resort. The first stretch is fairly level, but then the trail starts to climb as it heads northwest away from the road. You'll cross a creek, the only water source before you reach the lake. Continue climbing steadily upwards through lodgepole pine forest. About 2 km (1.2 mi) from the car, your route will **cross several ski runs**. Next, pass under the chairlift and follow the signed **Poland Lake Trail** leaving the road on the left.

Follow the trail as it switchbacks steeply up the hill for 1 km (0.6 mi) through beautiful meadows bright with paintbrush and lupine. Be sure to turn around and admire the view behind you. You can see the rounded tops of Snow Camp and Lone Goat Mountains on the Skyline Trail (Trip 38) as well as the 70-m (230-ft) cascade of Nepopekum Falls.

As the grade eases, the meadows give way to open forest dotted with berry bushes. About 3.5 km (2.2 mi) from the trailhead, **rejoin the access road** and turn left. A few hundred metres later, reach a map and signboard at the top of the Horseshoe ski run. At this point, you'll have gained most of the elevation on this hike. The rest of the way to the lake is nearly flat.

NATURE NOTE

Watch for bears grazing on the grass in the open ski runs, especially early and late in the day. Although bears have a reputation as fierce carnivores, they are actually omnivores, eating a wide-ranging diet of plants and animals in their quest to consume up to 30,000 calories a day. The young grasses that grow on open slopes, such as ski runs and avalanche chutes, are one of their favourite foods.

Keep hiking on the old road as it heads west across the shoulders of Grassy and Bojo Mountains. Your route passes through a few small meadows with lots of wildflowers. As you pass through rocky sections, watch for the tiny petals of spreading phlox clinging to clumps of soil. There are also a few peekaboo viewpoints of First Brother Mountain on the Heather Trail (Trip 35) to the north and the twin rocky pinnacles of Hozomeen Mountain to the south.

The **old road ends** at a hitching post. Cyclists and horseback riders must leave their steeds here. Follow the trail up a small rise beside a creek towards the lake. Once you reach the shore, follow the trail around the east side of **Poland Lake**. At the northern end, cross a log bridge over a small stream and arrive at the campsite. Previously known as Paddy's Pond, the lake is named for a Mr. Poland who surveyed the area for a proposed Great Northern Railway line from Princeton. That plan never got off the ground because the terrain was too impractical.

The view south to Hozomeen Mountain.

CAMPING

The campsite is in a beautiful meadow. There is a small dirt-floored, lean-to shelter that can be used as a cooking shelter, but it is showing its age, so don't plan to sleep in it.

Campsites: Flat clearings for at least 6 tents at the north end of the lake
Toilet: Outhouse
Water: Collect from the creek that runs through camp.
Food Storage: In a metal food locker
Other Amenities: A metal fire ring, benches, and lean-to-style cooking shelter

Lupines carpet the meadows near Poland Lake campground.

EXTENDING YOUR TRIP

Poland Lake Loop: A rough, overgrown, and often marshy anglers' trail leads around the west side of the lake to make a 1-km (0.6-mi) loop.

Memaloose Trail: This overgrown trail leads from the northeast corner of Poland Lake down to Highway 3 at Allison Pass. It's a 9-km (5.6-mi) hike that loses 410 m (1345 ft) of elevation. Leave a car at each trailhead to make a one-way traverse.

FURTHER RESOURCES

E.C. Manning Provincial Park: info and fees http://bcparks.ca/explore/parkpgs/ecmanning/

Trail Map: Manning Park and Skagit Valley by Clark Geomatics

NTS Map: 092H02

40
CATHEDRAL LAKES

Difficulty: ◆
Duration: 3 to 4 days
Distance: 29 to 31 km (18 to 19.3 mi)

Elevation Gain: 1360 m (4462 ft)
High Point: 2190 m (7185 ft)
Best Months: July to September

Fees and Reservations: Camping fees are $10/person/night, payable online. All campsites are first-come, first-served.

Regulations: No drones. No dogs. No smoking, vaping, or cannabis. Fires permitted at Quiniscoe Lake campground only.

Caution: Keep your distance from the mountain goats as they can become aggressive and territorial.

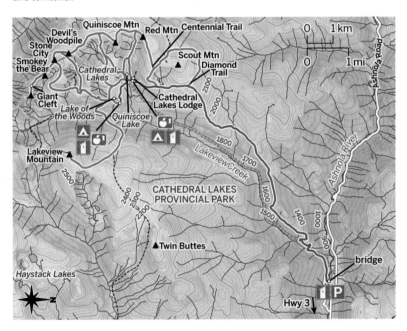

CATHEDRAL PROVINCIAL PARK is sandwiched between the temperate Cascade Mountains and the dry Okanagan Valley. Hikers who make the long climb through the forest into the core area of the park will be handsomely rewarded. A network of alpine lakes sits cradled amongst rocky peaks. Base yourself at one of two different lakeside campgrounds for a few days and take day hikes up along the ridgeline or through meadows of wildflowers.

The resident mountain goat population is thriving, and this is one of the best places in BC to spot them.

GETTING THERE

From Princeton, follow Highway 3 east for 62 km (38.5 mi). Turn right onto Ashnola River Road, following signs for Cathedral Lakes. Follow the road for about 24 km (14.9 mi). It starts paved but soon turns to 2WD-accessible gravel with some washboard sections. Just past the Cathedral Lakes Lodge parking lot, turn left for the Lakeview trailhead and campground. There is a parking lot here, several campsites, and an outhouse. If you want to skip the trek into the core area, you can also book a spot on the Cathedral Lakes Lodge Unimog shuttle. It operates on a steep and narrow private road that is closed to the public. Most campers use this option, so do not be surprised to see some elaborate set-ups in the campground.

TRAIL

TRIP PLANNER

0 km (0 mi)	Lakeview trailhead
0.5 km (0.3 mi)	Cross access road
1.5 km (0.9 mi)	Cross access road
1.6 km (1 mi)	Walk on road
2.6 km (1.6 mi)	Junction with Lakeview Trail
11.5 km (7.1 mi)	Junction with Diamond Trail (8-km/5-mi loop)
12.7 km (7.9 mi)	Junction with Centennial Trail to Cathedral Rim (16-km/9.9-mi loop)
14 km (8.7 mi)	Cathedral Lakes Lodge
14.5 km (9 mi)	Quiniscoe Lake campground
15.5 km (9.6 mi)	Lake of the Woods campground
16 km (9.9 mi)	Junction with Lakeview Mountain Trail (6 km/3.7 mi to summit) and Cathedral Rim Trail (16-km/9.9-mi loop)

Three trails access the core of the Cathedral Lakes area: Ewart Creek Trail, Wall Creek Trail, and Lakeview Trail. The Lakeview Trail is the shortest and most direct route. It is also the most common option, so it is described below. From the trailhead, cross a footbridge over the Ashnola River. There are few water sources on the long and steep climb up to the core area, so make sure you fill up here.

Follow the trail up the hill and reach a **dirt road**. This is the private road to Cathedral Lakes Lodge. You will cross this road several times on your hike.

Ladyslipper Lake and the trail up to Cathedral Rim.

It sees very little traffic; still, use caution when crossing. Turn right and walk a few metres down the road, then pick up the trail on the other side at a Lakeview Trail sign. The trail continues climbing, **crossing the road** again about 1.5 km (0.9 mi) from the trailhead. A few minutes later, arrive at the road again. The original trail from this point is washed out, so you must **follow the road** for a short distance. Watch for vehicle traffic.

After about 1 km (0.6 mi) of road walking, **leave the road** on a signed trail to the right. This is the last time you will see the road. About 5.5 km (3.4 mi) from the trailhead, reach an open ridge covered in sagebrush and low shrubs with great views of Crater Mountain to the north. The trail heads back into the trees and continues climbing steadily. Cross a boggy patch, then continue through the forest. In a few places, the trail becomes less distinct. Watch for orange diamond-shaped markers to stay on track.

Near the 11-km (6.8-mi) mark, the vegetation thins out and you'll begin to get views of the bare and rocky summit of Scout Mountain ahead. Congratulate yourself on having gained a staggering 1360 m (4462 ft) of elevation. Soon you'll reach a **junction with the Diamond Trail**. Go left to remain on the Lakeview Trail. Keep hiking for another kilometre (0.6 mi), ignoring a side trail on the right to Scout Lake. Reach a **junction with the Centennial Trail** and go straight to reach **Cathedral Lakes Lodge**.

Hikers on the Cathedral Rim Trail.

You will notice that, lower down, Douglas-fir was common. Midway through your hike, you were walking through lodgepole pine and spruce. And now that you've arrived in the subalpine, you'll see lots of balsam fir and larch. If you brave the cold temperatures, fall is a beautiful time to visit Cathedral Lakes to watch the larches change colour.

Follow signs to head left through the lodge complex towards the **Quiniscoe Lake campground** at the east end of the lake. For a quieter camping experience, turn left at the junction in the Quiniscoe Lake campground and follow the trail 1 km (0.6 mi) farther to **Lake of the Woods campground**.

CAMPING

QUINISCOE LAKE CAMPGROUND

This compact campground at the east end of Quiniscoe Lake is just a few minutes past the Cathedral Lakes Lodge and close to lots of trails. It is the only campground in the park that allows campfires.

Campsites: 30 sites on framed-earth pads. The campsites farthest from the lodge have great water views.
Toilets: 4 outhouses scattered throughout the campground
Water: Collect from the lake or the lake outlet creek.

Food Storage: In 4 large wire-mesh storage caches to protect your food from birds and rodents. They aren't weatherproof, so pack your food in a water-proof bag.

Other Amenities: Shared picnic tables, shared metal fire rings, and free firewood

LAKE OF THE WOODS CAMPGROUND

Located 1 km (0.6 mi) from Quiniscoe Lake, this campground is in open forest along the north and east shorelines of Lake of the Woods. It has beautiful views of the peaks along the Cathedral Rim Trail, including Quiniscoe and Grimface Mountains, as well as Lakeview Mountain to the southeast.

Campsites: 28 campsites on framed-earth pads
Toilets: 2 outhouses (one at each end of the campground)
Water: Collect from the lake.
Food Storage: In 2 large wire-mesh storage caches to protect your food from birds and rodents. They aren't weatherproof, so pack your food in a water-proof bag.

EXTENDING YOUR TRIP

Plan to spend a day or two doing day hikes from your base camp. The core area of the park has a huge network of hiking trails, making multiple loop options possible. Here are some suggestions to get you started.

Quiniscoe Lake Trail: A flat and easy 2-km (1.2-mi) loop around Quiniscoe Lake, past a waterfall.
Diamond Trail: An 8-km (5-mi) circuit around Scout Mountain, gaining 250 m (820 ft). Enjoy wildflowers on the rock bluffs and views down to the Ashnola River.
Cathedral Rim Trail: This is the park's signature hike along a crescent-shaped ridge encircling a cluster of lakes. The trail follows a ridgetop through alpine

NATURE NOTE

The 30 resident mountain goats often hang out at both campgrounds. Several of the animals are wearing GPS tracking collars as part of a BC Parks study to better understand their behaviour. The goats crave salt and they come into the campground to lick pee and dishwater or chew on sweaty clothing. Goats assert dominance over each other at natural mineral licks, and these ones have been using this behaviour to block humans on trails in the area. Keep your campsite clean and use outhouses to avoid attracting territorial goats to the campground. Show respect by keeping your distance when you view these majestic ungulates.

Mountain goats at Lake of the Woods campground.

terrain and over the rocky summits of Red Mountain, Quiniscoe Mountain, Devil's Woodpile, and Stone City. The west end terminates at unique rock formations called Smokey the Bear and Giant Cleft. The circuit is 16 km (9.9 mi) long with 540 m (1772 ft) of elevation gain. But with four separate trails accessing the rim, you can tackle it in shorter sections.

Lakeview Mountain Trail: Leave the busy core area behind and head to Lakeview Mountain, the highest peak in the park at 2628 m (8622 ft). The views from the summit are unparalleled. Look south into the roadless expanse of Washington's Pasayten Wilderness, speckled with snowy summits. West across the valley are the sparking lakes in the park's core area, with the impressive ridge of the Cathedral Rim behind them. It's a 12-km (7.5-mi) round trip with 600 m (1969 ft) of elevation gain.

FURTHER RESOURCES

Cathedral Provincial Park: info and fees http://bcparks.ca/explore/parkpgs/cathedral/
Cathedral Lakes Lodge: shuttle info http://cathedrallakes.ca/
Driving Map: Thompson Okanagan BC Backroad Mapbook
NTS Map: 092H01

BONUS TRIPS

IF YOU'VE COMPLETED all the hikes in the book, you're ready to start planning your own backpacking trips. Here are five more ideas to get you started. Do your own research online before heading to any of these destinations.

41. PHELIX CREEK

On this trip, you'll climb through the forest next to Phelix Creek to reach the UBC Varsity Outdoor Club's beautiful Brian Waddington Hut. From the shores of picturesque subalpine Long Lake, scramble up slopes blanketed in wildflowers to the summits of impressive peaks named for characters in *The Lord of the Rings*. It's a 5-km (3.1-mi) hike from the trailhead, plus another 5 km (3.1 mi) of road walking from a washout on the rough logging road that comes up from Birkenhead Lake Provincial Park near D'Arcy. Although the snow stays late here and the area is closed from August 15 to October 15 each year while grizzly bears are feeding, it's a quiet wilderness spot with lots of options for exploring.

42. MOUNT TROUBRIDGE

Mount Troubridge is the highest point on the Sunshine Coast Trail at 1305 m (4281 ft). Your 6-km (3.7-mi) route to the peak starts at Rainy Day Lake and passes through one of the largest patches of old-growth forest remaining on the Sunshine Coast. Sleep in a little log cabin near the summit and wake up to incredible sunrise views. The pond below the hut has a small dock that is a great place to spend a lazy afternoon. The trail starts near Rainy Day Lake, which can be reached on rugged logging roads. Or start hiking right from the ferry dock by combining this hike with Trip 17 (Saltery Bay Loop).

43. PIERCE LAKE

The Recreation Sites and Trails BC route to Pierce Lake in the Chilliwack River valley is steep! It gains 1000 m (3281 ft) in just 8 km (5 mi). There are informal campsites at the lake, and at Upper Pierce Lake, which is 2.5 km (1.6 mi) farther and 350 m (1148 ft) higher. None of the campsites have toilets or food lockers, so be prepared to use your Leave No Trace skills. Use the campsites as a base to scramble to the summit of 2091-m-high (6860 ft) Mount MacFarlane for panoramic views. Look for Slesse Mountain to the south with Mount Shuksan behind it across border, Mount Rexford to the southeast, and the Cheam Range to the north. Caution: the trailhead just off Chilliwack Lake Road is notorious for frequent vehicle break-ins and vandalism.

44. DEWDNEY TRAIL

With 36 km (22 mi) of trail and connections to the Whatcom Trail, HBC Heritage Trail (Trips 30 and 31), and a network of logging roads, the less-travelled Dewdney Trail provides several options for multi-day backpacking trips. Located in the quiet northwest portion of E.C. Manning Provincial Park, this historic route was built in the 1860s to transport mule teams from Hope to the gold fields in the Interior. The trail climbs over 1100 m (3609 ft) to reach Paradise Valley and the headwaters of the Tulameen River. Volunteers from equestrian clubs maintain the trail and several backcountry campsites, but some sections can be very overgrown.

45. HOPE PASS

This historic trail in E.C. Manning Provincial Park dates to the gold rush era of the 1860s and equestrians still use it today. The 23.5-km-long (14.6 mi) trail climbs 1000 m (3281 ft) along the Skaist River from Cayuse Flats on Highway 3 to the wildflower meadows of Hope Pass, with two backcountry campsites along the way. With connections to the Grainger Creek and Nicomen Lake Trails, you can make a 45-km (28-mi) loop over several days. You can also combine this trip with the Heather Trail (Trip 35) to explore a huge swath of Manning Park.

ACKNOWLEDGEMENTS

WRITING AND RESEARCHING this book has consumed my life for the past five years. I'm so excited to see it out in the world, but I know I wouldn't be here without a lot of help.

I am especially grateful to the friends and fellow hikers who accompanied me on research trips: Andre Chang, Michael Coughlin, Laurel Eyton, Sophie Fugulin, Steve Ingold, Brooke Kinniburgh, Cynthia Lim, Urszula Lipsztajn, Geniva Liu, Tudor Oprea, Sarah Pawliuk, Brenda Remedios, Debra Richardson, Nicole Smith, Greg Smolyn, Shannon Thibault, and Marianne Williams. Thanks also to the late Scott Helmer whose wonderful collection of BC natural history guides I drew upon during my research. I also owe thanks to the photographers who contributed their work to this book: Jaime Adams, Andy Gibb, Stephen Hui, Steve Ingold, Sarah Pawliuk, and Romeo Taras.

The team at Greystone has also been so helpful. In particular, my editor Lucy Kenward buoyed my confidence as a first-time author. Without her direction and local trail familiarity, writing this guide would have been a much less efficient process. I'd also like to thank fellow guidebook author Stephen Hui for his advice and encouragement.

Without the hard work that outdoor clubs and advocacy organizations do, we would not have trails to hike. Consider giving back by volunteering your time or making a donation to one of these organizations. The trips in this book would not be possible without the following groups: Alpine Club of Canada, Back Country Horsemen of BC, British Columbia Mountaineering Club, Burke Mountain Naturalists, Chilliwack Outdoor Club, Federation of Mountain Clubs of British Columbia, Friends of Cypress Provincial Park, Friends of Garibaldi Park Society, Friends of Manning Park, Hope Mountain Centre for Outdoor Learning, Okanagan Similkameen Parks Society, Pemberton Wildlife Association, Powell River Parks and Wilderness Society, Ridge Meadows

Outdoor Club, Stein Valley Wardens, Tetrahedron Outdoor Club, Vancouver Korean Hiking Club, Varsity Outdoor Club (University of British Columbia), and the Wilderness Committee.

My parents deserve thanks for their support over the years, especially my dad, who fostered a love of the outdoors in my sisters and me from a young age by taking us on adventures well off the beaten path. My cat Audrey was also instrumental in the success of this book, supervising nearly every writing session. Lastly, and most importantly, this book would not have been possible without the support of my husband, Greg Smolyn. He hiked over half the trails with me, provided tech support, gave up his home office, and has always been my biggest cheerleader. Deepest thanks and love always, Greg.

INDEX

Note: Trip details are indicated by page ranges in **bold**

ABOUT THE AUTHOR

TARYN EYTON is a born and raised Vancouverite who has been hiking all her life and backpacking for over 15 years. She runs an all-things-outdoor website, HappiestOutdoors.ca, and works as a freelance outdoor and adventure travel writer.

Eyton is a certified Leave No Trace Master Educator and has been volunteering with Leave No Trace Canada to teach Awareness Workshops for the last decade. She is also a member of the Board of Directors for Leave No Trace Canada and the Friends of Garibaldi Park Society. *Backpacking in Southwestern British Columbia: The Essential Guide to Overnight Hiking Trips* is her first book.

- Facebook.com/HappiestOutdoors
- @happiestoutdoors
- @happiestoutdoor
- HappiestOutdoorsBlog@gmail.com
- HappiestOutdoors.ca/BackpackinginSWBC